PLACES WE SWIM
California

PLACES WE

Calif

Caroline Clements   Dillon Seitchik-Reardon

SWIM

ornia

A GUIDE TO THE BEST RIVERS, LAKES, WATERFALLS, BEACHES, GORGES, AND HOT SPRINGS

Hardie Grant

EXPLORE

Northern
California

N

Gold
Country

Bay
Area

SAN FRANCISCO

Sierra
Nevada

Central
California

Southern
California

LOS ANGELES

NORTH PACIFIC OCEAN

Contents

Introduction   vii
Important Ideas   ix
Top 5s   xiv

Northern California

McCloud River Falls Trail   5
Vichy Springs   9
Women's Grove   13
Devil's Elbow   15
Smith River Confluence   19
Castle Lake   23
Big Chico Creek   27
Potem Falls   31
Shadow Lake   35
Road Trip: Redwood Coast, Mendocino to Smith River   38

Sierra Nevada

Emerald Bay State Park   45
Island Lake   49
The Potholes   53
Carlon Falls   55
Budd Lake   59
Grecian Pools   63
Pamoo (Travertine Hot Springs)   67
Green Lake/East Lake   71
Minaret Lake   75
Wild Willy's Hot Springs   77
Little Lakes Valley   81
Keough's Hot Springs   85
Muir Rock   87
Road Trip: Sierra Cross-Section, Truckee to Groveland   90

The Bay Area

Gualala River Redwood Park   97
Indian Springs   101
Del Rio Woods   105
Mother's Beach   109
Angel Island State Park   111
Sunny Cove   115
Road Trip: Wine Country, San Francisco to Napa Valley   118

Gold Country

Finney's Hole   125
Emerald Pools   129
Purdon Crossing to China Wall   133
Highway 49 Crossing to Hoyts Crossing   137
Buttermilk Bend   141
Prospector's Pool   145
American River Confluence   149
Camp Nine   153
Cleo's Bath   157
Road Trip: Boomtown Legacy, Auburn to Emerald Pools   158

Central California

Red Rock Pools   165
Santa Cruz Island   169
Pismo Beach   171
Upper Salmon Creek Falls   175
Big Sur River Gorge   179
Lovers Point   181
Mercey Hot Springs   185
The Cliffs   189
Middle Fork Tule River Falls   193
Remington Hot Springs   197
Road Trip: Central Coast, Santa Barbara to Monterey   198

Southern California

Tecopa Hot Springs   205
Two Bunch Palms   209
Point Dume State Beach   213
Annenberg Community Beach House   217
Manhattan Beach   219
Santa Catalina Island   223
Crystal Cove   227
Treasure Island Beach   229
Black's Beach   233
La Jolla   237
Road Trip: Sunshine Coast, LA to San Diego   240

Index   242
About the Authors   247
Acknowledgements   247

Introduction

When I was 18, I moved from New Mexico into a 10-by-10-foot tent cabin in Yosemite National Park. My roommate slept two feet away from me and snored so loud that I would often jolt awake in the night thinking there'd been a rockslide. It was the best summer of my life.

The Sierras forever altered my trajectory. As they became my summer home, I met brilliant, hilarious, optimistic people living nomadic lifestyles, "dirtbags" who had proudly pulled out of a traditional career path to live in the wilderness—to climb, hike, swim, and surf. They followed the seasons across California and around the world. The experience rewired my young brain. I didn't know you were allowed to live that way.

What is it about California that changes generation after generation of visitors? What is so special about being immersed in nature? In many ways, that is the question we set out to answer in this book. There is something so profoundly addictive and awe-inspiring about the California wilderness that it changes your life. It demands that you savor every moment.

It set me off on a path of exploration that ultimately led to Australia, where Caroline and I met. We found a connection in our love of travel and were soon planning trips together. Surf trips. Road trips. Backpacking trips. We began writing books. We've been lucky to have spent much of our time together exploring new places and writing travel guides. Yet California is the place that always draws us back.

At first, we couldn't resist the pull of the High Sierra. Desperate to share what I knew; I dragged Caroline up mountains and into freezing lakes—often joined by our family and friends. We soaked in hot springs and slept under the stars. Soon we found ourselves exploring further afield. Driving up and down the coast, camping among peaceful redwoods, floating down rivers drinking beer. Gradually, it shifted from my place to our place.

When the world changed in 2020, we suddenly found ourselves unable to leave Australia. As an American, I had to go years without seeing family. During this time Caroline and I had a baby. We had a lot to share with our loved ones back in the US.

As the restrictions began to loosen, we started to do what we've always done together: plan an adventure. We decided to write our next book about California. Just the idea filled us with hope. In a short period of time, travel had become so fraught with danger and fear that we wanted to reclaim it—the joy of it—for ourselves.

We bought an old 24-foot motor home sight unseen on Craigslist and moved in for six months with our two-year-old son, Leo, wondering what the hell we'd gotten ourselves into.

This is all a long way of saying that what you see in these pages is a snapshot from this period of our lives, but it is also the culmination of decades of informal research. It's the result, as well, of many hundreds of people who helped guide our adventures, by sharing their own experiences and advice. The kind strangers who fed us and gave us a place to park.

People we chatted with in hot springs and bars. Mechanics who got us back on the road as quickly as possible. Our friends and family who joined us throughout the journey. All of them helped us to capture the California that we know and love.

The variety of environments here continues to amaze us. Each one of California's landscapes is special in its own right. From dusty chaparral to sun-drenched beaches. The calm of ancient redwood forests. Granite canyons and emerald pools, volcanic peaks, and thermal springs. The many long, slow river miles that wind through oak forests, boomtowns, and vineyards.

We have tried to capture the very best possible cross-section of the state. In our choices, we've been guided by some core ideas—that places should be eye-poppingly beautiful, be enjoyable for all types of people, be reasonably safe in good conditions, and not be prohibitively difficult or expensive to access. When deciding on a spot to feature, we'd ask ourselves: Is this place special or unique to the region? Would we want to spend a whole day here? If a friend was visiting from far away, would we want to show this off?

The result is a collection of our favorite swims across the state—the best beaches, rivers, lakes, waterfalls, rock pools, and hot springs. It's a book for locals who want to explore new regions, as well as visitors who want to get a sense of what California is all about. Water is the most precious and endangered resource on the planet, and it is the key to understanding and exploring California. Where it goes, life follows. We treat swimming as an access point to exploring the many wild and diverse identities of the state.

Along the way, we may have found the answer to our question. What makes California so special? It gives us permission to be small. To be dwarfed by places that are so much greater than us, and feel awe at being part of it all. Being in nature, and better yet alone in nature, allows us to unburden our cluttered minds and become totally engrossed in the present. It's an increasingly rare gift to be able to focus our senses, whether in the concentrated effort of hiking up a steep hill or in the crushing exhilaration of cold water squeezing the air from your lungs. These moments make us feel truly alive.

It was our great joy to research this book, and we put a lot of ourselves into it. It gave us a deeper understanding and love for California's wilderness, as well as for each other. Things didn't always turn out as expected, but we always woke up with a sense of wonder and curiosity for the next adventure around the corner. This book is a reminder that the best of what our world has to offer lies in the things we cannot make. Enjoy these precious, beautiful places. Take care of them and protect them. Drink them in with joy and share them with the people you love.

Dillon

Important Ideas

Acknowledgment of Ancestral Lands

Caroline Clements and Dillon Seitchik-Reardon acknowledge the many Indigenous Peoples who are the traditional custodians of the lands now known as California, and pay our respects to Elders past, present, and emerging. These ancestral homelands continue to be of great importance to the Indigenous Peoples of California today.

The public and private lands described in this book hold creation stories, burial grounds, and ceremonies of Indigenous Peoples who have lived in this area for many thousands of years. These lands form an important part of customary law, tradition, spirituality, history, knowledge, belief, language, and practices. All places should be visited with respect, appreciation, and acknowledgment of the Indigenous Peoples of California who are the traditional custodians. Treat these lands as sacred places because they are.

Environmental Impact

Everyone should enjoy being outdoors, but more people does not have to mean more impact. We just need to be better and more conscious of the effects our actions may have on plants, animals, other people, and even entire ecosystems. Unfortunately, it's not enough to clean up only after yourself. To help sustain the health of the environment, it's important to leave it even cleaner than you found it. Bring a small bag to collect any bits of trash you encounter throughout the day. (See p.x for Leave No Trace principles.)

General Etiquette

It's really quite simple—don't be a jerk, and don't leave a mess behind. Be respectful and considerate of these shared spaces and the locals who love them. If you are open and friendly, people will normally reciprocate. It's everyone's responsibility to maintain a good vibe—which can mean different things in different places. Some swims are quiet, peaceful escapes; some are nudie spots; while others may be rowdy and sociable. Assess your surroundings and go with the flow.

Our Favorite Travel Resources

CALIFORNIA STATE PARKS PASS: The best investment you'll ever make. The annual pass provides vehicle entrance at 134 state parks.

AMERICA THE BEAUTIFUL PASS/NATIONAL PARKS PASS/ INTERAGENCY PASS: The second-best investment you'll ever make. Covers entrance fees and day use fees (with some exceptions) to lands managed by the National Park Service, Forest Service, and Bureau of Land Management, among others. That's a lot of land.

RECREATION.GOV: For reserving campsites and obtaining trail permits on federal lands up to six months in advance. The app works surprisingly well.

RESERVECALIFORNIA.COM: For all California state parks and reserves. Book sites up to six months in advance. This includes 279 parks, over 340 miles of coastline, 970 miles of lake and river frontage, 15,000 campsites, 5,200 miles of trails, 3,195 historic buildings, and more than 11,000 known prehistoric and historic archeological sites.

Both RECREATION.GOV and RESERVECALIFORNIA. COM are essential resources for navigating public lands and campgrounds. Search functions work well and booking is easy. While most campsites are booked far in advance, cancellations are common. If you don't know you'll be somewhere until two days beforehand, give them a try. We've had a lot of luck with last-minute bookings.

CAL FIRE (CA.FIRE.GOV): Because swimming season is often fire season, we use this website to track active fires and their smoke.

VISITOR CENTERS: The best local resource. Staff are passionate and knowledgeable about the area they serve, often providing answers to questions you didn't know to ask. We always stop in to get advice about trip planning, including maps and permits. In areas where wilderness permits are required, there are often quotas at trailheads; however, park staff can usually recommend alternate routes that will get you to where you want to go if a particular trailhead is booked up.

GOOGLE MAPS: Have you heard of it? The majority of places in this book can be found in Google Maps (or your preferred mapping app), but connectivity can be spotty. Plan ahead and download map sections for offline use in remote areas.

IOVERLANDER: This app allows you to filter a ton of different points on a map. We use it mostly to find established and wild campsites, rest areas, and sanitation dump stations. There are a lot of apps like this, but this one has served us well.

ALLTRAILS: The most comprehensive database of hiking trails. We still use paper maps when we hike, but we always reference AllTrails for descriptions and directions. It's good for getting the lay of the land while you're planning your trip.

Planning Your Trip

The most important part of any adventure is planning. A little research before you leave can save time, money, and discomfort later:

- Know the regulations and any special restrictions for the area that you plan to visit. Permits, vehicle access, dog restrictions, fire restrictions, fuel stove restrictions, and food storage (bear canisters) are all common considerations in California.

- Understand the weather conditions, which can change suddenly. Extreme heat is common in the summer and should dictate when and where you go. Sudden rain and snow are common in the mountains. Tides and swell can make or break your beach experience. Wildfire, including smoke, should be avoided at all costs.

- Pack appropriately for the weather and duration of your trip.

- Try to schedule your trip to avoid times of high use. The best time for you is when you have the most time available. The second best time is midweek.

- Understand the ability of your party and consider factors like climate, fitness, distance, elevation, and logistics.

- Travel in small groups to reduce impact and simplify logistics.

- Repackage food to minimize waste and reduce bulk.

- In more remote areas, carry a topo map or take photos of a map.

Day Trip Packing Ideas

We always regard a day swimming and walking as a sum of its parts: the journey getting there, the company you're with, and the meals along the way. We like to travel light and fast, with the bulk of what we carry being food and water. Ideally, you'll consume that weight throughout the day. Listed below are the essential items that we never leave home without.

- **FOOD:** The best way to keep spirits high is to always have snacks on hand. Apples, canned fish, nuts, energy bars, dried fruit, hard-boiled eggs, tortillas, and cheddar cheese are our staple foods that travel particularly well. Chocolate is less resilient but good for the soul. For day hikes we always choose flavor over weight. We also pack one extra meal in case we take longer than expected.

- **WATER PACK:** A minimum of two liters per person per day. Bring more if access to refills is likely to be restricted. We use 2L water bladders on long days, and stainless steel, insulated bottles on shorter hikes.

- **WATER PURIFICATION:** Often not necessary on day trips. We always bring a pack of Katadyn Micropur Forte tablets as an emergency stash. There are excellent, compact filters on the market, but they are heavier and more bulky than tablets.

- **HAND SANITIZER:** Self-explanatory.

- **POCKET KNIFE:** Mostly for cutting food and spreading peanut butter. We use an Opinel No. 8.

- **SUN PROTECTION:** Hat, sunglasses, and SPF50+ sunscreen (applied regularly). We use biodegradable, mineral-based sunscreen because it's gentle on the skin and doesn't contaminate waterways.

- **BREATHABLE, LONG-SLEEVED SHIRT:** Ideally matching so we look like a team.

- **BOOK OR E-READER:** A luxury item for those who like to rest in companiable silence.

- **CAMERA** If you don't document it, did it even happen?

- **SWIMSUIT:** Because we are Places We Swim.

- **SARONG:** Used as a compact, lightweight towel that doubles as sun protection. Can be worn longyi-style for extra street cred.

- **A WARM TOP LAYER:** It's good to have layers so you can adjust your temperature as needed. This is especially true in the mountains, where weather can change rapidly. The best thing we ever bought was merino wool tops—lightweight, breathable, and warm. Most importantly, wool doesn't hold odors like synthetic fabric.

- **RAIN PROTECTION:** There is nothing worse or more dangerous than being caught in the rain. We carry a lightweight waterproof shell, which serves as a windbreaker and an extra warm layer as well.

- **LONG SOCKS:** They protect your ankles and catch burrs before they fall into your shoes.

- **RUNNING SHOES:** Not as clunky as hiking boots. Runners are nimble, breathable, and give good support for long walks, but are also easy to carry if you're walking on a beach (shoes, like jeans, are generally considered taboo on the beach).

- **PHONE:** It's a map, light, camera, and connection to emergency services—plus, you can text your friends: Look where I am!

- **TRASH BAGS:** Not just for your own waste, but to collect the bits you find along the way. Can be used as an emergency shelter if you get into a tight spot.

- **HEADLAMP:** You never know when your hike will become an "epic."

- **PLASTIC HAND TROWEL:** For digging a hole when you need to poop (see p.xi). We bring this when we know there won't be any toilets nearby. Sold in most outdoor stores.

Leave No Trace

These are universal principles for all outdoor travel and form a solid foundation for anyone seeking adventures. More detail can be found at LNT.org.

1. **PLAN AHEAD AND PREPARE:** Understand the conditions, trails, and fitness of your group and pack appropriately.

2. **TRAVEL AND CAMP ON DURABLE SURFACES:** Stay on defined paths as much as possible.

3. **DISPOSE OF WASTE PROPERLY:** We endorse the maxim "pack it in, pack it out." This applies to your personal trash, food containers and scraps, and hygiene products, including toilet paper. If there is one thing we hate, it's seeing people's shitty TP when we are trying to enjoy a beautiful place.

4. **LEAVE WHAT YOU FIND:** Don't take any plants, rocks, animals, or artifacts from the wilderness.

5. **MINIMIZE CAMPFIRE IMPACTS:** Campfire restrictions are often in effect throughout California. Where fires are permitted, use established fire rings or fire grates.

6. **RESPECT WILDLIFE:** Don't touch or feed animals (even if they are super cute).

7. **BE CONSIDERATE OF OTHER VISITORS** (see p.ix, General Etiquette).

8. **LEAVE IT BETTER:** Not everyone is as considerate and responsible as the readers of this book. You are the best. Please help make California even more beautiful by collecting a little more than your share.

Pooping Outside

Knowing how to poop in the woods is one of the most important outdoor skills you can have. It's also something that many people get wrong. Knowing the correct technique before the need arises will make for a better outdoor experience for all.

- Choose a place at least 200 feet (70 large steps) from any water source, campsite, trail, or dwelling. You get extra points for finding a place to poop that has a great view.

- Dig a hole at least four inches wide and six to eight inches deep (we carry a plastic hand trowel for this purpose). If possible, find loose, rich soil and a sunny site. If the ground is too hard or rocky to dig, try lifting a rock and use that spot.

- Poop in the hole. If you wipe with leaves, sticks, or any other found material, you can place them in the hole too.

- If you wipe with toilet paper, place it in a sealable plastic bag and carry it out with you. Yes. Carry it out with you. People pick up their dog's poop every day but get squeamish about putting their own toilet paper in a bag. Sure, it's kind of gross—but not nearly as gross as finding someone else's used TP.

- Backfill the hole and tamp it down with your foot. Replace any rocks that you moved, to discourage digging critters. You can place an upright stick in the spot to discourage the next humans in need of a hole.

- Use hand sanitizer to clean your hands. Rub vigorously, paying close attention to your fingers. The most common source of intestinal sickness while hiking/backpacking is people self-contaminating with their own fecal matter.

- Describe your scenic view and the quality of your movement in unsparing detail to your companions. They will appreciate it.

Swimming Best Practices

If you are reading this book, then you agree that swimming is an essential part of any outdoor adventure. We've done our best to curate a group of swims and hikes that are safe in good conditions. But nothing is guaranteed. It is up to you to assess the water, any potential hazards, and the weather. Know your own swimming ability and, more importantly, know your limitations. Your safety is your own responsibility, and a little bit of common sense will go a long way. Here are a few rules we try to follow:

- Read all nearby signs.

- Sit and look for a while before getting in the water.

- Ask other swimmers about warnings and local information.

- On patrolled beaches, speak with a lifeguard before getting in the water.

- Check the water temperature before jumping in.

- Check the depth (can be very deceptive).

- Swim with a buddy.

- Enter the water slowly and feet first.

- Young children should wear life jackets.

- Look for natural hazards, such as snags and submerged objects.

- Identify currents and rips.

- Be aware that even in sleepy-looking rivers, currents may be much stronger than they appear.

- If it doesn't look safe, don't swim.

- Don't swim in fast-flowing water.

- Don't swim when impaired by alcohol or other drugs.

- Don't swim during a thunderstorm.

- Don't swim in water with algal blooms. These are common toward the end of the summer in low-elevation rivers and lakes where the water temperature is warm.

- Always. Have. Fun.

Wild Hot Springs Best Practices

Wild hot springs are a big part of the life and culture of California. Although we have tried to only include places that are well known, they are no less fragile. As always, it is important to be respectful of both the environment and other users. Here are our best practices:

- **BE QUIET:** Hot springs are a quiet place, not a party place. Keep your voice low and don't play music.

- **BE WELCOMING:** Say hello, make space, and give everyone their turn.

- **CLEAN UP:** Pick up any trash that you see, even if it is not yours. See Leave No Trace principles (p.x).

- **HYDRATE:** drink plenty of water while you are bathing.

- **NUDITY IS COMMON AT MANY WILD HOT SPRINGS:** Be respectful of other people's bodies and personal space, whichever way they/you choose to bathe.

- **AVOID SUBMERGING YOUR HEAD:** There is always a (tiny) risk of the presence of Naegleria fowleri, a lethal brain-eating amoeba, which thrives in hot temperatures.

- **No soap, no candles, no fragrances in the springs:** It's not your personal bathtub.

- **No glass:** Glass breaks and is difficult to clean up.

- **No alcohol and no smoking:** These are fun activities for other places.

- **No dogs:** We love dogs, but not at hot springs. Nobody wants to hear barking or have them scrambling in and out of the pool with weird, excited energy. Unwatched animals may shit near the springs, contaminating the water and making the surroundings unpleasant for other visitors.

- **Kids can go either way:** We're parents and recognize that kids can be just as disruptive as dogs (or more so). If they can follow the above guidelines, they can stay. Otherwise, leave them at home with your dog.

- **Don't camp within 300 feet of a spring:** Camping or parking nearby can have negative impacts on the hot springs themselves, and it will disrupt the peaceful experience of other visitors.

Cliff-Jumping Best Practices

Cliff-jumping is great fun, but it does come with serious risks (like injury or death). The key is knowing your own abilities and assessing the environment. You don't have to do the highest jump to have a good day. You don't even have to jump at all. You do need to act responsibly and not get hurt.

- Respect local regulations and only jump where permitted.

- Always bring a friend or make sure that there are other people around.

- Watch others jump first.

- Ask others if there are any hazards (we usually talk to a few local people).

- Swim around the landing zone and inspect for depth and submerged hazards before jumping (even if you have been there many times before).

- Remember that river bottoms are constantly changing due to swift currents and heavy seasonal flows.

- Wear shoes to protect your feet and assist with climbing.

- Start small: Jump feet first with your arms tucked in.

- Quickly swim away from the landing zone.

- Don't let people pressure you; it's okay to just watch.

Hiking Best Practices

California is one of the best places in the world for hiking. The abundance of public lands and diversity of environments means that you never have to travel too far to find a great trail. Many of the destinations in this book include at least a little bit of a walk, but very little hiking experience is required to have a great time. The most important thing is to be adequately prepared. These are some of the basic rules that we follow:

- Research where you are going before leaving home and pack accordingly (see our Day Trip Packing Ideas, p.x).

- Pick an appropriate route and destination for the weather conditions, allocated time, and ability of your group.

- Bring a friend and/or tell someone where you are going.

- Bring a paper map or a photo of the map. It takes up hardly any room and could be a life-saver. Many of our hikes have limited phone service, so we prefer not to rely on an app.

- Start early to avoid crowded trailheads and give yourself the most time possible to enjoy the day.

- If you feel like you have lost the trail, you probably have. Trails are really obvious when you are on them, so try to backtrack to where it was best defined. You'll usually find that you took a wrong turn, and the path will become apparent from a fresh perspective.

Poison oak, rattlesnakes, and bears, oh my!

By far the most hazardous part of any outdoor adventure will be driving in your car to get there. Next up is the sun—UV rays and heat. However, there are a couple of common plants and animals that are good to be aware of. Our best advice is to recognize and avoid them using a few commonsense methods.

Pacific Poison Oak is probably the most common hazard you will encounter in California, from sea level up to 5,400 feet. New leaves are shiny and reddish, maturing into a dull green in summer, and back to yellow or scarlet red before dropping in the fall. The leaves are lobed (resembling oak leaves), 1–6 inches long, and typically arranged as triple leaflets on stems ("leaves of three, let it be"). If you brush against poison oak, wash the affected area as soon as possible with a poison oak cleanser (e.g. Tecnu) or soap and water. Most people will break out into an itchy, burn-like red rash within hours to a few days after contact with the urushiol oil in poison oak. Long pants and long sleeves are helpful in avoiding contact. More poison oak information is available on the Cal Poison website, calpoison.org/about-poison-oak.

Rattlesnakes are the most common venomous snake and an important component of the California ecosystem, as they help to control rodent populations. Rattlesnakes are found in a variety of habitat types up to about 9,000 feet elevation, usually near or under cover, such as rocks, logs, and woodpiles. They are seen year round, but particularly in the prime swimming season from April to October. If you do see or hear a rattlesnake while hiking, stop and wait until the snake leaves the area. It has most likely felt you coming from the vibrations you've made walking on the trail. Snakes generally avoid humans and will move away when they have space. Bites mainly occur when the snake is disturbed or otherwise provoked. If the snake continues to obstruct the path, seek an alternate way around, keeping a wide berth. Some useful rattlesnake information is available on the Cal Poison website, calpoison.org/about-rattlesnakes.

Black bears are common in the foothills and mountains, often appearing brown, blond, or reddish. Because they are big and strong, people have an outsized fear of bears. While bears have very occasionally charged hikers, it is usually because the person unknowingly came between a mother and cub. Most bear encounters occur because bears come close in search of food. This is common around Sierra cabins, campsites, and busy parking areas. Metal bear boxes to store scented items are always available in areas with high activity. Portable bear canisters are required in many backcountry areas. Be sure to place your canister at least 10 yards away from where you cook and sleep.

If you encounter a bear, keep your distance, both for safety and out of respect for the animal. In undeveloped areas, at least 50 yards is recommended. If you encounter a bear in a developed area or if it is approaching, stand your ground and scare the bear away by waving your arms and making loud noises.

Stingrays are common in southern California during the summer and fall when coastal water temperatures are their warmest. The best way to avoid getting stung is by doing the "stingray shuffle": drag your feet through the sand as you enter the water to warn the stingray you're coming and give it time to swim away.

Stings can be extremely painful and serious if not treated properly—though often, all you need to do is soak the wound in hot water for 30 to 40 minutes to neutralize the toxin. On a patrolled beach, speak to a lifeguard if you're stung, or else seek immediate medical attention. There is a risk of severe infection if any spines remain in your skin.

Ticks are active year round but are most common during warm months. In California, the western black-legged tick transmits the bacteria that cause Lyme disease (among others). Most common in the coastal regions and along the western slope of the Sierra Nevada range, it prefers cool, moist environments in shaded grasses, shrubs, and leaf litter in oak woodlands.

Ticks rest on plants and attach to their hosts when you brush up against them. Our best advice is to avoid being bitten in the first place. Try to stick to the middle of trails to avoid contact with plants. We wear insect repellent when travelling in dense foliage, natural stuff on our skin (Oil of Lemon Eucalyptus, OLE) or hardcore chemical repellent on our clothes (DEET or picaridin). Some people even treat their outdoor clothes with 0.5% permethrin.

After spending a day in higher risk environments, it's worth inspecting your body (or getting a friend to do it for you). Most common tick hiding places are in and around the ears and hairline, under the armpits, inside the belly button, around the waistline and crotch, and behind the knees. We freeze ticks before removing to help prevent the release of toxins. Products like Tick Tox and ArcTick are good for this.

Early diagnosis and treatment of any tick-born diseases is important. The CDC (www.cdc.gov/lyme/index) has a lot of useful information and advice.

Other hazards: We recommend familiarizing yourself with any specific local dangers as part of your trip planning. Visitor centers will often have useful information and advice. First aid is outside the scope of this book, but it is important to familiarize yourself with best practices from reputable sources. REI has a good overview at www.rei.com/learn/expert-advice/wilderness-first-aid-basics. There is no substitute for proper training.

Please Note

We have made every effort to provide clear and correct information. Nevertheless, information is subject to change, and conditions on any given day are unpredictable. *Places We Swim California* is intended as an inspirational guide to swimming and hiking but is by no means comprehensive or authoritative.

Be sure to check official websites before visiting the places described in this book to get the most up-to-date information you need for your visit. We wish you the best of weather and all the enjoyment in the world as you explore these very special places.

Top 5s

People often ask us which are our favorite swimming spots. We find it easier to answer when we focus on a specific theme. So during our travels we keep lists of our top fives—best roadside meals, best saloons, cutest towns, worst sunburns, most interesting people, and yes, best swims. Here are the very best, in no particular order. They are a great place to start your own swimming wish list.

Best Beaches

California has some of the most diverse landscapes, and hence some of the most diverse swims. The best beaches range from sunny coves to bays with sandstone bluffs, to inland river beaches with impossibly clear water. Some are sandy, some are rocky, and all are truly world-class.

Treasure Island Beach, Laguna Beach (p.229)

Lovers Point, Pacific Grove (p.179)

La Jolla, San Diego (p.237)

Del Rio Woods, Russian River (p.105)

Buttermilk Bend, South Fork Yuba River (p.141)

Most Secluded

Quiet swimming spots are ones that people cherish and even pride themselves on knowing about. There is a sense that having a place to yourself is the highlight of the swim. If that is you, then you will enjoy these hidden, out-of-the-way locations, whether high up or down in a valley. Some require a hike to get to, but they are all worth the mission.

Shadow Lake, Lassen Volcanic National Park (p.35)

Minaret Lake, Ansel Adams Wilderness (p.75)

Upper Salmon Creek Falls, Big Sur (p.175)

Devil's Elbow, Trinity River (p.15)

Middle Fork Tule River Falls, Sequoia National Forest (p.193)

Best Skinny Dips

Skinny dip. Nudie swim. Bare bathing. By any name, the joy is the same. There is something thrilling and invigorating about swimming au naturel. We love these spots for their unique landscape and the privacy they offer. Some are sanctioned "clothing-optional" swims, while others are places where the spirit overtakes any sense of propriety.

**Wild Willy's,
Long Valley (p.77)**

Black's Beach, Torrey Pines State Park (p.233)

Budd Lake, Yosemite National Park (p.59)

Purdon Crossing, Yuba River South Fork (p.133)

Remington Hot Springs, Kern River (p.197)

Best River Swims

Probably the hardest list to whittle down, but for that reason the strongest. These rivers hold some of the most pristine water in the world. In our opinion, rivers are the best places to swim in California.

**Smith River Confluence,
Six Rivers National Forest (p.19)**

Highway 49, Yuba River South Fork (p.137)

Carlon Falls, Tuolumne River South Fork (p.55)

Big Sur River Gorge, Big Sur (p.179)

**Gualala River Redwood State Park,
Gualala (p.97)**

Northern
CALIFOR

Northern California

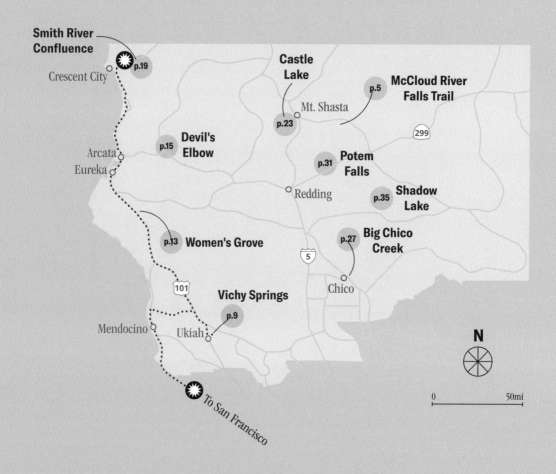

Smith River
Confluence

p.19

Crescent City

Castle
Lake

p.23

Mt. Shasta

McCloud River
Falls Trail

p.5

299

Devil's
Elbow

p.15

Arcata

Eureka

Potem
Falls

p.31

Redding

Shadow
Lake

p.35

p.13 Women's Grove

5

Big Chico
Creek

p.27

101

Vichy Springs

p.9

Mendocino

Ukiah

Chico

To San Francisco

N

0   50mi

Favorite Swim

Smith River Confluence (p.19)

Best Hike

Heart Lake,
Mt Shasta (p.23)

When to visit

Swimming season along the coast and in inland valleys is May to August, before water levels get too low and algal blooms become a risk. The eastern, mountainous side of the state thaws out from July to October. This is when roads open up and swimming holes warm up.

Northern California is a vast and wild part of the state that includes some of the most unique and varied wilderness areas in America. Driving along Highway 101 it often feels like you are a visitor to an ancient kingdom. Redwoods hug the coast and, indeed, the road, in an unbroken band that stretches into southern Oregon. Hike and swim beneath these giants at Women's Grove (p.13). The cool, foggy environment imbues the world with a sense of peaceful timelessness. Walking in the old forests and meticulously preserved towns, you can easily forget not only the time of day, but the century you're in.

Inland, the sun burns bright and strong. Wet winters meet Mediterranean summers in an intoxicating combination for water lovers. Wild rivers surge through remote valleys under blue skies. The famed Six Rivers region comprises over a million acres of diverse ecosystems and landscapes, providing vital salmon and steelhead habitats. For us, the pristine Smith River (p.38) and resurgent Trinity River (p.15) are the jewels of the area and the perfect access points to countless adventures.

Along the eastern flank of the state, the land rises to a high plateau. This little-visited area is shaped by ongoing volcanic activity in the Southern Cascade Range. Enormous monoliths dominate the landscape, their glacial slopes feeding secluded perennial streams and springs. Castle Lake (p.23) offers a front row seat to the magnetic power of Mount Shasta. Hidden waterfalls (Potem Falls, p.31) and pristine alpine lakes (Lassen Volcanic National Park, p.35) reward travelers who veer from the beaten path.

All across Northern California, there is a sense of remoteness that hardly exists anywhere else. It is a place to be completely immersed in nature. This chapter comes with a warning: Many residents came here as visitors and have never left. It could happen to you.

Favorite Redwood Grove

Rockefeller Forest, Humboldt Redwoods State Park (p.13)

Cutest Town

Mendocino (p.39)

Road Trip

Redwood Coast (p.38)

McCloud River Falls Trail

Shasta-Trinity National Forest

Three incredible waterfalls in a basalt canyon

⊙ **ANCESTRAL HOMELANDS**
Winnemem Wintu, Shasta, and Pit River

⊖ **TYPE OF SWIM**
River and waterfalls

✳ **ACTIVITIES**
Swim, rock jump, fish, camp, hike

⊘ Kid friendly, yes-ish. The water is very cold and access can be steep. Dog friendly on leash.

◐ **BEST TIME TO VISIT**
July to October

⋀ **CLOSEST CAMPSITE**
Fowlers Campground is located between Middle and Lower McCloud Falls on the McCloud River.

⊕ **CLOSEST TOWN OF INTEREST**
McCloud (7.5 miles)

⊘ **HOW TO GET THERE**
McCloud Falls turnoff is located about six miles southeast of McCloud town on Highway 89 (Volcanic Legacy Scenic Byway). You will see a Forest Service sign pointing to Fowlers and Lower Falls. Turn right and continue along this road for about 1.2 miles to arrive at the Lower Falls Day Use and parking area.

⊖ **ACCESS**
Easy-ish. Follow the River Trail from Lower Falls for a four-mile round trip to Upper Falls and back, with about 500 feet of elevation gain. The section between Lower Falls and Fowlers Campground is suitable for wheelchairs, while the remaining sections of trail have some steep inclines.

✳ **LOCAL KNOWLEDGE**
For the Indigenous Peoples of this area, the river offered water, protection, food, and spiritual connection to the land. From late spring to fall, the Winnemem Wintu, Shasta, and Pit River People came up from their permanent valley homes to hunt elk and to fish. The area has abundant acorns, pine nuts, wild onions, wild plums, chokecherries, mushrooms, elderberries, currants, watercress, and wild tubers.

Our young son is very fond of "Goldilocks and the Three Bears," particularly the idea that there can be distinct choices available to suit any taste. In the case of the McCloud, we find ourselves in a real-life Goldilocks situation. As the river carves through two miles of basalt lava rock and volcanic mudflows, it forms three falls—Upper, Middle, and Lower—each of which has a distinct personality and unique traits that are "just right" for someone.

We start our walk at *Nurunwitipom*, the Winnemem Wintu name for Lower Falls, which roughly translates to "falls where the salmon turn back." It is the most easily accessed swimming hole, and the modest round pool features a friendly drop of about 15 feet at its highest point. Nearby, small tubs in the riverbed heat up quickly in the summer sun, making this a favorite destination for those who might recoil at the otherwise icy water.

We follow the River Trail upstream, skirting Fowlers Campground, for just over a mile to reach Middle Falls. Campers swing from hammocks, eagerly consuming both books and drinks. Access to Middle Falls is past the top corner of the campground, just before a set of steep switchbacks to the lookout. Take the trails toward the water and be prepared to scramble over a few boulders.

At Middle Falls, the McCloud River surges over a 50-foot cliff into the deep pool below. Rainbows explode from the base of the waterfall as delicate ferns bathe in the cooling mist. The spray of freshwater mixes with the dry summer air to produce the distinct smell of recent rain. This is the perfect place for experienced swimmers and thrill seekers.

The river is fed by deep springs and snowmelt from Mt. Shasta and rarely warms above 53°F. It's so cold that you can feel it pushing on you, sending your blood deep into your organs and leaving your limbs to operate with clumsy, irregular movements. The water is both freezing and exhilarating. We all laugh and shriek as we plunge into the pool. Seasoned visitors bring floaties and skim along the surface. Teens jump from a 35-foot ledge as people cheer and clap, though most of us hold our breath anxiously. Even the dogs look nervous.

From here, it's a steep climb up to the Middle Falls lookout and a further half mile to Upper Falls. This is the perfect swimming hole for people seeking privacy and tranquility. It is the largest swimming hole, but because the access is more challenging, it's rarely busy. At the far end of the pool, water gushes from a narrow slot in the canyon to fill this wide, deep basin. All around, smooth, polished boulders shimmer like metal in the sun. As we lay down our towels on the edge of the river we agree that this stop is "just right" for us.

NEARBY

AXE & ROSE PUBLIC HOUSE
424 Main St, McCloud

Once a cafeteria and later a dance hall, this grand corner property is now a pub and restaurant. The bar menu includes sandwiches that go well with a beer or a cocktail, while the bistro serves mains such as a rib eye, duck breast, and pastrami primavera. Or sit out back in the beer garden with some logger fries while the Eagles play on the stereo.

WHITE MOUNTAIN CAFE
423 Main St, McCloud

The Mercantile Building, an iconic feature of this quaint historic town, is home to several local businesses, including the classic American diner White Mountain. Staff welcome you to low-rider counter seating or booths, where you can settle in for bottomless coffee and large plates of chicken and waffles, pancakes, and omelets big enough to share.

MEAT MARKET & TAVERN
231 Main St, McCloud

What was once the old town butcher shop today is a bar paying homage to the original venue. The menu is meat focused, taking inspiration from various global cuisines. Sit up at high bench tables to eat Spanish spiced mussels, "pig and peaches" (a modern take on a taco), and Portuguese pork and clams.

Vichy Springs

Ukiah

◎ **ANCESTRAL HOMELANDS**
Northern Pomo

〰 **TYPE OF SWIM**
Hot spring tubs, swimming pool

⋈ **DRESS CODE**
Clothing required in shared spaces

✳ **ACTIVITIES**
Swim, soak, massage, hike

⊘ Kid friendly

⊗ No dogs

☽ **BEST TIME TO VISIT**
It's nice here year-round, but the shoulder months
March to May and September to November have mild
weather and are not crowded.

⊙ **OPEN HOURS**
9am–5pm for day use.
24 hours for overnight guests.

⑤ **COST OF ENTRY**
Day use rates start at $35 per person for two hours.
Overnight lodging starts at $215 a night and includes
soaking.

⟁ **CLOSEST CAMPSITE**
Vichy Resort offers RV parking on-site for $30 a night.
Next-closest option: Bushay Recreation Area
(14.5 miles).

⊕ **CLOSEST TOWN OF INTEREST**
Ukiah (3.5 miles)

⬀ **HOW TO GET THERE**
Vichy Springs resort is located 3.5 miles east of Ukiah
at 2605 Vichy Springs Road.

⊖ **ACCESS**
Easy

✳ **LOCAL KNOWLEDGE**
The serenity of Vichy has long drawn artists and
writers to this place of refuge, Mark Twain among
them. Journalist, novelist, and activist Jack London
would bring friends, renting a series of cabins for the
weekend to get inspired. Presidents Teddy Roosevelt
and Benjamin Harrison also came to Vichy to soak and
find respite.

This enchanting property on the outskirts of Ukiah has long been a popular destination for travelers from afar. Like artists, writers, and US presidents before them, they come to soak in the only natural warm and carbonated mineral bath in North America. Opened in 1854, Vichy (pronounced vish-ee) is also the oldest spa in California. Though (like its mineral-soaked patrons) its age does not show.

The youth-giving waters affect not only swimmers, but also the gardens. Arrive at the 700-acre resort and be enveloped by expansive lawns under delicate maples. The lush oasis-like plantings and copious water supply at Vichy make for a much cooler ambient temperature on hot summer days, when the surrounding hills and walking trails can easily exceed 100 degrees (as we experienced).

A 50-meter pool will be the first body of water you see, though it's not for swimming laps. Here, you will find relaxed swimmers of all ages, floating quietly, clad in bathing suits (a Vichy requirement in all facilities). This pool is the coolest on the property, solar heated and surrounded by lounge chairs. To find the bubbly Champagne springs, continue down the shaded path, past the cabins, and over a vine-covered wooden bridge. It is here that Vichy Springs' warm and effervescent, mineral-filled water surges from six miles deep in the ground—the same type of water discovered by Julius Caesar in Vichy, France. Rustic, one-person baths, still fed by the original pipes, are built side-by-side into the ground, stained ochre from the minerals in the water.

Unlike other springs we've encountered, Vichy's are less sulfurous in taste and odor. The water contains lithium, calcium, magnesium, potassium, and sodium among other trace minerals. Healthful qualities are said to help with stomach acidity and ulcers, and we are encouraged to drink a cup straight from the source, which is under lock and key, only accessible with the caretakers. They tell us they consume one themselves every day, as their complexion seems to attest. So with open minds we gulp down a cup of this miracle juice, hoping the benefits are more palatable than the taste.

Devotees of the Champagne water, including the local Northern Pomo tribe, have long been using it to soothe cuts, burns, and run-ins with poison oak. As well as healing, the bubbly water has an invigorating fizzing effect on your skin. Submerging in it initially feels lukewarm, but once you settle in, you'll notice a warm tingle as tiny bubbles collect around you. This is carbon dilating your capillaries. Meanwhile, madrone and buckeye trees sway in the light summer breeze. The whole experience will likely lull you into a meditative state. You will leave with soft hair, glowing skin, and a sense of renewal.

NEARBY

BLACK OAK COFFEE ROASTERS
467 North State St, Ukiah

Black Oak roasts premium single-origin beans, which go into their espresso and filter coffee blends. Their HQ in Ukiah acts as a tasting room and cafe, but they supply coffee all over Sonoma and Mendocino Counties, so you'll likely see their beans pop up in cafes throughout the region.

SCHAT'S BAKERY
113 West Perkins St, Ukiah

This family-run institution, with ties back to Holland, has bakeries around the US and Canada. Pastries, loaves of bread, and desserts are available from the counter, and there is a diner-style menu. We always grab a cheese and jalapeno loaf stuffed with bacon to go for some hefty hike/swim sustenance.

THAI DISH
801 North State St, Ukiah

We'd heard that Thai Dish does some of the best Thai food in Northern California. Classic, authentic dishes such as eggplant pork, pork massaman, pumpkin curry, fried rice, pad thai, and tapioca pudding fill the menu, served in a quaint garden setting. It is a no-frills, casual place for a good meal, and sometimes that's all you need.

"With open minds we gulp down a cup of this miracle juice, hoping the benefits are more palatable than the taste."

A deep, cool pool among the tallest trees in the world

Women's Grove

South Fork Eel River, Humboldt Redwoods State Park

⊙ **ANCESTRAL HOMELANDS**
Lolangkok Sinkyone

⊖ **TYPE OF SWIM**
River

✦ **ACTIVITIES**
Swim, hike, mountain bike, horseback ride

⊘ Kid friendly, Dog friendly on leash

◐ **BEST TIME TO VISIT**
May to August. Be aware of toxic algal blooms late in the summer.

⊗ **CLOSEST CAMPSITE**
Albee Creek Campground (5 miles)

⊕ **CLOSEST TOWN OF INTEREST**
Ferndale (34 miles)

↗ **HOW TO GET THERE**
The California Federation of Women's Clubs Grove is located on the Avenue of the Giants about three miles north of the Humboldt Redwoods State Park visitor center. Watch for the sign on the west side of the road. It is about a quarter mile south of Founders Grove and the Highway 101 crossing.

⊖ **ACCESS**
Easy. The swimming hole is accessed directly from the Women's Grove parking area. Look for the well-established trail toward the river and walk along the pebbly streambank.

✳ **LOCAL KNOWLEDGE**
The Rockefeller Forest is the largest remaining contiguous old-growth redwood forest in the world, encompassing 10,000 acres of diverse life. "Old growth" is a term that refers not to individual trees, but to the entire forest community. Historically, it has been used to describe a forest that has never been logged. Most of these wild forests are actually "all-aged," with old and young trees growing together.

The South Fork of the Eel River is one of the most beautiful and accessible stretches of river in Northern California. Rich in both swimming holes and redwood forests, it is fed by rugged interior mountains and fog-shrouded coastal rainforest. As the river meanders north, it cuts a path of sandy beaches and deep pools for its entire 105-mile journey from Laytonville to its confluence with the Eel River proper. You can easily spend a whole summer crawling up Highways 101 and 254 in search of the perfect swimming hole, but if we have to choose one spot, it's the river beach at California Federation of Women's Clubs Grove (aka Women's Grove) in Humboldt Redwoods State Park.

Sandwiched between some of the most impressive and ancient redwood groves in the world, this section of the river is easily accessed and uncrowded. The wide, pebbly beach leads to a deep bend in the South Fork where the water is cool and clear late into the summer. A fallen tree marks the swimming hole, and visitors scramble up this natural pier to lie in the sun briefly before diving back into the dark water below.

High above, redwoods sway in the windless afternoon, the tiniest vibrations amplified along the length of their towering trunks. The coast redwoods here are the tallest trees on the planet. The King Range to the west blocks much of the summer fog, and in winter protects the forest from powerful storms and wind, so the trees can put energy into growing taller instead of regrowing broken tops.

Crossing the seasonal footbridge or driving Mattole Road into the Rockefeller Forest is an invitation to time travel. Many of these trees are 300 feet tall. Sixty generations of human anxiety and toil instantly evaporate with one look at a 2,000-year-old tree. There is comfort in the continuity of nature.

Sunshine occasionally pierces the many-layered canopy like a spotlight, but mostly we walk in twilight shade. The forest trails are dusted with soft redwood branchlets and needles, sorrel and ferns. The silence here is so complete that it becomes addictive. It spreads across the forest like freshly fallen snow, distorting our sense of time and recalibrating our focus. This grove will make you pay attention to trees. To see them as individuals.

We follow the Bull Creek Flats Trail on the south side of the creek and the Big Tree Trail on the north to complete an 8.5-mile loop. In the distance, other hikers pick their way among the trees—seen but seldom heard. We come here to walk, to swim, and to rest. Under the spell of these big trees we sleep like it's our job. We sleep like two people who are not living in an RV with a small child. This place is the remedy to a disease we didn't know we had.

NEARBY

STANDISH-HICKEY STATE RECREATION AREA AND THE PEG HOUSE
69501 Highway 101, Leggett

Standish-Hickey is a redwood campground on a slow-moving section of the Eel River. Riffles, deep holes, and calm shallow areas make this stop appealing to swimmers of all levels. The rustic cafe and general store, the Peg House, is conveniently positioned just across the highway. Have a burger or oysters with beer and enjoy live music.

RICHARDSON GROVE STATE PARK
1600 Highway 101, Garberville

The 2,000-acre Richardson Grove State Park, gateway to the north coast redwoods, has more than 160 sites across three campgrounds. Here you can enjoy hiking trails, swimming holes, and picnic areas under the shade of redwoods and maple trees. A visit here truly puts things into perspective and is a balm for the weary traveler.

EEL RIVER CAFE
801 Redwood Dr, Garberville

As you drive through Garberville it's hard to miss the Eel River Cafe's large neon sign featuring a chef and frying pan. On the inside this cozy diner, furnished with checkerboard floors and trout paraphernalia, counter seating and red leather booths, offers breakfast and lunch, with classic diner meals—pancakes, omelets, burgers, and salads.

Devil's Elbow

Trinity River, Willow Creek

⊙ **ANCESTRAL HOMELANDS**
Na:tini-xwe (Hupa)

⊖ **TYPE OF SWIM**
River

⊛ **ACTIVITIES**
Swim, paddle, fish

⊘ Dog friendly on leash

⊗ No kids

◖ **BEST TIME TO VISIT**
June to October

⊼ **CLOSEST CAMPSITE**
Tish Tang Campground (4 miles)

⊕ **CLOSEST TOWN OF INTEREST**
Willow Creek (4.8 miles)

⊘ **HOW TO GET THERE**
The pullout for Devil's Elbow is about 4.8 miles north of Willow Creek and 6.5 miles south of Hoopa on Highway 96 (Trinity Highway). Look for the large dirt parking area on the east side of the road at a big bend. The trail is marked by a single tall stake.

⊖ **ACCESS**
Moderate. From the roadside pullout, a short but steep trail leads you down to this swimming hole. It'll take about 15 minutes to get to the beach from the pullout, a bit longer coming back up.

⊛ **LOCAL KNOWLEDGE**
This rugged mountain community is (allegedly) home to Bigfoot, also known as Sasquatch. In the first week of July, the town holds the annual Bigfoot Daze festival, bringing crowds from all over. This lively 60-plus-year tradition includes an ice cream social, a horseshoe tournament, a watermelon eating contest, and a Bigfoot calling contest, among other outdoor festivities.

Six Rivers National Forest extends over 130 miles south from the Oregon border into California's Humboldt County. The namesake rivers being the Eel, Klamath, Mad, Smith, Trinity, and Van Duzen. They say you are not a true local until you have swum in all of them.

From our experience, it is hard to beat the swimming holes around the small town of Willow Creek, on the Trinity River. This area, the Hoopa Valley, benefits from a relatively temperate climate, with high winter rainfall and warm, dry summers. It's reliably sunny and about 20°F warmer than on the coast. The river is a vital salmon and steelhead habitat, carving a serpentine path through the rugged Trinity Alps, nourishing the many small communities along its course.

Just north of Willow Creek is our favorite swimming hole, Devil's Elbow. The spot is defined by a sudden, sharp river bend that slows down its flow and dredges a deep green pool at the tip of the "elbow." It's a classic summertime spot enjoyed by locals and nearby coastal dwellers who travel inland to escape the summer fog.

A steep trail of tight switchbacks delivers you to the sandy beach below where smooth limestone slabs channel the river into its tight bend. The water is so glassy you almost feel guilty breaking its surface. We float quietly, trying our best not to disturb the hovering peregrine falcons overhead and the Chinook salmon darting underneath us. It's like sitting on the lens between two worlds.

This stretch of the Trinity River, known as the Hoopa Valley—or Na:tiniw, "The place where the trails return"—is considered the spiritual center of the Hupa people's world, though it encompasses only a small part of their ancestral territories. The pristine, fertile lands are nestled at the base of steep mountain walls, evoking the feeling of a *beyul*—in Tibetan lore, a hidden, otherworldly paradise that is revealed only at certain times. Think Shangri-La, but with redwoods, salmon, and blackberries. The Trinity River is a place of both ceremony and celebration. It's no wonder it's a focus for so many tribal nations, including the Tsnungwe, Karuk, Yurok, Chilula, and Whilkut.

This intersection of nature and culture is where we find the most interesting travel experiences. The nearby Hoopa Valley Reservation is the largest Indian reservation in California. Today, Na:tini-xwe are endeavoring to revive the Hupa language. It is said to have a completely different thought process than English, expressing a complex understanding of the land and nature. Indeed, you'll find tribal members throughout the region bringing their knowledge to everything from fishery and land management to climate resilience projects.

NEARBY
TRINITY RIVER FARM
2443 Highway 96, Willow Creek

A family-run farm stand and nursery growing fresh, delicious produce and flowers. Open during the summer months from April until the end of October, Trinity River Farm sells apples and pears from their orchard, eggplants, and chilies, jams, jellies, and sauces. You can also pick your own bouquet of flowers for $10.

RIVER SONG NATURAL FOODS
80 Country Club Dr, Willow Creek

The local health food grocer in town, River Song offers organic produce and ethically made products (homewares, kids' toys, kitchen equipment) to Willow Creek and the wider Humboldt County region. It also has a little cafe and juice bar inside serving fresh smoothies, sandwiches, and salads.

OSPREY CAFE
39010 Highway 299, Willow Creek

A tiny but popular hole-in-the-wall organic cafe with limited bar seating along the front window, Osprey does mostly grab 'n' go food. Ice cream, espresso, and organic breakfast and lunch are served, with specials such as Brazilian black bean chili, turkey mushroom melts, golden milk lattes, and strawberry tea cake.

Smith River Confluence

Six Rivers National Forest

Iridescent water and pebble beaches along California's most wild and scenic river

⊙ **ANCESTRAL HOMELANDS**
Tolowa Dee-Ni'

⊖ **TYPE OF SWIM**
River

✾ **ACTIVITIES**
Swim, rock jump, paddle, hike

⊘ Kid friendly, Dog friendly

☾ **BEST TIME TO VISIT**
June to October

⊗ **CLOSEST CAMPSITE**
Jedediah Smith Campground (3 miles)

⊕ **CLOSEST TOWN OF INTEREST**
Hiouchi (1.5 miles) and Crescent City (12 miles)

⊘ **HOW TO GET THERE**
From Crescent City, take Highway 199 inland for 11.5 miles to the South Fork Road turnoff at Myrtle Beach. It's a further quarter mile to the Forks River Access and Boat Ramp parking lot.

⊖ **ACCESS**
Easy. From the parking lot the trails split to Second Bridge and further downstream to the cliffs at the confluence. Either direction is about 200 yards and relatively flat. Keep an eye out for poison oak. Carefully inspect water levels and river currents before jumping in.

✳ **LOCAL KNOWLEDGE**
From the Klamath Mountains in Oregon to the river mouth at Crescent City, more than 315 miles of the Smith River drainage are designated Wild and Scenic, making it one of the most complete natural river systems in America. The river flows freely, without a single dam for its entire length. The only major wild river system in California, it is a vital nursery for Chinook and coho salmon as well as cutthroat and steelhead trout.

Driving along Highway 199 is an exercise in divided attention and self-control. Our awareness is constantly drawn to the shimmering form of the Smith River, in tantalizing glimpses that threaten to pull us off the road. This river is irresistible. Iridescent blues and greens swirl into view through groves of fragrant bay trees, Doug firs, and coastal redwoods. As we turn onto South Fork Road and cross the first bridge at Myrtle Beach we see a solitary kayaker pierce the still pool below. Many days we don't make it past this turnout, the urge to stop is so great.

Our favorite swimming holes are around the confluence of the North and South Forks. Locals call this area "Second Bridge," but the official name is Nels Christensen Memorial Bridge, and it's easily recognizable by the long rope swing that hangs from the arching span. Here, the relatively warm waters of the South Fork gently lap along the shallow, pebble beach as the river bends downstream. People of all ages howl with a mixture of joy and fear as they leap from blocky cliffs into the deep water below. The most popular jumping rocks are just above the confluence. Blue and green come together after their long journeys apart and you can feel the warm and cold water mixing around you. The water is so clear that you can see pebbles tumbling and fish searching for food deep below the surface.

A lush, mixed evergreen forest surrounds the serpentine river, and includes Jedediah Smith Redwoods State Park and Redwood National Park. This area contains nearly half of all remaining old-growth coast redwoods in the world, which rise some 300 feet above the forest floor. The ancient groves are accessible via nearby trails and are an essential part of any visit to the area.

With caution and respect, visitors can forge a connection to this place by jumping into the water for a swim. Early in the summer and after heavy rain, flows can be wild and unpredictable. Be aware of strong currents and always inspect landings before jumping from any height. Confluences are powerful sections of river. That's also what makes them special.

NEARBY

JEDEDIAH SMITH REDWOODS STATE PARK
(*CHVN-SU'LH-DVN*)

Any visit to this area should include a stop to walk among the giant trees. Cross the Smith River on seasonal footbridges from Jedediah Smith Redwoods campground to Stout Grove. A short, 0.6-mile loop passes among some of the largest and oldest redwoods in the area. Those seeking more will enjoy the 5.6-mile return trip to the Boy Scout Tree and Fern Falls.

HIOUCHI CAFE
2095 Highway 199, Crescent City

This historic roadside diner is just a mile from the Smith River swimming spots. Its red-and-white exterior appeals to all our classic diner fantasies. Come for hearty homestyle breakfasts, burritos, sandwiches, and good vibes. Bag lunches are available to go for fishermen and travelers.

PERLITA'S MEXICAN RESTAURANT
297 Highway 101, Crescent City

Near the harbor in Crescent City, this small eatery doesn't look like much from the outside, but it's always busy. They make authentic pork and cheese tamales, offer daily tortas specials, and serve other traditional Mexican dishes alongside colorful Jarritos soft drinks. It's a simple, no-frills setting, as some of the best places are.

Castle Lake

Shasta-Trinity National Forest

◎ **ANCESTRAL HOMELANDS**
Shasta and Wintu

⊖ **TYPE OF SWIM**
Lake

✦ **ACTIVITIES**
Swim, paddle, fish, hike

⊘ Kid friendly, Dog friendly on leash

◑ **BEST TIME TO VISIT**
July to October

⌂ **CLOSEST CAMPSITE**
Castle Lake Campground (0.25 mile)

⊕ **CLOSEST TOWN OF INTEREST**
Mount Shasta City (about 11 miles)

⬈ **HOW TO GET THERE**
From Mount Shasta City, head south on Ream Avenue. The road will bend and cross the freeway. Turn left (south) on W. A. Barr Road. In about two miles you will cross the dam at Lake Siskiyou and then you will see the turnoff for Castle Lake (Ney Springs Road). Turn left and then make a quick right on Castle Lake Road. Drive the paved road seven miles to the lake. The road dead-ends at the parking lot.

⊖ **ACCESS**
Easy. The road to Castle Lake is typically cleared by Memorial Day weekend, but you may want to wait a few weeks for the water to warm up. Parking is less than a hundred feet from the lakeshore, and a series of well-established trails line its perimeter.

✳ **LOCAL KNOWLEDGE**
Within academic circles, Castle Lake is one of the most famous alpine lakes in the world. It has been the subject of continuous ecological research since 1959, one of many small mountain lakes monitored to study the effects of climate change on aquatic ecosystems as part of the California Mountain Lake Network. UC Davis and the University of Nevada Reno operate a permanent research station on the western shore of Castle Lake.

After months of navigating forest fires and road closures in Northern California, we needed to catch a break. And one day, we saw our opportunity. For the first time all summer, the smoke was blowing away from Castle Lake. But for how long?

We raced across the state, hurtling through the night on a diet of gas station drip coffee and dark chocolate peanut butter cups. The smokey haze stretched behind us like a trail of squid ink until stars pierced the black sky with shocking clarity. We gratefully breathed in the mountains around us. We had scored.

Even at the height of summer, the morning air is sharp. Cool, blue light spills across Castle Lake, then blushes as it climbs the steep granite walls. It's a perfect glacial cirque, a bowl-shaped basin left behind by a retreating ancient glacier. Today, birdsong carries across this natural amphitheater, but in the winter and spring you are just as likely to hear the booms of rockfall on the western shore. "Castle Peak" is the informal name for a blocky outcrop some 1,500 feet above the lake. It's a moderate climb and the perfect morning activity while we wait for the sun to warm the water.

From the parking area, the trail to Heart Lake and Castle Peak traces the eastern shore, then, after crossing the water outlet, steadily climbs about half a mile to the saddle. Continuing south, it's another mile up to Heart Lake. You can happily stop here, or follow a series of steep, informal trails and cairns along the ridgeline to "Castle Peak" (about 1.5 miles one way). There are no signs, but keep walking uphill and you will get there.

The views of Mt. Shasta just get better the higher you go. The mountain is absolutely magnetic. A singular reference point in northeastern California, it is visible for about 100 miles in every direction. Unlike the mountain ranges further south, these solitary volcanoes of the Cascade Range are of a different genesis. The view of Mt. Shasta above Castle Lake is more a pilgrimage than a hike.

By the time we get back down to the lake, the sun is high overhead. The Shore Trail follows the western edge of the water to a number of secluded beaches. Our favorites are just past Castle Station. During the summer, researchers float a large pontoon platform in the middle of the lake as part of their ongoing ecological studies. It's open to the public and a worthy destination for any swim or paddle. On this tiny wooden island, people sprawl across the deck like reptiles, drinking in the warmth before they dive back in. Castle Lake is far from everything, and we think it's the remoteness that allows the body to truly relax and unwind here.

NEARBY

MIKE & TONY'S
501 South Mt. Shasta Blvd, Mount Shasta

Resembling a scene from *The Sopranos*, this Italian diner and cocktail bar has real character. The interior is all dark wood and low lighting, with Italian movie posters on the walls. Families eat giant entrees with bread, veggies, and a side of pasta. Desserts include cheesecake, chocolate mousse, and tiramisu.

YAK'S SHACK
401 North Mt. Shasta Blvd, Mount Shasta

An all-day coffee shop on the main street that looks like an alpine ski hut, with indoor and outdoor seating, Yak's serves coffee, breakfast sandwiches, and burritos, alongside peanut butter lattes and green smoothies. There is beer on tap and a burger menu, making this place and any-time-of-day stop.

DEADWOOD SUPPLY
408 North Mt. Shasta Blvd, Mount Shasta

The ultimate multipurpose venue, Deadwood is an equipment supply store for your kayak and bike rental needs, but they also have a bottle shop, lounge, and taproom with beers served until 8pm. Brews rotate regularly, and include ales from the local Redwood Curtain Brewing, Falls River Brewing Co., and Urban Roots.

Big Chico Creek

Bidwell Park, Chico

ANCESTRAL HOMELANDS
Mechoopda

TYPE OF SWIM
Rock pools and swimming pool

ACTIVITIES
Swim, hike, fish, horseback ride, bike ride

Kid friendly, Dog friendly

BEST TIME TO VISIT
May to October

OPEN HOURS
UPPER BIDWELL PARK
Gates are open 5:30am to 9pm April–September,
closing at 7pm October–March.

SYCAMORE POOL
24-hour access, but night swimming is not
recommended. Lifeguards are on duty daily from noon
to 7pm between Memorial Day and Labor Day. Pool is
closed on Thursdays, when it is drained and cleaned.

CLOSEST CAMPSITE
Woodson Bridge State Recreation Area (20 miles)

CLOSEST TOWN OF INTEREST
Chico

HOW TO GET THERE
You can park in Lot E, Bidwell Hiking Area, on
Upper Park Road and walk up the riverside Yahi Trail
to reach Salmon Hole and Bear Hole. From Tuesday
to Saturday the road is open further to Parking Areas
K and L, which are directly above the swimming
holes. Sycamore Pool is located near the corner of
Vallombrosa Avenue and Vallombrosa Way in One
Mile Recreation Area, Lower Bidwell Park.

ACCESS
Upper Bidwell Park is accessible by trail or road (see
directions above). We prefer the Yahi Trail, which
follows Big Chico Creek along a mostly shaded single-
track trail. It's about 1.5 miles from the start of the
Yahi Trail to Salmon Hole, and a few hundred yards
further up to Bear Hole. For Sycamore Pool, park in
the surrounding neighborhoods. Paths are all paved,
with ramp and ladder access to the pool.

LOCAL KNOWLEDGE
On New Year's Day, hundreds of people gather at
Sycamore Pool for the annual Polar Bear Swim—a
ritual to wash off the previous year and start afresh.

Chico is known for three things: Cal State Chico, Sierra Nevada Brewing Company, and—the city's true superpower—Bidwell Park. The sprawling 3,670-acre open space stretches almost 11 miles, from the rocky buttes above the city to the heart of its leafy downtown. It is one of the largest municipal parks in the world (Manhattan's Central Park is 843 acres, San Francisco's Golden Gate Park 1,017), yet it serves a community of only 100,000. The outdoor life and culture of Chico revolves around Bidwell Park, and at the center of it all is Big Chico Creek.

The perennial stream, which draws its waters from Colby Mountain in Lassen National Park, forms the demarcation between the Sierra Nevada and the Cascade range. Relatively cool year-round, it is an ideal spawning ground for endangered Chinook salmon, not to mention a welcome respite from the intense heat of the Sacramento Valley, where summer temperatures regularly exceed 100°F. Big Chico Creek provides the perfect escape.

After the 35-mile journey from its headwaters, cool water surges through Upper Bidwell Park, sculpting the black rock of the iconic Lovejoy Basalt into architectural swimming holes. The most popular are Bear Hole and Salmon Hole, just off the trail. These deep, sparkling pools are surrounded by high rock walls and pedestals—the favored territory of rock jumpers and sun worshipers. Currents here can be hazardous, so it is critical to check conditions before jumping in.

Immediately downstream, Big Chico Creek sprawls between wide banks and becomes an entirely different experience. Under a canopy of willow, oak, and sycamore you can spend a day lounging in the water without fear of the summer sun. The Yahi Trail traces the water's edge for miles, providing access to countless secluded beaches and shallow pools. Eddies swirl behind fallen trees to scour small swimming holes. It's the perfect environment to sit waist deep and read a book or get lost in meandering conversations with friends.

A few blocks from downtown, Big Chico Creek spills into a large concrete basin to form Sycamore Pool, about 180 yards long by 30 yards wide—one of the largest public pools in California. This is the most accessible swimming destination on the creek. The grassy lawns and hulking trees of Lower Bidwell Park give the pool the feeling of a grand old estate. It's the proper swimming pool experience without the chlorine.

No matter how hot it gets, Big Chico Creek is the cooling force that sustains the land and people of this small city. It is where we gather with friends or go to be by ourselves. For Chico, nature and culture cannot be separated.

NEARBY
STOBLE COFFEE ROASTERS
418 Broadway St, Chico

As so-called digital nomads, we are
particularly drawn to cafes with good coffee
and easy working conditions. Yes, we're those
annoying people who are always scoping
out the nearest power outlet to accompany
our latte. Stoble is the ultimate hybrid cafe,
conceptualized by some locals as the place to
come work and stay caffeinated.

SIERRA NEVADA BREWERY
1075 East 20th St, Chico

It would be sacrilege to come to Chico and not
visit family-owned Sierra Nevada Brewery, the
town's greatest export (and one of our favorite
American beers). The pungent scent of hops
is intoxicating as you enter the large, open
brewing and dining sheds. Food in the beer
hall is served casually—think pizzas, burgers,
and share plates with a pint of beer.

GRANA
198 2nd St, Chico

A modern Italian farm-to-table bistro serving
wood-fired pizza, charcuterie, and daily
specials—which in summer might be a bowl of
roasted shishito peppers, a porchetta roll, and
a peach and burrata salad. Sit in the courtyard
under vines and sip Italian wine.

"It's the perfect environment to sit waist deep
and read a book or get lost in meandering
conversations with friends."

Potem Falls

Shasta-Trinity National Forest

A secluded perennial waterfall deep in volcano country

⊚ **ANCESTRAL HOMELANDS**
Atsugewi, Yana, and Wintu

◒ **TYPE OF SWIM**
Waterfall

✳ **ACTIVITIES**
Swim

⊘ Kid friendly, Dog friendly

☾ **BEST TIME TO VISIT**
July to October

◬ **CLOSEST CAMPSITE**
Cassel Campground (40 miles)

⊕ **CLOSEST TOWN OF INTEREST**
Burney (29 miles)

↗ **HOW TO GET THERE**
Potem Falls is located 35 miles northeast of Redding via Highway 299. The turnoff is at Fenders Ferry Road, halfway between Round Mountain and Montgomery Creek. Follow Fenders Ferry Road for about nine miles to the canyon bottom, cross a bridge, and continue a further three-quarters of a mile up to reach the trailhead. It is marked by a pullout on the left and a Forest Service sign stating "Potem Falls."

⊖ **ACCESS**
Moderate. From the pullout it's a short but steep hike with good footing, about 200 yards down to the falls. The path has been improved with the construction of switchbacks and is a much gentler grade than previously.

✳ **LOCAL KNOWLEDGE**
We'd heard warnings about the bad road—six miles of dusty gravel—and although it was a bit bumpy in our 24-foot motorhome, it's easily passable by most vehicles in dry conditions. What we usually find is that the places that require a bit of time and perseverance often pay the best dividends. Potem Falls is certainly such a place.

People often ask us how we feel about revealing the locals' favorite swimming spots. It's a good question, though many of the places we cover—in Yosemite, Tahoe, and Southern California, say—are no secrets. We're not pioneering any new ground here; we are simply documenting some of our favorite swims. Ones that very much deserve a page or two in a book like this. The lesser-known spots like Potem Falls, though, fall into a different category. Fortunately, thanks to its discreet location, a place like this remains relatively quiet, even in summer, and comes with a sense of personal discovery.

Potem Falls is a small, semi-secret waterfall and wide plunge pool deep down a winding road in Shasta County. We arrive on a weekend morning in summer expecting to find it busy with locals, but we have this spectacular swimming hole mostly to ourselves for a couple of hours. Narrow at the top, the waterfall fans out as it tumbles 70 feet into the pebble-bottom pool below. With a nice, gradual entry for easy wading, it is not deep until you get much closer to the falls.

A large rock on the left seems perfectly positioned to swim out to, lie on, or jump off of. On the same side a few threadbare rope swings tied to tree branches hang down over the water. One is sturdy enough to hold our weight and we shriek as we clear the rocks and plunge into the water below. Yelps and screams become part of the natural soundtrack here, as we enter the icy, mountain-fed waters with exhilaration, and emerge with spiked heart rates.

Cracks in sheer rock walls around the falls burst with greenery. The water flows at Potem year-round, and it is immaculately clean and clear—we're sure you can drink it. When other swimmers arrive, one tells us a dip here wakes him up better than his morning coffee.

Hikers come and go as the afternoon arrives. Some have dogs and wander around the edges, some bring picnic lunches, others dive into the pool, emerging clear-eyed and pink-skinned. One woman sits on the edge for 20 minutes, watching as her son and teenage granddaughter timidly approach the cold water, as though she is there for moral support only. Then, after meditating on the decision, she, too, enters the water, swims straight out to the falls, and vanishes behind it. She doesn't leave the water for an hour.

It's a nice reminder that at any age, we can still jump into a body of water and swim around under a waterfall, laughing and yelping like children, and revel in the feelings of freedom, joy, and wonder that nature gives us. A lot of things will change in the world, but this simple act will always remain the same. And if just one other person experiences these things at Potem Falls because they read about it here, then our job is done.

NEARBY

McArthur-Burney Falls
McArthur-Burney Falls Memorial State Park

Just off Highway 89 near the town of Burney is the eponymous 129-foot waterfall. An extremely popular drive-up, the spot is bumper-to-bumper busy over weekends in spring and summer (April–October). Arrive early to secure a parking spot. Day use is 8am to sunset and a small fee is required.

Hatchet Creek Falls
Big Bend Road, off Highway 299

Located along the Pitt River, Hatchet Creek Falls (aka Lion Slide) is a swimming hole and 25-foot waterfall located between Burney and Redding. This spot is identified by a large fir tree that has fallen over the pool, with steps cut into the toppled trunk to climb and jump from into the water.

Alpine Drive Inn
37148 State Highway 299, Burney

This nostalgic pink-and-white A-frame serving classic road trip fast food—burgers, chips, milkshakes, tater tots—really spoke to us as we drove through the town of Burney. Order a sundae or a soft-serve in a cone, and sit out front in the shade to recount your trip to the falls.

The prized lake in the shadow of an active volcano

Shadow Lake

Lassen Volcanic National Park

⊙ **ANCESTRAL HOMELANDS**
Atsugewi, Yana, and Maidu

⌣ **TYPE OF SWIM**
Lake

✳ **ACTIVITIES**
Swim, camp, fish, hike

⊘ Kid friendly

⊗ No dogs

◖ **BEST TIME TO VISIT**
July to October

◔ **OPEN HOURS**
Open all hours, but road access is typically from May to early November.

⑤ **COST OF ENTRY**
$30 vehicle pass valid for 7 days. Free entry with an Interagency Pass.

△ **CLOSEST CAMPSITE**
Summit Lake North and South (6.5 miles)

⊕ **CLOSEST TOWN OF INTEREST**
Shingletown (19 miles from park's Northwest Entrance); Chester (30 miles from the Southwest Entrance).

↗ **HOW TO GET THERE**
Park at the Terrace Lake Trailhead, located on Lassen Volcanic National Park Highway about halfway between the Lassen Peak parking area and Kings Creek Meadow parking area. There are a few pullouts on either side of the highway.

⊖ **ACCESS**
Easy. A rocky but well-maintained, single-track trail from the Terrace Lake Trailhead makes for a 3.8-mile round trip. Keep in mind that the road is typically open only from May to early November.

✳ **LOCAL KNOWLEDGE**
Lassen Volcanic National Park is one of the rare places on Earth that contains all four different types of volcanoes—shield, composite, cinder cone, and plug dome. Every part of this landscape is shaped by three million years of volcanic events, with the last eruption of Kohm Yah-mah-nee (Lassen Peak) as recently as 1921.

While California is known for some of the busiest and most iconic national parks in the country, it also contains some of the least visited. Lassen Volcanic National Park is of the latter category. This is entirely a reflection of its remote location, rather than the quality of the park itself. In fact, the lack of traffic makes it all the more enjoyable. Those who make the effort will be delighted by one of America's most peaceful and diverse natural wonders.

The story of creation is so visibly written on the land that the barrier between geology and time does not seem to exist here. The hissing fumaroles of steam, boiling water, and bubbling mud found at hydrothermal features are a testament to volatile forces that are still active today. And yet, for all this drama, the visitor experience is one of calmness and beauty.

The park is known for its abundant summertime wildflowers, thanks to a diversity of soils and microclimates, and for miles of quiet trails leading to peaceful glacial lakes. Of these, Shadow Lake is our favorite. Situated between Reading Peak and Kohm Yah-mah-nee, it is just far enough from the highway to not suffer from crowds, but close enough to make for an easy day trip.

Start out on the short, downhill trail to teacup-sized Terrace Lake. From here, you'll catch your first glimpses of Shadow Lake through the trees. Viewed from above, the water sparkles pure blue. Sunlight pierces the surface and dives deep into the impossibly clear water. As we descend to the lakeshore the water becomes a polished mirror of mountains and sky. All alone here, we feel like we are breaking an unspoken rule. Are we worthy of such perfection? Best to just dive in rather than trigger an existential crisis.

The water is refreshingly cool, even on the hottest days. The gently sloping beach soon drops away and we are floating above a void. Infinite gradients of blue spread out below us, broken only by the shadows of long-fallen trees. We rest here in stillness for a long time. We watch clouds race past Kohm Yah-mah-nee. Red firs sway as a light breeze brushes the basin.

Back on the lakeshore we eat handfuls of trail mix and allow warmth to bloom across our bodies. Life in this rugged landscape is constantly changing, but we are grateful to have caught it at this exact moment.

NEARBY
LASSEN PEAK TRAIL (4.8 MILES ROUND TRIP)
Lassen Volcanic National Park

The sacred Kohm Yah-mah-nee (Lassen Peak) is one of the largest plug dome volcanoes in the world. At 10,457 feet, it's the marquee feature of the park, providing a bird's-eye view of the surrounding area. The trail is short, steep, and exposed as it climbs 1,957 feet to the summit. Start early to avoid too much sun.

BROKEOFF MOUNTAIN TRAIL
(7.8 MILES ROUND TRIP)
Lassen Volcanic National Park

When you chat to park staff about hiking, the favorite summit mentioned is invariably Brokeoff Peak. It's not the highest in the park, so doesn't draw the same crowds. For sheer alpine beauty, though, it's the best. The trail passes through a multitude of mountain environments as it climbs 2,600 feet from open meadows to the summit.

BUMPASS HELL
Lassen Volcanic National Park

Bumpass Hell sits in the eroded vent of an extinct dome volcano. More than 75 fumaroles, hot springs, and mud pots occur within this 16-acre hydrothermal area, where water temps can reach 322°F. A flat 2.6-mile round-trip trail starts at Bumpass Hell parking area and takes you to the basin via a boardwalk.

REDWOOD COAST

MENDOCINO
TO SMITH RIVER

The coastline of Northern California is simply enchanting, with bluff-top villages perched amid rolling hills, redwood forests, and jagged cliffs overlooking the Pacific Ocean. You've come far enough from the bustling Bay Area to slip into a slower pace of life filled with leisurely sun-kissed days and romantic foggy nights. This road trip is one of our longest, and includes beaches, hot springs, and river swims. You'll need the time to unwind and relax into this unforgettable landscape.

Day 1

SF to Mendocino

170 MILES / 4 HRS 30 MINS + STOPS

It's a big day of driving, but we think it is the most beautiful stretch of coast in all of California. Plan a lunch break at **Cafe Aquatica** in Jenner and enjoy the views across the mouth of the Russian River. Even the agnostic will be impressed by the architecture of **Sea Ranch Chapel**. If the weather is good and the sea is calm, stop for a refreshing dip at **Cook's Beach** before continuing on to Mendocino.

Day 2

Mendocino and Surrounds

NO DRIVING REQUIRED

Walk around the Mendocino Headland until the fog burns off, then head down to Big River Estuary for an afternoon on the water. Enjoy a long, pre-dinner stroll through the Mendocino back streets, admiring the fetishized preservation of Victorian homes. Finish the day with a meal at Fog Eater Cafe, where you can pick up some wine from their bottle shop.

Day 3

Mendocino to Vichy Springs

50 MILES / 1 HR 30 MINS + STOPS

Grab a coffee at Good Life Bakery and food supplies at **Harvest Market** in Mendocino, then follow the winding mountain road inland past redwood forests and remote homesteads. This region seems perfectly suited to weather a zombie apocalypse—something to consider while driving. Spend the day in the Champagne mineral baths at **Vichy Springs** (p.9)—or stay the night to make the most of all-hours access to the baths. Be sure to BYO food and drink: there is a communal kitchen but no food service.

Day 4

Vichy Springs to Standish-Hickey

71 MILES / 1 HR 15 MINS + STOPS

An outstanding stretch of highway that takes you behind the "Redwood Curtain." Spend the day swimming in the South Fork of the Eel River down in the canyon below **Standish-Hickey State Recreation Area** (p. 13) campground. In the evening, cross the road to the **Peg House** for burgers, oysters, and live music. It's an institution you shouldn't miss.

Day 5

Standish-Hickey to Humboldt Redwoods SP

45 MILES / 50 MINS

Drive 20 miles north to Garberville for breakfast at the Eel River Cafe, a classic diner pitstop. Continue north along 101 to the **California Federation of Women's Clubs Grove** (p.13) for a swim, before you hit the Rockefeller Forest in **Humboldt Redwoods State Park**. Sustained for 2,000 years by Pacific Coast fog, trees stand 300 feet tall here, forming the world's largest old-growth forest of coast redwoods. Spend the afternoon reveling in human insignificance among these majestic creatures.

Day 6

Humboldt Redwoods SP to Arcata

86 MILES / 1 HR 45 MINS + STOPS

Stop in the town of Ferndale for breakfast and a stroll, then take an inland detour to the Van Duzen River. Swimmers Delight is one of the most popular swimming holes in Humboldt County, with a campground and picnic tables for day use. Its shallow entrance and proximity to parking is appealing to families, but more secluded pools await upriver. After a day in the sun, drive an hour north to the charming university town of Arcata and settle into the modern American eatery Campground (yes, that's its name), where they cook food over a wood fire.

Day 7

Arcata to Smith River Confluence

85 MILES / 1 HR 30 MINS

Set off early with a bagel from Los Bagels in Arcata and drive north to Prairie Creek Redwoods State Park. Start at **Gold Bluffs Beach** or take hiking trails beyond the end of the road into Fern Canyon. Scenes from *The Lost World: Jurassic Park* were filmed here, and you'll see why with its 60-foot-high sheer rock walls exploding with lush ferns of emerald green. Continue on to the **Smith River Confluence**, where you can jump from rocks and swim in the icy water of this sparkling, pebble-beach river.

Day 8

Smith River Confluence to Jedediah Smith Redwoods SP

1 MILE / 2 MINS

Start strong with breakfast at **Hiouchi Diner**, where diner dreams are made. Order pancakes and enjoy the tunes—you've got a day in **Jedediah Smith Redwoods State Park** ahead. The redwoods are so dense here, you can hardly see the sky as you wander under the gargantuan trunks. The Boy Scout Tree Trail is the signature hike—a 5.3-mile round trip through Tdiverse woodlands. It's a great place to cap off your weeklong Northern California redwood crusade.

Sierra
NEVADA

Sierra Nevada

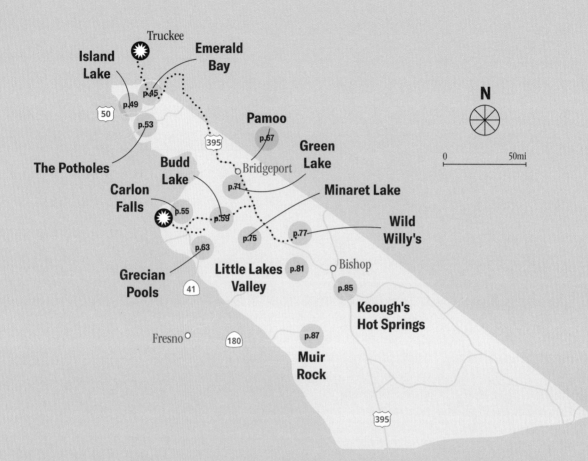

Truckee

Island Lake

Emerald Bay

p.45

p.49

50

p.53

The Potholes

Pamoo

p.67

Green Lake

Bridgeport

Budd Lake

395

p.71

Minaret Lake

Carlon Falls

p.55

p.59

Wild Willy's

p.75

p.77

p.63

Little Lakes Valley

p.81

Bishop

Grecian Pools

41

Keough's Hot Springs

p.85

Fresno

180

p.87

Muir Rock

395

N

0   50mi

When to visit

May to October,
depending on the snowpack

Favorite Swim

**Carlon Falls
(p.55)**

Best Hike

**The Grand Canyon of the
Tuolumne (p.59)**

Cutest Town

**Groveland
(p.55)**

The Sierra Nevada will ruin your life. It is a masterpiece of gravity, water, and stone. Exploring this mountain range can become a singular, unending obsession that is 450 miles long and 60 miles wide. Once you realize how easily accessible this wilderness is, it's impossible to get enough of it. Suddenly you are sleeping under a boulder, living off Fritos, instant mashed potatoes, and dented cans of tuna. You are in the best shape of your life and have never been happier. It happens to people all the time, and some never recover.

As long as humans have inhabited North America, the Sierras have been a summer home, with evidence of camps going back at least 13,000 years. There is water everywhere in the range, from the inland sea that is Lake Tahoe (Emerald Bay, p.45) to the hidden paradise of Minaret Lake (p.75). These mountains are truly playful. John Muir called them a "gentle wilderness." The land was glaciated just deep enough to create cosmic canyons like Yosemite, Hetch Hetchy (RIP), and Kings (Muir Rock, p.87), but also lightly enough to leave behind countless interconnecting high basins like Desolation Wilderness (Island Lake, p.49).

Long dry summers are what make the Sierra legendary, throwing open a wide window of opportunity to endless peaks, valleys, meadows, rivers, streams, lakes, waterfalls, and oh so many granite slabs. Slabs for walking. Slabs for climbing. Slabs for lying in the sun after a swim. Endless polished expanses of treeless playground: that is the Sierra Nevada.

In this chapter, we include the sagebrush steppe and high desert of the "East Side," the sprawling basin east of the mountains where innumerable hot springs gurgle to the surface. No Sierra trip is complete without a rejuvenating soak at Wild Willy's (p.77) or a dip at Keough's (p.85) humble bathhouse. This is by no means a comprehensive guide, but we hope it provides just the right mix of our favorite places to launch your own Sierra obsession.

Favorite Lake

Minaret Lake
(p.75)

Best Barbeque

Copper Top BBQ
(p.85)

Road Trip

Sierra Cross-Section
(p.90)

Emerald Bay State Park

Lake Tahoe

⊙ **ANCESTRAL HOMELANDS**
Wá-šiw (Washoe)

⊖ **TYPE OF SWIM**
Lake

✳ **ACTIVITIES**
Swim, hike, paddle, boat

⊘ Kid friendly

⊗ No dogs

◖ **BEST TIME TO VISIT**
July to October

◷ **OPEN HOURS**
7am to 7pm

⊘ **CLOSEST CAMPSITE**
Emerald Bay Boat Camp

⊕ **CLOSEST TOWN OF INTEREST**
South Lake Tahoe (21 miles)

⊘ **HOW TO GET THERE**
Emerald Bay is 21 miles north of South Lake Tahoe
on Highway 89. Park at Vikingsholm or Eagle Falls
parking areas.

⊖ **ACCESS**
Easy to moderate. It's a steep one-mile descent from
the parking areas down the paved path to reach the
water.

✳ **LOCAL KNOWLEDGE**
We know why Lake Tahoe is popular—it's truly
magnificent. But our best advice is to avoid visiting
during holiday weekends in summer (Memorial Day,
Fourth of July, Labor Day), when crowds descend on
the lake from all directions and it's virtually impossible
to get anywhere after 8am.

Lake Tahoe is one of the most memorable places from our past
California trips together. We return with bright eyes and fond
memories, rebooting our conversation about living here in winter,
when Tahoe becomes a tantalizing snow-covered temptation. For the
purpose of swimming, though, summer is the best time to visit, and
Emerald Bay is our location of choice every time.

Tahoe is so big that it is easy to feel lost in its immensity. This
two-million-year-old blue sea, sitting at 6,225 feet of elevation, is the
largest alpine lake in North America, stretching 12 miles across and
nearly 22 miles in length—75 miles all around. Which can make it
feel a little intimidating.

That's why we love Emerald Bay. Located in the southwest corner
of Tahoe, Emerald Bay is a lake within a lake, a great glacial scoop of
a bay separated by a narrow strait. Part of the allure is that it is just
small enough to create a sense of scale. Whereas Tahoe can feel like
an ocean, Emerald Bay feels like a sheltered cove.

Every morning, people gather on the rocks above the bay to watch
the sunrise. Sitting in quiet knots of friends and family, we share hot
drinks and hushed stories, a ritual of communion. And then it's time
to take the trail down to the water, a 500-foot descent. Some carry
large paddleboards or heavy ice chests, and we salute you. Our goal,
though, is simply the water, clear and beautiful.

Once on the sparkling bay itself, you'll glance past Vikingsholm
(see Nearby) over to Fannette Island and the ruins of a small stone
castle. Motorboats whizz about, some pulling waterskiers or inflatable
donuts with kids flying high out the back. Meanwhile, those dedicated
stand-up paddleboarders glide peacefully around the edges.

Entry to the water is made via small sandy beaches. Our favorite
is just beyond Boat Camp, a seductive section along the north edge
scattered with large boulders ideal for lying on—or jumping off of,
to dive deep into the clear blue water. We've spent fresh mornings
and lazy afternoons meditating on life's big questions here, taking in
the stunning scenery of the bay, the mountains rising on all sides. It's
enough to make anyone feel like a drop in the ocean.

NEARBY

VIKINGSHOLM

In 1928 a parcel of land at the head of Emerald
Bay (including Fannette Island) was purchased
privately by philanthropist Lora Knight
for $250,000. Shortly after, the 38-room
Vikingsholm castle was built as one of the first
summer homes on Lake Tahoe. This incredible
example of Scandinavian architecture still
stands today and is well worth a guided tour.

EMERALD BAY BOAT CAMP

A picturesque summer campground on the
north side of Emerald Bay along the Rubicon
Trail. The 20 sites can be accessed via boat from
the jetty or walked into. From May 22 to June
12, sites are first come first serve. Otherwise
they must be reserved, and advanced bookings
are essential.

THE RUBICON TRAIL, D. L. BLISS STATE PARK

A five-mile trail takes you north from Emerald
Bay to the Rubicon Point Lighthouse in D.
L. Bliss State Park. As the trail rises from the
shore, you'll find opportunities to scramble
down and plunge into the sparkling turquoise
lake, before the sudden drop-off into the deep
blue abyss.

EMERALD BAY STATE PARK

"Emerald Bay is a lake within a lake, a great glacial scoop of a bay separated by a narrow strait."

Island Lake

Desolation Wilderness/Eldorado National Forest

Large alpine lakes in a pocket-sized wilderness

◎ **ANCESTRAL HOMELANDS**
Wá-šiw (Washoe) and Nisenan

☺ **TYPE OF SWIM**
Lake

✿ **ACTIVITIES**
Swim, hike, climb

✓ **Kid friendly, Dog friendly on leash**

◖ **BEST TIME TO VISIT**
July to late September

$ **COST OF ENTRY**
$8 per vehicle per day. This fee is waived for overnight permit holders (see below).

△ **CLOSEST CAMPSITE**
You can camp around Twin Lakes and Island Lake with a valid overnight permit. Car camping at Wrights Lake Campground (1 mile).

⊕ **CLOSEST TOWN OF INTEREST**
Strawberry (13.5 miles)

▥ **BEST MAP**
Tom Harrison Maps: Hoover Wilderness

⊖ **PERMITS**
There is an overnight quota from the Friday before Memorial Day to September 30th. Wilderness permits are required for both day use (self-registration at trailhead) and overnight use (recreation.gov or Placerville Ranger Station in Camino, CA). Bear canisters are required in Desolation Wilderness.

↗ **HOW TO GET THERE**
From Placerville, drive 35 miles east on Highway 50 to Wrights Lake Road (about 4.5 miles before Strawberry). Turn left and continue for about 8.5 miles. The road forks at the southwest corner of Wrights Lake; turn right and follow the south side of the lake about 1.5 miles until it dead-ends at the parking area and Twin Lakes Trailhead.

⊖ **ACCESS**
Moderate. Park at the trailhead and follow the well-signed path to Twin Lakes. From there, route-finding is choose-your-own-adventure up to Island Lake (about half a mile).

✱ **LOCAL KNOWLEDGE**
If you don't want to rough it in a tent, many of the cabins around Wrights Lake are available for rent to base yourself for day hikes in Desolation Wilderness.

Desolation Wilderness, located between the southwest shore of Lake Tahoe and Highway 50, is a playground of forest, granite peaks, and glacially formed valleys and lakes—a microcosm of the entire Sierra Nevada. The landscape changes dramatically over short distances, making it one of the friendliest and most rewarding wilderness areas to explore. Island Lake is an easy 3.5-mile walk (one way) and offers a snapshot of everything the High Sierra has to offer. It's perfect for hikers with small kids.

The hike starts from Wrights Lake, a forested subalpine lake surrounded by a small holding of private property dating back to 1850s homesteaders.

From the parking area, walk around a locked gate to the Twin Lakes Trailhead. There is a welcome sign with trail information and wilderness permit self-registration for day hikers. As we attach the permit to our backpack and step across the wooden footbridge, it feels like crossing into another country.

The trail follows a long meadow. On this perfectly clear, early-September morning, the sun not having yet topped the crest, there is a blanket of overnight frost. The trail splits to the right and we follow signs to Twin Lakes, crossing another small footbridge and traversing the top of the meadow. The land tilts upward, and soon sunlight spills into the basin. We strip away layers of steaming clothing as we pick our way up the rocky trail, the Crystal Range opening up around us.

Trail ducks mark the path over open slabs, and a few well-defined use-trails cut along the north shore of Twin Lakes. We jump in briefly, then walk the last half mile in our bathing suits to where the long, skinny Island Lake inhabits the uppermost part of the basin. A few solitary pines are scattered around, but it's the hearty alpine shrubs that catch our eye. Dense flushes of red, orange, yellow, and green spread along the lakeshore and push against granite beaches. We choose one and lay our packs down. The water is silky in its stillness. We dive in and swim out to the small islands, which are mercifully close, ferrying across bags of dried apricots and almonds to complete our personal Shangri-La.

Island Lake feels like it is about 12,000 feet, but in fact it's just over 8,000—low by Sierra standards. This is the magic of Desolation Wilderness: the way that it dwarfs distance and elevation. In a few easy miles we have passed through multiple subalpine and alpine biomes. Hike up a few hundred feet, and it feels like a thousand. Is that Mt. Whitney towering above us? No, just the modest Mt. Price (9,975 feet). For us, coming here is about finding feelings and experiences rather than chasing numbers. To feel like you are on top of the world is enough.

NEARBY

STRAWBERRY GENERAL STORE
17481 Hwy 50, Twin Bridges

A business since 1946, the Strawberry store, ten minutes from Desolation Wilderness, is a place you feel like lingering awhile after buying a bag of chips and some Reese's Peanut Butter Cups for the road. Luckily, there's a cozy nook to enjoy a cup of coffee or read a book, and picnic tables outside.

LOVERS LEAP
Twin Bridges

Just across the road from Strawberry General Store is the Lovers Leap Campground and the beginning of a 5.7-mile loop hike through the high country. Gaining more than 1,300 feet, the trail provides impressive views of Eldorado National Forest.

THE GETAWAY CAFE
3140 Hwy 50, Meyers

This local institution serves a hearty mix of Californian fare for breakfast/brunch and lunch. We love the chilaquiles with eggs over easy and the coconut-crusted French toast. They make most things in-house, creating their own brand of "comfort alpine cuisine."

"We dive in and swim out to the small islands,
which are mercifully close, ferrying
across bags of dried apricots and almonds
to complete our personal Shangri-La."

The Potholes

Silver Fork American River, Eldorado National Forest

Slip-and-slide mountain tubs overlooking Eldorado National Forest

⊙ **ANCESTRAL HOMELANDS**
Wá-šiw (Washoe) and Nisenan

⊖ **TYPE OF SWIM**
Rock pools

✳ **ACTIVITIES**
Swim, hike

⊘ Kid friendly, Dog friendly on leash

☾ **BEST TIME TO VISIT**
March to October

⌂ **CLOSEST CAMPSITE**
Silver Lake West Campground (1 mile)

⊕ **CLOSEST TOWN OF INTEREST**
South Lake Tahoe (39 miles)

⊘ **HOW TO GET THERE**
The trailhead is located on Highway 88 (Carson Pass Highway) about five miles west of Kirkwood, directly across the road from Silver Lake.

⊖ **ACCESS**
Easy. The trail starts at the southwest corner of the Highway 88 bridge in Silver Lake, not far from the Silver Lake West campground. There's limited signage, but an easy one-mile trail will take you along the river, through forest regrowth, to the swimming holes.

✳ **LOCAL KNOWLEDGE**
A pothole is a cylindrical crater formed in the rocky channel of a turbulent stream or river. When small pebbles and sand are carried downstream, the force of the water can create whirlpools that scrape the walls with the sediment, enlarging the pit over time. Centuries (at least!) of this erosion have carved out dozens of potholes in Silver Lake, including one known as the Bottomless Pit.

Our check engine light came on just a mile from the Silver Lake campground—and it really meant business. As we lurched onto the gravel shoulder, the engine died, the brakes seized, and our power steering cut out. We had no phone reception. Luckily, the road had just leveled out, but it was a tense stretch of highway as we coasted down into Silver Lake.

With our vehicle out of action, we gave in to our surroundings and parked for a couple of days. Fortunately, we had plenty of food onboard, and our welcoming camp hosts offered a satellite phone and water. For $15 a night, this might be some of the best value in California.

And of course we did some exploring—which led to this fortuitous discovery.

The gentle, one-mile walk into the Potholes begins at the bridge just south of the Silver Lake West campground. (It used to start in the campground, but after a popular travel magazine named it in the top 10 best Sierra swims, it got too busy. So they had to relocate the trailhead for public day use access.)

An unmarked trail follows the babbling creek—in fact, it's the American River, though at this point it's just a small stream. The path winds through a forest of sapling lodgepole pines recovering from the Caldor Fire burn of 2021. As the forest ends and the dramatic, sloping valley opens up, you arrive at a wide expanse of exfoliated granite, onion-like layers peeled back by water pouring through the cracks. Hulking bristlecone pines stand like giants, their twisted trunks stubbornly withstanding the relentless winds and snows of winter.

During summer, this place is a swimmer's delight, a many-tiered stream system that has been patiently awaiting our arrival for thousands of years. People dip in and find their own pothole, while others slide over small waterfalls into pools below. We're the first to arrive this midmorning, but small groups of other hikers soon join us, finding their own places to settle and swim. Although this elevated valley doesn't offer much shade, the sun's warm kiss is a necessary element to brave the snowmelt-fed freshwater pools at 7,000-plus feet.

As we revel in this distinct Sierra landscape, we are reminded that these mountains, rivers, and lakes are both winter and summer destinations. It's hard to imagine that only a few months from now, snow will start to settle on the exact place we sit in our swimsuits, and ice will cover the surface of the water.

Silver Lake is unmistakably quieter than neighboring Lake Tahoe, which is our next stop, and the place where the tow truck will deposit our weary family. But for the moment, we're happy to be stuck here for a couple of halcyon days to enjoy the Potholes to the fullest.

NEARBY

HIKES AROUND SILVER LAKE

There are various long and short hikes you can do in the area surrounding Silver Lake and up in Carson Pass. The classic around-the-lake is a six-mile loop. Start anywhere and go in either direction, hugging the water closely for most of the way. Halfway around, stop for an ice cream at Plasse's Resort or Kit Carson Lodge.

KIT CARSON LODGE
32161 Kit Carson Rd, Kit Carson

Named after legendary mountain man Kit Carson, this nearly 100-year-old lodge is a rustic accommodation on the edge of Silver Lake. Available early June to early October, basic cabins house two to eight people, with outdoor decks and lake views. The property also offers a restaurant, boat hire, an art gallery, a general store, and a forest wedding chapel.

KIRKWOOD INN
Highway 88, Kirkwood

A historic log cabin, Kirkwood Inn dates back to the 1800s as one of the first accommodations in the area. The saloon bar is a fun place for a meal, serving cocktails, burgers, and BBQ. (Not to be confused with Kirkwood Ski Resort, where you can ski/snowboard in winter, and hike and mountain bike the rest of the year.)

Carlon Falls

Tuolumne River South Fork, Stanislaus National Forest

A glistening waterfall and emerald-clear pools creating a natural waterpark

ANCESTRAL HOMELANDS
Central Sierra Me-Wuk, Northern Paiute, and Miwok

TYPE OF SWIM
River pools and waterfalls

ACTIVITIES
Hike, swim

Kid friendly, Dog friendly

BEST TIME TO VISIT
May to October

COST OF ENTRY
$8 day use fee; free with state parks pass

CLOSEST CAMPSITE
Hodgdon Meadow Campground (2.7 miles)

CLOSEST TOWN OF INTEREST
Groveland (24 miles)

HOW TO GET THERE
From Groveland, take Hwy 120 (Big Oak Flat Road) east for 24 miles. Turn left at Evergreen Road and follow for one mile to a pullout with a gate and a sign that marks the Carlon Falls Trailhead.

ACCESS
Easy. A mostly flat one-mile walk along a well-established riverside trail through pine forest. It takes around 20 minutes to hike in to the falls, with two small uphill sections.

Although we'd spent many summers in Yosemite National Park, it wasn't until we had family move to Sonora that we started exploring the western Sierra foothills. Like many, we always treated the Hetch Hetchy area as a quick access point to the park from San Francisco, a place to drive through, not stop in. It's not on too many people's swim radars.

To us, Carlon Falls is the perfect swimming hole: the clear, green water so clean you could drink it (yes, we may have filled our water bottles here); easy to access (a one-mile walk in) but just far enough that it's not too busy; with shady spots to sit, but the water surface warm from direct sun. You can easily spend a whole day here.

There are several places to swim at Carlon Falls. The first pool you arrive at is idyllic and shallow, certainly a good place to get wet. But just a little ways on, the second is the real jewel, where you can sit right under the tiered 35-foot waterfall. In between the pools, small circular tubs have been created by the water movement over thousands of years, an unsung work of nature's genius. We slip into the large pool and swim over to smooth rocks, submerged like seats around a hotel pool bar. In deeper sections you can claim one of these and stay perched for hours.

Couples swim over to the falls for high-pressure showers. The water pouring down from above is slightly warmer than the pool, the heavy deluge like a nourishing deep-tissue massage. The water is remarkably clear here. Fed by snowmelt high in the Sierra, the perennial South Fork of the Tuolumne River cascades down the mountains as one of the cleanest waterways in the state.

As the name of the road that accesses Carlon Falls suggests, the surrounding landscape is evergreen, evolving with the seasons but always maintaining its deep hue. Big, leafy umbrella plants grow between rock slabs as water leaks from every crack and crevice. Puffy green plume-like shrubs remind us of the Truffula trees in Dr. Seuss's *The Lorax*. It feels otherworldly.

With family in tow (three generations), we spend a relaxed, sun-kissed afternoon at this mystical waterfall wonderland—diving off rocks, sitting under the whitewater, scrambling up to the top of the falls to walk across fallen tree trunks, and competing in underwater swimming races with the rainbow trout that live here. Then we pull our slippery bodies onto hunks of hot black rock to warm up and dry ourselves without towels. It is a truly memorable place. We leave with glowing cheeks, warm hearts, and an acknowledgment that waterfalls and swimming holes this special are rarely so accessible.

NEARBY
HOTEL CHARLOTTE
18736 Main St, Groveland

Stop for a drink and sit out on the second-floor veranda overlooking Main Street, or play cornhole in the beer garden out back. Hotel Charlotte is a charming spot, good for a casual meal, with basic hotel rooms upstairs. For live music, drop by the Iron Door Saloon across the road, the oldest continuously running saloon in California.

COCINA MICHOACANA
18730 Main St, Groveland

Authentic Mexican is not hard to find in California, even in the smallest of towns. (Groveland's population is just under 500.) Cocina Michoacana is a classic example. The drinks menu includes micheladas, agua de Jamaica, and horchata, all made in-house, and among the main dishes are enchiladas, fish, and shrimp tacos.

RAINBOW POOL
Highway 120, Groveland

An established swimming hole just off the highway in Stanislaus National Forest. Once a toll stop for stagecoaches, and then a bathhouse resort, these days Rainbow Pool is open to the public from 8am to 8pm daily for a $8 day use fee. It's perfect if you need a quick dip and a toilet break.

Budd Lake

Tuolumne Meadows, Yosemite National Park

A stunning alpine lake nestled in Yosemite's Cathedral Range

ANCESTRAL HOMELANDS
Central Sierra Miwoe-wuk

TYPE OF SWIM
Lake

ACTIVITIES
Swim, hike, climb

Kid friendly

No dogs

BEST TIME TO VISIT
Late July to mid-October. Late in the summer is best, to avoid mosquitoes.

OPEN HOURS
Park entry is 24/7, but Tioga Road is generally only open June to October (depending on snowfall).

COST OF ENTRY
$35 entry fee to Yosemite National Park, valid for seven days. Free entry with an America the Beautiful or similar annual interagency pass.

CLOSEST CAMPSITE
Tuolumne Meadows (4 miles). Backcountry camping south of Cathedral Pass with a valid wilderness permit.

CLOSEST TOWN OF INTEREST
Tuolumne Meadows General Store (4 miles)

BEST MAP
Tom Harrison Maps: Tuolumne Meadows & High Sierra Camps

PERMITS
None required for day hiking

HOW TO GET THERE
The Cathedral Lakes Trailhead/John Muir Trail is about half a mile west of the Tuolumne Meadows Visitor Center on Tioga Road (Highway 120). Be sure to place any food, toiletries, and other scented items in the bear lockers at the trailhead, even if you are only out for the day.

ACCESS
Advanced. This is a mostly off-trail hike and map reading skills are required.

One of the greatest joys of the Sierra Nevada is backcountry hiking. Getting away from the roads and the main trails is also the secret to avoiding Yosemite crowds. Once you get comfortable traveling overland, using map and compass, a whole new world of unique mountain experiences comes to life. The good news is that you don't have to go far. Budd Lake is the perfect entry-level backcountry hike and a favorite among park employees and climbers.

This hike starts at the John Muir Trail/Cathedral Lakes Trailhead in Tuolumne Meadows and follows the well-trafficked path for about 0.8 miles. After a couple of switchbacks, look for a single-track climbers' trail on the left, marked with a carabiner signpost. This informal path cuts through the forest and then follows Budd Creek up the drainage. It's a popular approach route for climbers heading to Cathedral Peak, so it's well worn.

The trail meanders near the creek through thinning forest, over rock outcrops marked by small cairns, and becomes less visible as the basin opens up at higher elevations. Stick close to the streambed, eventually crossing to the left (east) bank, and it will lead you directly to Budd Lake. (It's easy to follow climbers' trails and end up close to Cathedral Peak. Not a problem. Just keep walking uphill until you see the lake, then traverse over to collect your prize).

Budd Lake is a blue jewel sitting in a bowl of polished granite below Echo Peaks and Cockscomb. The water is clear and cool, with broken slabs extending outward in all directions. We've been coming here for 20 years, and it never changes. It's a vault for our nostalgia. The sweet, dry smell of summer. The easy stillness of the surface before our first plunge. There is a deep comfort in the relative permanence of geologic time. We come here to lose ourselves. To be part of something bigger.

It's easy to spend the day dipping in and out of the lake and watching parties of climbers summit Cathedral Peak. A light breeze carries the occasional laughter and yells of "climb on!" The perfect Yosemite soundtrack.

When we are feeling particularly motivated, we scramble up the saddle to Echo Ridge for a panoramic view of the Cathedral Range. Matthes Crest extends like a mile-long knife blade to the south. Endless backcountry adventures lie just beyond. Budd Lake is a portal to another world. It brings your map to life. Let it become familiar. Run along the ridges and sit on top of a blocky peak. Or just read a book by the lake. You cannot experience this place all at once. That's why we keep coming back.

NEARBY

Tuolumne General Store
Tuolumne Meadows

This seasonal spot serves as a grocery store, restaurant, post office, and town square, and it is well stocked for your backpacking needs. The message board outside reads like early Craigslist, with gear for sale, rides sought and offered, and people signaling their whereabouts to friends. Keep an eye out for grizzled PCT hikers ogling new shoes as if they were gold bullion.

The Mobil/Woah Nellie Deli
22 Vista Point Dr, Lee Vining

This may be one of the only gas stations in America to have cult status. Aside from the normal roadside amenities, its kitchen serves quality pub-style food, pizzas, and pitchers of margaritas. During summer, Thursday-night live music draws a crowd who dance under the starlit sky. Open May–November (depending on snowpack).

Grand Canyon of the Tuolumne
(34 miles one way)

This multi-day adventure follows the Tuolumne River deep into one of the great, less-traveled parts of Yosemite. Starting from Tuolumne Meadows, hike down to Pate Valley, then out at White Wolf Lodge. The Grand Canyon has everything we love about the Sierra—alpine meadows, waterfalls, granite walls, natural waterslides, and deep swimming holes. Allow three or four days.

Grecian Pools

Wawona, Yosemite National Park

⊙ **ANCESTRAL HOMELANDS**
Southern Sierra Me-Wuk, Nüümü (Northern Paiute)
and Miwok

⊖ **TYPE OF SWIM**
Rock pools

⊕ **ACTIVITIES**
Swim, hike

⊗ No kids, No dogs

◖ **BEST TIME TO VISIT**
June to September

Ⓢ **COST OF ENTRY**
$35 entry fee to Yosemite National Park, valid for
7 days. Free entry with an America the Beautiful or
similar annual interagency pass.

⊘ **CLOSEST CAMPSITE**
Wawona campground (2.6 miles)

⊕ **CLOSEST TOWN OF INTEREST**
Wawona (2.2 miles)

⊘ **HOW TO GET THERE**
From Wawona Village, turn right at Chilnualna Falls
Road and follow to the end, passing through the
residential enclave of North Wawona before reaching
the trailhead parking lot.

⊖ **ACCESS**
Challenging. Steep but short, with some shaded
sections of trail. The pools are off-trail and require
some bushwhacking to access.

✳ **LOCAL KNOWLEDGE**
It's unclear how the nearby community and hotel
of Wawona got their name. One story says that it
represents the sound of an owl (in Mewuk dialect,
"Wawŏ'na"), considered the guardian spirit of the
surrounding giant sequoia trees. Another story says it
means "Big Tree" in Miwok.

For all the millions of visitors who come to Yosemite National Park every year, we're sure that plenty of others write it off, deterred by its popularity. This is a huge mistake. Despite its fame, it remains a life-changing place. For us, it was the gateway drug to the Sierra Nevada. Plus, any seasoned campaigner knows that there is a lot more to Yosemite than the Valley. Wawona, in particular, is often overlooked.

Located just a few miles from Yosemite's southern entrance station, Wawona sits quite low by Sierra standards, at 4,000 feet. This means that the air and water temperatures are typically much warmer than in the rest of the park. Ideal swimming conditions.

If you Google Grecian Pools for directions, you'll probably come up short. This knowledge has been passed down by generations of park staff. You see, Grecian Pools is the traditional recovery spot after the annual employee lū'au. It's just far enough to be private but close enough for people to get here after a bad night's sleep.

The hike into Grecian Pools begins along the Chilnualna Falls Trail, which weaves a steep four miles up into the tiered waterfall system along Chilnualna Creek. To reach this swimming hole, however, you peel off about a mile up the same path.

The trail takes you through a shady habitat of oak woodlands that gets denser with elevation. As you breathe more heavily, inhale the resinous earthy scent of endemic bear clover (aka mountain misery). Soon enough, the trail becomes a series of sharp switchbacks with stairs hand cut into the granite bedrock. When you reach a rusty trail sign showing locations and distances, you are about halfway to Grecian Pools.

It's a blink-and-you-might-miss-it situation, so we're going to get specific now. Once you start heading away from the creek, there's a switchback where you'll get an expansive view over Wawona Valley. Here, you've emerged from the forest into a drier, manzanita-covered landscape. Look for the unsigned path to the pools about 300 feet up on the right, just before a set of three or four man-made stairs.

Step off the trail to the right and veer downhill to the left, following a use-path to the creek. Head upstream around some larger boulders. (If you get to a cliff edge, you've gone the wrong way.) Soon the pools will reveal themselves, cascading over large slabs of granite, nourishing the earth with their cool water flow. You have arrived.

Chilnualna Creek pours through cracks in the rocks to sculpt this series of swimming holes. Ease into the shallower pools, plunge into deeper ones, and air-dry on flat sun-warmed slabs. Find shade in the shadow of bigger formations where you can unpack lunch and feast like a god.

NEARBY
SWINGING BRIDGE
Wawona

After your Grecian Pools hike, visit Swinging Bridge, just down the road. The trailhead is at the end of Forest Drive in Wawona. From there, walk in half a mile, and you will find a 40-foot bridge over the river that rocks and sways with each step. You can swim right under the bridge.

WAWONA HOTEL
8308 Wawona Rd, Yosemite Valley

This charming Victorian-era bastion, the oldest operating hotel in California (since 1879), has 104 rooms, and the white-tablecloth restaurant serves breakfast, lunch, and dinner (reservations recommended).

MARIPOSA GROVE
Wawona

Mariposa Grove is the largest sequoia grove in Yosemite, with about 500 mature trees, many of which are over 300 feet tall. Walk the two-mile Grizzly Loop Trail that circles the grove for the best vantage of these epic giants.

Sculptural natural hot springs in the Bodie Hills

Pamoo (Travertine Hot Springs)

Bridgeport

⊙ **ANCESTRAL HOMELANDS**
Nüümü Witu (Eastern Mono), Newe Sogobia (Western Shoshone), Nüümü (Northern Paiute), and Wá-šiw (Washoe)

≈ **TYPE OF SWIM**
Hot springs

⊠ **DRESS CODE**
Nudity is common

‖ **ETIQUETTE**
Wild hot springs are fragile and sacred places. Please be respectful of the environment and other users by practicing Leave No Trace (p.x) ethics. Likewise, allow the springs to be a quiet place, not a party place. Keep your voice low and avoid playing any music. Strictly no glass or soap in the springs.

⊘ Kid friendly and dog friendly if they are quiet.

☾ **BEST TIME TO VISIT**
Spring or fall, when the weather is cooler and the summer crowds have thinned out.

⚠ **CLOSEST CAMPSITE**
Strictly no camping at the hot springs. Limited dispersed campsites can be found about a half mile before Pamoo on the north side of the road.

⊕ **CLOSEST TOWN OF INTEREST**
Bridgeport (1.8 miles)

⬀ **HOW TO GET THERE**
From Bridgeport, drive south on Highway 395 for about half a mile and turn left on Jack Sawyer Road. Continue for 1.2 miles as the road winds into the hills, dead-ending at the Pamoo parking area. In winter, the dirt road is impassable by car, but you can walk in.

⊖ **ACCESS**
Easy. From the designated parking area, walk about 200 yards to access the main springs. There are a few more springs another 500 yards down the hill.

✳ **LOCAL KNOWLEDGE**
The Bodie Hills are low mountains in the transition zone between the Sierra Nevada and the Great Basin. While they appear unassuming, they harbor a diverse assemblage of natural and cultural sites, including a high density of Native American heritage sites, from permanent settlements to seasonal gathering places. The transitional environment fosters a huge variety of sagebrush as well as lodgepole pine, Sierra juniper, and Utah juniper. Here, animals like the pronghorn antelope, mule deer, and the bi-state sage grouse find sanctuary.

Over the years, Pamoo has become one of our favorite hot springs on the East Side. Unlike many other springs, which typically are in a valley or adjacent to a stream or river, Pamoo's pools are in the hills, with views across Bridgeport Valley and up into the Hoover Wilderness. It's a great soak in its own right, but the ease of access and proximity to many of our favorite hikes and swims is what has made this place an essential stop on all our trips.

We often arrive late at night, achy from a long hike or drive—and it's the perfect remedy for both. The high desert is always cool at night, and the clean, soft smell of sage mixes with the earthy musk of the springs. Stars shine so brightly on this side of the range that you hardly need a headlamp to find the pools below. After a short walk, we grope the ground for a dry place to put our clothing and towels, then lower our bodies into the water with a groan of relief. Our minds wander into the sky, returning just in time to send us off to bed.

There is strictly no camping at the springs proper, but there is often space at one of the dispersed sites along the road. People roll out sleeping bags under the stars, while others sleep in parked cars and vans. All are quiet and respectful. We set an alarm for dawn and hope it doesn't disturb our neighbors.

Sunrise is our favorite time for a soak and is often less busy than other parts of the day. The high-desert steppe is a sea of sage, with a few low-slung piñon trees for good measure. Around the springs we see antelope bitterbrush, in the rose family, and rabbitbrush and mule-ears, in the sunflower family. All through the summer flowers burst from the pale bushes and paint the hills with a profusion of brilliant yellows.

The morning light throws the intricate detail of the namesake travertine into full relief. One of the youngest types of rock on Earth, travertine (made of calcium carbonate) forms as heated groundwater percolates slowly to the surface through small fissures, creating colorful, mineral-rich deposits. Layer upon incremental layer have built up to form tall ridges, while a steady flow of hot water rolls down etched channels to fill the four pools below. These tubs are a masterpiece, many tens of thousands of years in the making.

Down the hill, springs discharge into a small wetland where grass and reeds grow in vibrant shades of green. It's the definition of an oasis. A close inspection will reveal a few sand-bottomed pools that are large enough for one or two people. We sit and quietly take it all in, staying until the sun becomes too strong and our stomachs begin to grumble. Rejuvenated, we're now ready for the next adventure, even if it's just a breakfast burrito in Bridgeport.

NEARBY

JOLLY KONE
178 Main St, Bridgeport

This outdoor burger shack is a fast-food institution, and it's hard to miss the curious sign that proclaims "Burgers, Burritos, Ice Cream, Massage." We order one of each and sit out front in the sunshine.

BIG MEADOW BREWING COMPANY
241 Main St Suite C, Bridgeport

Bridgeport's craft nanobrewery may not seem like much, but if you see them cooking pizza out front on a portable wood-fired oven, you might want to give it a try. This rustic, small-town brewery has about five beers on tap and a rotating menu of pizza and BBQ. Open year round.

BODIE STATE HISTORIC PARK
Highway 270, Bridgeport

Bodie was the site of one of the richest gold strikes in California, with nearly 10,000 residents during its boom years, 1877–1880. Today it is preserved in a state of "arrested decay," with interiors as they were left—seemingly abruptly. It's fascinating to walk the dusty streets and peer in the windows of the once-thriving homes and businesses.

PAMOO (TRAVERTINE HOT SPRINGS)

Green Lake/East Lake

Hoover Wilderness/Inyo National Forest

Secluded mountain lakes in one of the Eastern Sierra's least-visited wilderness areas

ANCESTRAL HOMELANDS
Nüümü Witü (Eastern Mono/Monache), Me-Wuk (Central Sierra Miwok), Newe Sogobia (Western Shoshone), Nüümü (Northern Paiute), and Wá·šiw (Washoe)

TYPE OF SWIM
Lake

ACTIVITIES
Swim, hike, fish, horseback ride

HIKING DISTANCE
2.6 miles to Green Lake, 1.6 miles further to East Lake—4.2 miles altogether, one way

Kid friendly, Dog friendly

BEST TIME TO VISIT
June to October

OPEN HOURS
24 hours, but we recommend daylight hours for swimming.

CLOSEST CAMPSITE
Green Creek Campground, at the trailhead

CLOSEST TOWN OF INTEREST
Bridgeport (13.4 miles)

BEST MAP
Tom Harrison Maps: Hoover Wilderness

PERMITS
Permits are not required for day hikes, but wilderness visitors are encouraged to call or stop by the local Forest Service office in Bridgeport for current information. Wilderness permits and bear canisters are required year round for any overnight stay in the Hoover Wilderness.

HOW TO GET THERE
From Bridgeport, take 395 south for five miles. Turn right onto Green Creek Road, an unpaved, often very corrugated road. It's only 8.6 miles to the trailhead, but it might take you 30 minutes depending on current conditions.

ACCESS
Easy-ish. It's 2.6 miles up a gentle but consistent incline to Green Lake on a well-established trail, a further 1.6 miles up to East Lake.

LOCAL KNOWLEDGE
Weather conditions can change quickly at high elevation. Be prepared with proper clothing and supplies, even if the forecast is sunny. We always pack an emergency can of sardines, raincoats, and headlamps.

We saw a photo of Green Lake on a friend's wall showing two dogs frolicking blissfully. The setting was exquisite: hulking mountains with a scooped valley between them, white puffs of porcelain clouds in the blue July sky. It would, we decided, be the perfect destination for our son's first backpacking trip.

When the time came, we roped our brother Lee into this camping extravaganza. Straight off a fishing boat in Alaska, Lee had spent three months subsisting on salmon and rice. He needed to get his land legs back, and he was the crucial partner to our backpacking trip—a willing cold-water swimmer, able to carry a 30-plus-pound toddler.

The hike into Green Lake is a gentle 2.6 miles. The path is of the sturdiest Forest Service construction, large block steps painstakingly placed. When civilization ends, aliens will speculate about our curious arrangement of stones in the mountains. As we walk, several groups of handsome mules and their various cargos—humans, food, tents, fuel—pass us, off to a backcountry respite.

When we arrive at the lake, we choose a campsite with views up Glines Canyon, a giant stone half-pipe flanked by Gabbro Peak and Monument Ridge. It's an incredible backdrop to our afternoon swim. Fog swirls above the lake, occasionally pierced by bright bars of sunshine. The broody atmosphere feels like the Scottish Highlands, and we start calling it "Green Loch".

Determined, but admittedly fair-weather backpackers, we're buoyed by this perfect location and try to ignore the brooding storm clouds. The weather can and will change quickly up here, with nighttime temperatures dropping to near freezing even in summer. We huddle around our stove for dinner, jump into our tent when the sun goes down, and read until our books drop from our hands. It's probably all of 7pm.

Our son sleeps deeply, never waking. We, however, are not so lucky, for he also spends most of the night in motion, rooting around like a nocturnal truffle pig. Next time he can sleep in the vestibule.

We make breakfast and, after a cold swim and hot coffee to wash away our tiredness, head up the short 1.6 miles to East Lake. Rugged, treeless peaks climb steeply from the lakeshore. The water is cold, but our Alaskan ocean god is unimpressed. Even when lightning forks above us, he continues diving and swimming. Black clouds swirl over the pass ahead like the gates of Mordor. It's only another 5.5 miles to Virginia Lakes, but it's a slog with a toddler. Even in good weather.

We make a hasty retreat down the route we came as thunder booms overhead. Just as we reach the parking area, balls of hail are pinging off cars. We dub our first family backpacking trip a success.

NEARBY

BUCKEYE HOT SPRINGS
Buckeye Creek, Bridgeport

Permanent geothermal springs bubble from the grassy hill above, then cascade down the travertine dome to a series of small, shallow pools below. A cold stream runs along the edge of the springs, perfect for a cold plunge between hot soaks. Keep to the established trail and leave no trash.

MONO CONE, LEE VINING
51508 Highway 395, Lee Vining

When you're straight off a Sierra hike, Mono Cone is the perfect pick-me-up. This roadside burger joint serves to-go food, but it's best known for its soft-serve ice cream, choc dipped, and giant sundaes with whipped cream, Maraschino, cherries, and roasted peanuts on top. Pure decadence.

SILVER LAKE CAFE
6597 Highway 158, Silver Lake

Located along the scenic June Lake Loop of Highway 158 is this cozy diner and general store. There is almost always a line to get a seat. We like to rent a kayak and paddle around for an hour to build up an appetite, before devouring one of their famous three-egg omelets.

Minaret Lake

Ansel Adams Wilderness/Inyo National Forest

An immaculate glacial lake beneath jagged, otherwise otherworldly peaks

◎ **ANCESTRAL HOMELANDS**
Nyyhmy (Western Mono), Nim (North Fork Mono), Nüümü (Northern Paiute and Owens Valley Paiute)

◒ **TYPE OF SWIM**
Lake

✴ **ACTIVITIES**
Hike, swim, climb, fish

✕ No kids

✓ Dog friendly on leash

◖ **BEST TIME TO VISIT**
July to September

◔ **OPEN HOURS**
Entry roads are typically open between late June and September, depending on the snowpack.

⑤ **COST OF ENTRY**
$10 standard amenities fee, paid at Minaret Vista entrance station. No fees for overnight parking with a valid wilderness permit.

⌂ **CLOSEST CAMPSITE**
Minaret Falls Campground is about 1 mile from the trailhead. Backcountry camping at Minaret Lake.

⊕ **CLOSEST TOWN OF INTEREST**
Mammoth Lakes (22 miles)

ⓜ **BEST MAP**
Tom Harrison Maps: Devils Postpile—Minarets—Thousand Island Lake

⊖ **PERMITS**
None required for day use. Overnight wilderness permits can be obtained from recreation.gov or Mammoth Lakes Visitor Center.

↗ **HOW TO GET THERE**
This hike starts from Devils Postpile National Monument. During the summer there is a mandatory shuttle bus between Mammoth Mountain Adventure Center and Devils Postpile departing every half hour between 7:30am and 7pm. Tickets sold at the Adventure Center. Private vehicles may enter before 7am and after 7pm, or at any time with a valid wilderness permit or campsite reservation. Drive your own vehicle if you want to beat the crowds and get an early start.

⊖ **ACCESS**
Challenging. This can be a long day hike or a moderate multi-day backpacking trip.

One of the recurring themes of this book is the feeling of awe. It happens at the ocean, it happens among redwoods and sequoias, it happens in the mountains. It's the feeling of being connected to something bigger than yourself—things ancient, vast, powerful, and enduring. For us, Minaret Lake is one of the great mountain temples.

Here, the journey is as important as the destination. This can be a big day trip, or a much easier backpack. You can do an out-and-back from Devils Postpile (14.6 miles) or turn it into a 23.5-mile High Sierra lake loop (see Nearby for more detail). If, hypothetically, you are on a deranged and epic journey with your long-lost sibling, you can do the whole loop, adding unnecessary side trips up peaks, in a very long day that leaves you stumbling back to your car well after dark, ready to tear apart an XL pizza like a racoon on amphetamines. We have done it all different ways, and each option has its merit.

Starting from Devils Postpile, follow the trail south along the Middle Fork of the San Joaquin River less than half a mile to cross the footbridge and join the John Muir Trail (JMT). Hike north along the JMT for 1.8 miles as it veers above the river, past Minaret Falls, to a junction and a sign to Minaret Lake. Turn left (west) to follow Minaret Creek up the drainage to its headwaters. It's about 5.5 miles of steady climbing, with cascades, tubs, and plunge pools along the way. The trail steepens with a few switchbacks just before you pop over a ledge to spy the sparkling Minaret Lake.

Unlike the creamy blues and greens of higher lakes, Minaret shines with a distilled clarity. Glacial runoff is filtered through the surrounding meadows, leaving the water free of imperfections. Even on the hottest days the lake never feels warm, but it is always refreshing. Large slabs slope into the water, providing easy entry and a speedy exit. We kick-start our nervous system with a series of swims, and watch the clouds scrape past the many jagged spires of the Minarets.

These rugged mountains are highly unusual because they incorporate remnants of ancient, metamorphosed rock that rests above the iconic Sierra granite. Miraculously, the peaks survived erosion and glaciations over many millions of years as everything around them was excavated, smoothed, and polished. Great aprons of granite lead to the dark pinnacles above. This is a Sierra cathedral.

For us, the Minarets are the perfect Sierra place. They are an easily identifiable feature when viewed from far off, and even more incredible up close. You can spend a day here or a whole season. Sheltered campsites are scattered around the lakeshore, and you will rarely share the place with more than one other group. And from there, the surrounding wilderness invites exploration.

NEARBY

MINARET LAKE LOOP (23.5 MILES)

The ultimate lake loop. From Minaret, continue up to Cecile Lake, then down to Iceberg Lake. From there, follow the drainage down to Ediza Lake, where you pick up a maintained trail down to Shadow Lake to rejoin the JMT. Making your way south past Rosalie and Gladys Lakes, keep going until you arrive back at Devils Postpile.

SHEA SCHAT'S BAKERY
3305 Main St, Mammoth Lakes

Trays of freshly baked loaves and the scent of warm gluten will welcome you into Schat's, a much-loved name in California synonymous with bread and pastries baked in European stone-hearth ovens. Egg and bacon croissants, glazed donuts, freshly piped eclairs, and chile cheese bread fill the cabinets and stomachs of hungry outdoor enthusiasts.

YAMA RAMEN
The Village, 6201 Minaret Rd #101, Mammoth Lakes

A good ramen is a nourishing brothy noodle dish we can eat anytime, whether after a hike in summer or a ski in winter. Located in Mammoth Village, Yama is a small ramen bar where you can build your own. Choose a broth, add pork, prawns, tofu, or marinated chicken, and toppings. Specialty drinks include sake and Sabe cocktails.

Wild Willy's Hot Springs

Long Valley

ANCESTRAL HOMELANDS
Nüümü (Owens Valley Paiute)

TYPE OF SWIM
Hot spring

DRESS CODE
Nudity is common

ETIQUETTE
Wild hot springs are fragile and sacred places. Please be respectful of the environment and other users by practicing Leave No Trace (p.x) ethics. Likewise, allow the springs to be a quiet place, not a party place. Keep your voice low and avoid playing any music. Strictly no glass or soap in the springs.

Kid friendly, Dog friendly

BEST TIME TO VISIT
This is an incredible place to watch the Perseid meteor shower, between mid-July and late August.

OPEN HOURS
Entry roads are typically open between late June and September, depending on the snowpack.

CLOSEST CAMPSITE
This is Bureau of Land Management (BLM) land with dispersed camping allowed.

CLOSEST TOWN OF INTEREST
Mammoth Lakes (13 miles)

HOW TO GET THERE
Turn onto Benton Crossing Road, 5.5 miles south of Mammoth Lakes on Highway 395. Drive northeast for about three miles. The turnoff for Wild Willy's is an unmarked dirt road on the right-hand side just before the third cattle guard. Take this road 1.2 miles until you reach a parking area with a boardwalk. In dry conditions, this road is passable for most cars.

ACCESS
Easy. It's a short walk along the well-maintained boardwalk to reach the hot springs.

LOCAL KNOWLEDGE
Wild Willy's sits in the Long Valley, one of the biggest calderas in the world at 10 by 20 miles. About 760,000 years ago a volcanic eruption errupted and then collapsed in on itself, forming the oval-shaped depression that we see today. The calderas remains thermally active, with abundant hot springs and furmaroles throughout the valley.

This part of California is full of wild hot springs. The Owens Valley Paiute describe the region as *Payahuunadü*, "the Place of Flowing Water." Such features are closely guarded by locals for good reason—hot springs are precious, sacred places, easily destroyed and slow to restore. So much so that being introduced to a new spring is like an initiation into a secret society. First, you have to have lived in the area for at least thirty years. Second, locals will only take you at nighttime, blindfolded in the trunk of a car. Finally, you must swear a vow of silence on a loaf of Schat's Chile Cheese Bread.

Then there is Wild Willy's. This secret got out a long time ago, and it's as close to an institution as any hot spring can be. You might say it's the Yosemite of hot springs: well known and well trafficked, but no less spectacular or fragile.

If you are anything like us, you'll arrive in the dark, following a long hike, climb, or drive. The springs are not far from 395, but the route feels infinitely longer and more circuitous at nighttime. After navigating the bumpy dirt road, you arrive at a remote parking area filled with a motley assemblage of Subarus, vans, and RVs.

Wild Willy's famous wooden boardwalk crosses the salty landscape and down a small hill to the handful of pools below. The nights are always cold here, and plumes of steam serve as waypoints to the individual springs. The largest pools follow the creek on the right, with a couple of smaller and hotter tubs to the left. The water is around 100–105°F, depending on how close you sit to the source.

This is not a place for people seeking solitude, but neither is there any obligation to participate in the quiet conversation that inevitably passes. We enjoy eavesdropping on the day's adventures: a climbing club from Davis, a group of girlfriends from San Diego, mule packers from Bishop. On one occasion, an astronomer maps the sky with a green laser. On another, a naked couple play dueling fiddles in the moonlight (not an innuendo). It's (almost literally) a melting pot of people from all places and all walks of life. Each group is here to celebrate and enjoy the Eastern Sierra in their own way.

In the morning, frost covers everything. Mouths poke through the cinched hoods of mummy bags like snorkels. This is the witching hour, the precious sliver of time after the night owls have gone to sleep but before most people wake up. The White Mountains to the east prolong the alpine glow as warm hues of pink and orange inch down the towering Sierras to the west. Sunlight catches the steam in low golden clouds that spread across the entire valley. Soon the sound of zippers and distant rumble of engines break the silence as people pack their cars and disperse. We're grateful for these healing waters and are encouraged to see people treating them with respect.

NEARBY

HILLTOP HOT SPRINGS
Benton Crossing Rd, Mammoth Lakes

Down the road from Wild Willy's, this small, circular, man-made tub (aka Pulky's Pool) sits in the valley a few hundred feet down a wooden boardwalk. The tub is filled by two pipes pumping hot and cold water from an underground spring, which combine to create a temperature around 100°F. The tub fits up to five people and is clothing optional.

EAST SIDE BAKE SHOP
1561 Crowley Lake Dr, Mammoth Lakes

A community cafe and bakeshop serving hearty food made with whole grains, nuts, seeds, and some gluten-free options. Sweet bars include lemon, raspberry, and fig. Savory items—quiche and frittata, soups and salads—are served at lunch. On Saturday nights, dinner often comes with live music.

SHELTER DISTILLERY
100 Canyon Blvd #217, Mammoth Lakes

The shared vision of professional snowboarder turned coffee roaster Matt Hamer and brewers Jason Senior and Karl Anderson, Shelter Distillery serves up a portfolio of artisan spirits—whiskey, bourbon, gin, agave. Canned cocktails and beers are available to go.

"As our eyes adjust, the Milky Way pulses overhead, the stars electric in the clear dry air. No need for a headlamp."

Little Lakes Valley

John Muir Wilderness/Inyo National Forest

ANCESTRAL HOMELANDS
Nüümü (Northern Paiute), Nüümü (Owens Valley Paiute), and Nyyhmy (Western Mono)

TYPE OF SWIM
Lakes

ACTIVITIES
Hike, climb, swim, fish

Kid friendly, Dog friendly on leash.

BEST TIME TO VISIT
August into October

OPEN HOURS
Roads are typically open late June until the first major snowfall (October-ish).

CLOSEST CAMPSITE
Mosquito Flat walk-in (at trailhead)

CLOSEST TOWN OF INTEREST
Toms Place (10 miles)

BEST MAP
Tom Harrison Maps: Mono Divide High Country

PERMITS
Wilderness permits required for overnight trips.

HOW TO GET THERE
Turn off Highway 395 at Rock Creek Road in Toms Place, about halfway between Mammoth Lakes and Bishop. Follow Rock Creek Road for about 10 miles to Mosquito Flat. The road dead-ends at the parking area and trailhead.

ACCESS
Easy to moderate. This eight-mile out-and-back hike has about 1,200 feet of total elevation gain.

LOCAL KNOWLEDGE
This is a very popular trailhead because it is so accessible and the car does most of the steep climbing for you. On weekends or holidays, be sure to get there before 8am for a good parking place.

Little Lakes Valley is a reminder that not all great things require great effort. At 10,232 feet, the trailhead is the highest in the Sierra, landing visitors in the middle of an alpine meadow framed by lofty peaks. It is one of the best day hikes for lovers of water and wildflowers, not to mention a favorite mountain pass for those wanting to get deep into the backcountry in a hurry.

We like to wait until August or September to visit, once the meadows have sufficiently dried and there are fewer mosquitos. The hike starts from the aptly named Mosquito Flat and follows a stunning glacial valley to the edge of the Sierra Crest. There are at least two dozen lakes within a day's walk of the trailhead, and Little Lakes Valley is the perfect introduction to the area.

From the parking lot, the trail slopes gently upward for half a mile to meet the Mono Pass junction. (The pass is a key entry to the backcountry—but that's for another day.) Continue on to Mack Lake for the first incredible view of the surrounding peaks. Mt. Morgan, Pyramid Peak, Bear Creek Spire, and Mt. Dade watch over the valley and beckon you toward them.

Walking further up the basin, we soon arrive at a succession of marshy lakes. Marsh Lake (well named), Heart Lake, and Box Lake are surrounded by lush meadows. Keep an eye out for clusters of giant red paintbrush as you cross the creek.

Like the Hemsworth brothers, each lake is more beautiful than the last. About 2.5 miles from the trailhead the path skirts along the appropriately named Long Lake. And it's the best yet—a mile of rocky shoreline surrounds this slender pool of deep, clear water. In other circumstances this could easily be our final destination, but there is still more ahead.

The trail starts to climb more steeply for the final mile as it flirts with the treeline. Dwarf western white pines tell the tale of long, cold winters, while alpine columbines bloom like tiny supernovas among the blocky talus. You'll pass junctions to Chickenfoot Lake and Morgan Pass as you follow signs to Gem Lakes.

Although little creative license has been taken with the naming of these lakes, the simplicity fits. Gem Lakes sparkle with the alluring quality of glacial waters—a crystalline clarity that is both sapphire and emerald. This high up, swimming tends to be the domain of the cold water enthusiasts and alpine nudists. We find a discreet boulder on the far shore and submit to the siren's call.

You can easily spend a day alternating between the upper and lower Gem Lakes, or spend a month making side trips in adjacent basins. Little Lakes Valley is popular for good reason and should not be missed.

NEARBY

TOMS PLACE RESORT
8180 Crowley Lake Dr, Crowley Lake

This rustic retreat has been providing warm hospitality along El Camino Sierra for over a hundred years. Open year round, seven days a week, it offers a cafe, general store, bar, and lodging to service all your worldly needs, including hearty, country-style breakfast, lunch, and dinner.

ROCK CREEK LAKES RESORT
1 Upper Rock Creek Rd, Bishop

Rock Creek Lakes Resort is an alpine summer holiday setting surrounded by the John Muir Wilderness. Ensconced in nature, the resort provides cozy cabin accommodation, boat rental, hot public showers, a general store, and the Grill restaurant. Smoked meats, burgers, and sandwiches (vegetarian options too) fill the menu, and there's Mountain Rambler beer on tap.

MAMMOTH MOUNTAINEERING SUPPLY
GEAR EXCHANGE
106 S Main St #203, Bishop

This new and secondhand outdoor gear shop in Bishop is one of the best we've ever seen. Most of the space is a consignment store for sporting goods, athletic footwear, and outdoor clothing. Snowboards, skis, hiking boots, backpacks, camping gear, snow gear—basically, anything you might need for the Sierra: they have it.

Keough's Hot Springs

Bishop

ANCESTRAL HOMELANDS
Ütü'ütü witü of the Nüümü (Owen's Valley Paiute)

TYPE OF SWIM
Hot spring pool

ACTIVITIES
Swim, sauna, steam, massage

DRESS CODE
Bathing suits required

Kid friendly

No dogs

BEST TIME TO VISIT
Year-round

OPEN HOURS
11am–6pm Mon, Wed, Thurs, Fri;
9am–6pm Sat and Sun. Closed Tues.

COST OF ENTRY
$14 for adults, $10 for children 3–12,
$5 for kids under 2

CLOSEST CAMPSITE
You can camp at Keough's

CLOSEST TOWN OF INTEREST
Bishop (8.4 miles)

HOW TO GET THERE
Eight miles south of Bishop on Highway 395. A
similar distance north of Big Pine.

ACCESS
Easy

LOCAL KNOWLEDGE
There is nothing better than winter storm days
at Keough's. When it is dumping snow up in the
mountains, you can still get sunshine on the pool deck
and protection from the wind. Locals sit out here in
the sun and plot the next week of powder runs.

The Bishop area is world famous for its natural springs, and everyone has their favorite. Sometimes, however, you just want to float on a pool noodle in a giant concrete tub, dip a hot pretzel in cheese sauce, and finish up with a hot shower. No dirt roads. No polite conversation. No effort required. Just an unpretentious frontier resort that has hardly changed in over a hundred years. That's why we love Keough's Hot Springs, and why so many Eastern Sierra backpacking and climbing trips end here.

The Owen's Valley Piute called these springs *u'tu 'utu paya*. It's a sacred site for bathing and healing, and was once the center of a permanent Paiute village where a highly developed irrigation system allowed the growing of food.

The iconic structure that we know today was built in 1919, a classic art deco design, the cool mint facade a contrast to the (literally) piping hot water. The water source is 130°F and has to be cooled through a series of pipes and finally waterfalls to reach the main pool at a safe temperature.

There are two swimming pools at Keough's. The larger, main pool—measuring 100 by 40 feet—sits at a balmy 88–90°F. The small, warmer spa pool, which was once a kids pool, heats up to 104°F, which is like a giant bathtub, but probably a little hot for most children. Water is constantly moving through the pools, entering at one end and exiting at the other, which creates a natural flow that keeps the water clean and fresh. Open to the sky, but surrounded by covered lounging areas, the pools feel at once outdoors and sheltered. The surrounding mountains are never far from view.

At many California hot springs, staying on the property has always been part of the experience, and this is certainly true of Keough's. A history pasted on the walls tells of a time when it cost just $1.50 a night to stay in the cabins here. There was also a dance hall, a dining room—"connected with the plunge building . . . where excellent meals may be had at reasonable prices"—and a lunch counter. These days, camping on the property just a few hundred yards from the pool is possible, and a snack bar selling hot pretzels, chocolate bars, ice cream, chips, and fruit smoothies is open daily for visitors.

But it's the curative thermal waters we come for. Their medicinal properties have been said to help treat conditions affecting the stomach, the intestines, the urinary tract, and biliary passages. We haven't reviewed the research behind these claims, but can confirm that we feel rejuvenated and relaxed after a visit. With its proximity to the many great outdoor offerings of the Bishop area, Keough's has long been the go-to recovery place for weary bones and muscles.

NEARBY

COPPER TOP BBQ
442 N Main St, Big Pine

Fans rave about the baby back ribs, tri-tip, pulled pork, and mac and cheese at Copper Top. Some say it's the best BBQ in California. And now, so do we. You'll see the big wood-fired smokers out front and smell that delicious scent wafting down the highway. It's counter service, but there are some picnic table seats inside.

MOUNTAIN RAMBLER BREWERY
186 S Main St, Bishop

Set in an industrial warehouse space, this low-key, casual venue pours a selection of beers on tap, with a menu of burgers and pizza. There's a small stage for live music, often performed by bands visiting from out of state. Good beer, good vibes!

BISHOP PASS

At 11,900 feet, this is one of the great high passes into the backcountry. Starting at South Lake (9,300 feet), hike up the valley between the Inconsolable Range and Hurd Peak, six miles of granite terraces and soaring peaks. From Bishop Pass you can do a loop into Chocolate Lakes, rejoining the main trail at Long Lake. Then continue to eventually meet the John Muir Trail.

Muir Rock

Kings Canyon National Park

The iconic jump rock in this great California canyon

ANCESTRAL HOMELANDS
Nyyhmy (Western Mono), Yokuts, Tübatulabal, and Nüümü (Owens Valley Paiute)

TYPE OF SWIM
River

ACTIVITIES
Swim, hike, climb

Kid friendly

No dogs

BEST TIME TO VISIT
June to September. The road into Kings Canyon is generally open from the Wednesday before Memorial Day to the last Wednesday in October.

OPEN HOURS
24 hours, but we recommend visiting in daylight hours.

COST OF ENTRY
$35 entry fee to Kings Canyon National Park, valid for 7 days. Free entry with an America the Beautiful or similar annual interagency pass.

CLOSEST CAMPSITE
Several campgrounds—Moraine, Canyon View, Sentinel, and Sheep Creek—are located five miles back toward the King Canyon Visitor Center.

CLOSEST TOWN OF INTEREST
Grant Grove Village (35 miles)

HOW TO GET THERE
Take the breathtakingly scenic drive all the way through Kings Canyon National Park to the very end of Highway 180 (East Kings Canyon Road). Park at Road's End and walk 200 yards to Muir Rock.

ACCESS
Easy. There is a well-established trail south of the parking area leading directly to Muir Rock.

LOCAL KNOWLEDGE
Kings Canyon trails were no doubt more famous a century ago than they are today. Visitation numbers have been about the same for the last fifty years, while Yosemite has gotten busier and busier. Shhhh… The lack of notoriety makes for quiet, carefree days in the canyon, whether you're up in the high country or on a mellow day hike.

Muir Rock is located at "Road's End," the literal terminus of Highway 180 in Kings Canyon National Park. To get here, you drive along one of the most scenic, winding roads you'll ever encounter, culminating in a narrow valley bound by skyscraper granite cliffs and peaks. No number of photos or previous visits can dull the feeling of Kings Canyon. It's a new experience every time and something that will stay with you forever.

You can't miss the looping parking lot at the end of the road. A sign whimsically states that "where the road ends, the trails begin." Indeed, this is the main access point to exquisite backcountry, including the popular 41.4-mile Rae Lakes Loop. Lower-intensity day hikes to Mist Falls (3.9 miles) and Paradise Valley (5.7 miles) leave from here too.

Today, however, the main event is the huge granite rock on the edge of the Kings River. Follow the easy trail from the parking area some 200 yards along a dappled path of spongy branchlets and pine needles to reach the water. It's an easy scramble up the back of the rock from there. From this broad, idyllic perch it's not a stretch to imagine the namesake John Muir (who else?) writing a few notes in his journal or leaping 15 feet into the river below. You will see his name again and again as you explore the central and southern Sierra. Muir was a writer, ecological thinker, and founding member of the Sierra Club. He's a singular figure in the modern environmental movement, so called "Father of the National Parks," and his advocacy and essays continue to be a personal guide to nature for many.

Whether Muir's naked ass ever graced this particular rock we cannot confirm, but it is nonetheless an ideal platform for both contemplation and sunbathing. The clear, emerald green water below gently swirls and scours a deep pool where it meets the rock. Pebbled beaches at either side allow more direct entry to the river. Be sure to check that currents and water levels are safe before swimming.

Fly fishermen wave their wand-like rods over the rapids, as though casting a spell on the rainbow trout. Big fallen trees offer bench seats to sit on, and tiny mosquitoes buzz around your ears in the summer months. Always heard but seldom seen. There are certainly other pools up- and downstream to swim in, but this one is the most spectacular, and consistent. While we peer over the edge of the rock before a jump, an older couple approach, recalling summers here spent jumping from the rock in their youth. They tell us this rock was the destination for the summer. And we believe it. It's the highlight of this part of our trip too.

NEARBY

MIST FALLS HIKE
Land's End, Kings Canyon National Park

This 7.8-mile out-and-back trail leaves from Road's End, winding through woodland and meadows alongside the Kings River for a couple of miles before it climbs past a sequence of waterfalls and cascades. Black bears are seen here regularly.

BOYDEN CAVERN & KINGS CANYON LODGE
Highway 180

A marble cave, accessible only by 45–60-minute guided tours between April and November. The short but steep hike into the cave features spectacular views of the sheerest part of Kings Canyon, while the cavern itself is filled with stalactites, stalagmites, flowstone, pendants, and shields.

SEQUOIA NATIONAL PARK

Sequoia National Park, adjacent to Kings Canyon, is known for its giant trees, adapted to survive fire, drought, and beetle attacks. The General Sherman Tree in Giant Forest Grove is the most visited site, the largest tree in the world by volume. From the summit of Moro Rock you get panoramic views of the park.

"Whether Muir's naked ass ever graced
this particular rock we cannot confirm,
but it's nonetheless an ideal platform for
both contemplation and sunbathing."

SIERRA CROSS-SECTION

TRUCKEE TO GROVELAND

Everyone should visit the Sierra Nevada. Some say the experience is life-changing. Here is a week-long water tour of the lofty mountain region that takes you to Lake Tahoe and Yosemite National Park, sacred hot springs and dramatic river valleys.

Day 1

Truckee to Emerald Bay, Lake Tahoe

30 MILES / 45 MINS + STOPS

Drive south from Truckee via Highway 89 to Lake Tahoe and park at D. L. Bliss State Park. Hike the five miles to **Emerald Bay** (p.45) along the Rubicon Trail, stopping frequently to swim and take in the stunning views. Spend the day at Emerald Bay, diving in the clear water and exploring its protected sandy beaches along the north shore. Finish the afternoon with a tour of Vikingsholm, a 38-room Scandinavian-inspired summer home. Then head into South Lake Tahoe for dinner at **Freshies**, a casual, Hawaiian-themed rooftop restaurant.

Day 2

South Lake Tahoe to Bridgeport

116 MILES / 2 HRS 50 MINS + STOPS

The most direct route follows 395 south, but if you have the time, take Highway 50 to 89 through Markleeville and over Monitor Pass. Highway 395 has got to be one of the most beautiful stretches of road in America, and this stunning section connects the northern and central Sierra along river valleys and fragrant sagebrush steppe. Stop in Bridgeport for lunch— **Jolly Kone** has quintessential roadside burgers, fries, and milkshakes. Then spend the afternoon wandering around **Bodie State Historic Park**, a gold rush town preserved in a haunting state of "arrested decay." Head back to Bridgeport for an evening soak at **Pamoo** (Travertine Hot Springs, p.67), a small collection of hilltop thermal pools with mountain views.

Day 3

Bridgeport to Wild Willy's Hot Springs

115 MILES / 3 HRS + STOPS

From Bridgeport, head south on 395 past Mono Lake to the June Lake Loop, a 16-mile drive along four glistening blue lakes popular for fishing and kayaking. Stop at **Silver Lake Lodge** for their locally famous diner breakfast. With full bellies, head out on a day hike in the Little Lakes Valley (p.81). This alpine trail starts at **Mosquito Flats** and takes you up past a chain of pristine mountain lakes. After a day on your feet, rejuvenate your body with a dip at Wild Willy's Hot Springs (p.77) near Mammoth Lakes.

Day 4

Wild Willy's to Tuolumne Meadows

62 MILES / 1 HR 35 MINS + STOPS

Start the day at **Shea Schat's Bakery** in Mammoth to stock up on chili cheese bread and pastries. Head north on 395 back to Lee Vining and take Highway 120 west to enter Yosemite NP at Tioga Pass. Hike into the Cathedral Range via our favorite overland route to **Budd Lake** (p.59), or take the trail to **Cathedral Lakes**. After a steep hike in, you'll be ready for a cooling dip. Spend the night back in **Tuolumne Meadows** looking up at the stars and the monumental domes surrounding you.

Day 5

Tuolumne Meadows to Yosemite Valley

55 MILES / 1HR 45 MINS + STOPS

Get up early and head to Olmsted Point to watch the sun spill down Tenaya Canyon and illuminate Clouds Rest and Half Dome. Backtrack a mile to **Tenaya Lake** to walk the 2.5-mile loop trail along the shore, or sit on a sandy beach and enjoy this epic location. From there it's a glorious 1.5-hour drive to Yosemite Valley, where you can spend the rest of the day. Rent a bicycle and ride the valley loop, stopping often to take in the ever-changing views. Drop in for a cocktail at the historic Ahwahnee Hotel and spend the night in a tent cabin in Curry Village or camping at nearby Upper, Lower, or North Pines campgrounds.

Day 6

Yosemite Valley to Carlon Falls Trailhead

26 MILES / 55 MINS + STOPS

You could easily spend a week (or a lifetime) in Yosemite, but for this week-long itinerary, you'll have to skim the surface. Stop at El Cap Meadow to scan the rock for tiny climbers on the vast granite canvas above. Take a detour to Tunnel View on Wawona Road to see Yosemite Valley from one of the most photographed vantages in the world. You'll have to loop back into the valley to get to Highway 120. Exit the park from the west gate and head toward Groveland, stopping at **Carlon Falls** (p.55) for your final swim. A one-mile hike into this semi-secret tiered waterfall is the perfect way to end a road trip.

The
BAY AREA

The Bay Area

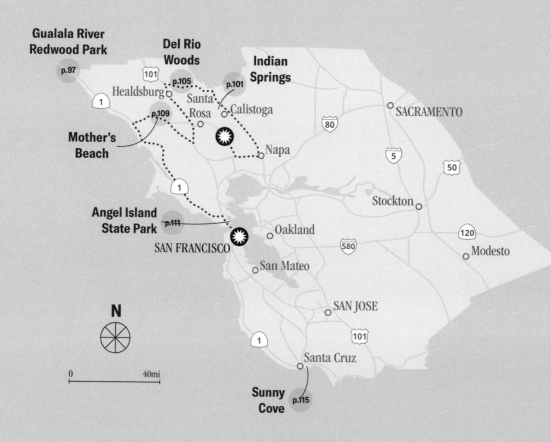

Gualala River
Redwood Park
p.97

Del Rio
Woods
p.105

Indian
Springs
p.101

101

Healdsburg

1

Santa
Rosa

Calistoga

SACRAMENTO

p.109

80

Mother's
Beach

Napa

5

50

Angel Island
State Park
p.111

Stockton

120

SAN FRANCISCO

Oakland

580

Modesto

San Mateo

N

SAN JOSE

101

0   40mi

1

Santa Cruz

Sunny
Cove
p.115

When to visit
April to June and September
to November

Favorite Swim
Gualala River Redwood Park
(p.97)

Favorite Meal
Casa de Mole, Healdsburg
(p.105)

Favorite Drink
Idlewild Wines, Healdsburg
(p.105)

The Bay Area—the rather nebulous term used to describe the region surrounding San Francisco Bay—is a place of big dreamers, the epicenter for everything from counterculture to social justice, environmental justice, and most recently, tech. These identities often overlap and contradict in ways that are intense and complicated, relaxed and beautiful, all at once. So perfectly Californian. Yet, for its infinite complexities, easy access to nature is what makes the Bay Area such a desirable place to live and visit.

For the sake of this book, we define the Bay Area as the part of the state that is within a reasonable day trip or overnighter from San Francisco. From quiet islands in the bay itself (Angel Island, p.111) to idyllic stretches of redwood-lined river (Mother's Beach, p.109), this diverse region extends up the Sonoma coast, inland to famed wineries and thermal springs (Indian Springs, p.101), and south along the moody Pacific to Santa Cruz (Sunny Cove, p.115).

This region features the perfect pairing of nature and culture. No matter how remote a place may feel, you are never far from world-class food and drink. The same range of microclimates and landscapes that make swimming such a joy also fosters some of the best produce in the country. This means that after a low-key day of drifting down a river, you can step straight into a booming culinary scene. There are very few other places in the world where you can travel so well without traveling very far.

Cutest Town

Calistoga
(p.101)

Favorite Bakery

Quail & Condor, Healdsburg
(p.105)

Road Trip

Wine Country
(p.118)

Gualala River Redwood Park

Gualala

Secluded redwood swimming hole with summer-camp vibes

⊙ **ANCESTRAL HOMELANDS**
Kashia Pomo

⊖ **TYPE OF SWIM**
River

✸ **ACTIVITIES**
Swim, hike

⊘ Kid friendly, Dog friendly

◖ **BEST TIME TO VISIT**
August to November

⊘ **OPEN HOURS**
24 hours, but we recommend swimming during daylight.

⑤ **COST OF ENTRY**
Free with nightly camping fee

⊘ **CLOSEST CAMPSITE**
Right here. Campground is open May to September; $74+ per night for a powered site.

⊕ **CLOSEST TOWN OF INTEREST**
Gualala (1 mile)

⊘ **HOW TO GET THERE**
From San Francisco, take Highway 1 north 110 miles to the town of Gualala. Turn right at Old Stage Road, then right again at Gualala Road. Gualala River Redwood Park is one mile from the highway.

⊖ **ACCESS**
Easy from the campground—though camping on-site is a requirement for access.

✳ **LOCAL KNOWLEDGE**
Edible kelp has long been harvested in the coastal regions of Northern California. In Gualala, licensed harvester Donna Murray Bishop gathers nori, kombu, wakame, and sea palm, which are dried and turned into salty snacks and supplemental powders. Donna also runs the Gualala Farmers Market (every Saturday through summer, 9:30am to 12:30pm), where you can find fresh local and organic produce, bread, coffee, pickles, and preserves, along with her seaweed products.

It might be a stretch to include Gualala (pronounced "wa-LAL-la") in this chapter, rather than the Northern California one, but we are feeling expansive. The locals know this area as "Mendonoma," a section of coast straddling Sonoma and Mendocino Counties. It possesses pasturelands that rise above sweeping Pacific Ocean views, quiet redwood state parks, quaint cliffside communities, and very little phone reception or capability to use a credit card—celebrated features, to many.

Just off the highway, a one-mile drive will deliver you into the town's campground, set along the Gualala River. The fern-draped timelessness of a redwood forest takes over as soon as the boom gate swings open. You get the feeling if you fell asleep here and woke up in 400 years, while you might be covered in a layer of soil and moss, things would otherwise be the same. Redwoods create genuine peace. They wrap the world in their soft branchlets like a spongy insulation, their understory never emerging from an eternal twilight.

The Gualala River extends inland from the coast a few miles before it splits into its major tributaries from the north and south. But for us, the Redwood Park campground offers the best swimming. You do need to be staying here to access it, though there are public entry points to the river less than a mile up along Gualala Road.

The property has an uncanny aesthetic, like something straight out of a Wes Anderson film. This is *Moonlight Kingdom* summer camp in all its perfect symmetrical glory. Hand-painted signs, patinaed basketball hoops, a rustic camp kiosk draped in festoon lights, and troupes of kids speeding around on bicycles bring to mind an idealized all-American childhood that we thought only existed in movies.

We pad on trails between campsites, then along the one-way road that weaves among trees up to 15 feet in diameter, and finally to the water's edge. The Gualala River embraces the campground, scouring a deep emerald trough along a smooth pebble beach. It's easy on the feet, and ideal for those who aren't crazy about sand. The water is cool, especially in the morning, before the sun has warmed it. Unlike the nearby ocean, however, the water here is so breathlessly still that it tricks the eyes. From far off, it looks like a shimmering green mirror. Up close, the water is so clear, it's impossible to gauge its depth. Salmon glide past far below the surface, and you can easily count individual stones in the riverbed.

Lost among the redwood trees, Gualala feels like an outlier, setting its own circadian rhythms. Even in the middle of July, we are snuggled around a campfire toasting marshmallows.

NEARBY

GUALALA SEAFOOD SHACK
38820 S Highway 1 #104, Gualala

This casual fish and chip shop offers such goodies as rockfish burritos, prawn sandwiches, line-caught tuna melts, and New England clam chowder, all best eaten with hot fries dipped in an umami seaweed sauce. There's some seating inside and out front, or you can order to-go and dine overlooking the water.

SEA RANCH

Known for its distinct collection of timber-framed houses, Sea Ranch, six miles south of Gualala, was developed in the 1960s by a group of notable American architects as a planned community. It boasts lodging, a dining room, bar and lounge, cafe, general store, clifftop golf course, and nondenominational chapel. A visit is highly recommended.

IZAKAYA GAMA
150 Main St, Point Arena

Twenty minutes north of Gualala in Point Arena is the warm wooden eatery Izakaya Gama, a Japanese-style pub. The rotating menu offers small plates such as seasonal pickles, miso turnips, and karaage, plus skewered meats, asparagus, and trumpet mushrooms cooked on the kushiyaki grill.

"The property has an uncanny aesthetic, like
something straight out of a Wes Anderson film."

California's original restorative
hot spring resort, tucked away in
picturesque Napa Valley

Indian Springs

Calistoga

⊙ **ANCESTRAL HOMELANDS**
Koliholmanok (Wappo) and Miwok

∼ **TYPE OF SWIM**
Thermal pool

✴ **ACTIVITIES**
Swim, massage

⊠ **DRESS CODE**
Bathing suits required

⊘ Kid friendly

⊗ No dogs

☾ **BEST TIME TO VISIT**
September to April (although it's open year round,
we prefer the cooler months).

⊙ **OPEN HOURS**
The pool hours change with the season. They are
typically open from 8:45am until midnight for hotel
guests and 10am to 6pm for day spa guests.

Ⓢ **COST OF ENTRY**
$50 for day spa guests (limited numbers) who book a
50-minute spa service. Free for resort guests.

⟁ **CLOSEST CAMPSITE**
Ritchey Creek Campground (4.4 miles)

⊕ **CLOSEST TOWN OF INTEREST**
Calistoga

⬈ **HOW TO GET THERE**
1712 Lincoln Ave, Calistoga. Calistoga is 75 miles
north of San Francisco.

⊖ **ACCESS**
Easy. For hotel or spa guests only.

✴ **LOCAL KNOWLEDGE**
Many of the cabins around Wrights Lake are available
for rent through the various vacation rental platforms
(AirBnB, VRBO, etc.). One of these houses would be a
great place to base yourself for day hikes in Desolation
Wilderness if you don't want to rough it in a tent.

Can a hot spring resort in California exist without tall palms? For centuries, these lanky trees have marked the land where oases and aquifers occur. In the town of Calistoga, none are more prominent than on the verdant parcel of land that is Indian Springs Resort.

Deep below ground, the Old Faithful Geyser (not that one) supplies mineralized water to Calistoga, a place known for its Cabernet Sauvignon, but also for its geothermal hot springs and mud baths. Here, relaxation and extravagance mix almost quixotically. If you are going to splash out, Indian Springs is the place to do it.

Spread out across 17 acres, the resort includes an eclectic assortment of cottages, bungalows, and Mission Revival–style buildings to accommodate guests, as well as a restaurant, a spa and boutique, and two large, iridescent mineral pools. Four thermal geysers supply a constant stream of water as well as volcanic rock to the property, perfect for mineral baths and muddy spa treatments.

Originally built in 1861 by a gold rush millionaire, Indian Springs is California's oldest geothermal resort. Long celebrated as a bohemian-style retreat, it now feels like the domain of the rich and famous. In the late 1980s new owners made extensive updates to the facilities, installing ponds, olive trees, rose bushes, lavender gardens, and paths to viewpoints over the nearby Palisades ridge, as well as croquet lawns, giant chessboards, and a restaurant (Sam's Social Club). Despite its genteel façade, Indian Springs is comfortably laid back and unglitzy.

The Main Pool, built in 1913 to replace the original 19th-century "plunge," is one of the biggest in California. External stairs take you up to a chalk-colored open-air building. Inside, the pool is graced by lounge chairs, striped umbrellas, and bronzed swimmers floating on buoyant pool mats. It is so spacious that it feels private and peaceful regardless of how many people are present. This is no ordinary hotel pool.

The highly mineralized geyser water escapes from the earth at 230°F. It is then cooled in a series of reservoirs until it is ready for human immersion. Pool temperatures fluctuate with the season, the Main Pool usually around 92–102°F, the smaller, intimate (and quieter) Adults Pool about 10 degrees cooler. Both are pristine.

A recognized American Viticulture Area (AVA), Calistoga lies at the far northern end of the Napa Valley. The historic downtown area brings travelers, wine drinkers, and thermal water devotees from all over the state to its abundance of pools and spas, wine bars and cellars. Calistoga is rich with all of these things, but for restorative indulgence, Indian Springs is unmatched.

NEARBY

Dr. Wilkinson's Backyard Resort and Mineral Springs
1507 Lincoln Ave, Calistoga

This restored old motel, with its original neon signage, offers mineral swimming, a day spa, and mud pools (to guests only), as well as a casual shipping-container cafe, open to the public. Run by the same family since 1952, this is one of Calistoga's original "wellness" resorts, and a fun alternative to Indian Springs.

Calistoga Roastery & Bakery
1426 Lincoln Ave, Calistoga

This local favorite has been operating on the main street of Calistoga since 1992. More rustic than many of the slicker venues along the strip, the Roastery & Bakery is also the only place open before 7am. Enjoy coffee with homemade pastries, bagels, or breakfast sandwiches, or for lunch, quiche and salad.

Calistoga Inn
1250 Lincoln Ave, Calistoga

At this popular restaurant and brewery, live music is featured every evening from May through October in the large outdoor patio overlooking the Napa River. The Napa Valley Brewing Company occupies the property's historic water towers, providing a rotating list of beers on tap. Rooms are available here too.

Del Rio Woods

Russian River, Healdsburg

⊙ **ANCESTRAL HOMELANDS**
Graton Rancheria, Wappo, and Southern Pomo

⊖ **TYPE OF SWIM**
River

⊕ **ACTIVITIES**
Swim, float, paddle

⊘ Kid friendly, Dog friendly

☽ **BEST TIME TO VISIT**
April to July

⊙ **OPEN HOURS**
Sunrise to sunset

⑨ **COST OF ENTRY**
$7 day use parking fee. Free for Sonoma County
Regional Parks members.

⊕ **CLOSEST TOWN OF INTEREST**
Healdsburg (2.6 miles)

↗ **HOW TO GET THERE**
Del Rio Woods Regional Park is located at 2656 S
Fitch Mountain Road, 2.7 miles east of Healdsburg.
Parking is limited (which means a limited number of
people), so get there early and settle in for the day.

⊖ **ACCESS**
Easy. From the parking area, cross the dry floodplain to
reach the river channel. It's never more than a couple
hundred yards away.

✳ **LOCAL KNOWLEDGE**
If you don't have your own tubes, Healdsburg-based
Russian River Adventures and River's Edge Kayak
and Canoe Trips both offer inflatable canoe rental and
shuttle services.

The Russian River is the lifeblood of Sonoma County, nourishing a long, fertile valley filled with organic farms and vineyards. The river is famously mellow as it meanders through oak woodlands around Healdsburg, past vineyards, historic riverside towns, and old-growth redwood groves, ultimately meeting the fog-shrouded Pacific at Jenner. During the summer, when water levels are lower, this entire 50-mile stretch of river is considered Class I—ideal for self-guided, "easy rider" floats.

The river is popular for good reason, and assumes many personalities. Some sections are crowded and rowdy, while others are quiet and relaxed. There are wide-open sunny sections and tree-lined narrow channels. Del Rio Woods is the perfect combination of relaxed and sunny. We love this spot—just above the busiest stretch of river, and with plenty of deep swimming holes and sand bars to enjoy a long, lazy day on the water.

We put in at Del Rio Woods and float 3.5 miles downstream to Healdsburg Veterans Memorial Beach for take-out. You can leave a car at each end or get a rideshare one way. If you don't stop, the float can take an hour, but this is an endurance race, which means taking as long as possible. Some people float coolers behind them. Some glide in sleek kayaks, or lazily spiral in simple tubes. There is no right way or wrong way. The only thing that is not welcome is a portable speaker. Leave that at home.

We bring camp chairs, books, food and drink (no glass containers), and stop frequently. It's a migrating picnic, where each sandy beach or gravel bar is better than the last. We sit under pale green willow trees or sunbathe on warm pebbled beaches. Mostly, though, we relax in waist-deep water, a book in one hand and a beer in the other. Is there a word for this activity? Marinating? Crawdadding? It is so highly refined on the Russian River that it's nearly an art form.

The river flows by rustic cabins, which we carefully examine in our slow drift. They look inviting and comfortable, the kinds of houses that people live in, not gilded weekend rentals. This is more of a Prius region than a Tesla one. You can feel the difference.

The beauty of this trip is that you end up in Healdsburg. It's the relaxed version of wine country, less glitzy than nearby Napa Valley, but still home to a thriving culinary scene. The town is charming and walkable, focused on a historic plaza with food and wine in every direction. Sun-kissed, famished, and lightly perfumed by the day's revelry, we set upon it like starved castaways. There is no better way to end the day.

NEARBY

IDLEWILD WINES
132 Plaza St, Healdsburg

This small wine bar hosts tastings of single varietals from three local vineyards, served alongside light snacks of salumi and Italian cheeses. You can walk in, but it's best to make a reservation. Check out their Ciao Bruto! shop next door for bottles and take-home provisions.

CASA DE MOLE
434 Center St, Healdsburg

A popular food market selling all your Latino kitchen needs—dry goods like masa harina or blue corn tortillas, deli items like jamon and queso, dried chilis, and bottled salsas. And in the cantina out back, you can order plates of tacos with their signature housemade mole. It's like being transported to Oaxaca.

QUAIL & CONDOR
149 Healdsburg Ave, Healdsburg

Croissants, cardamom knots, passionfruit tarts, and chocolate Florentines—if that has your mouth watering, then Quail & Condor is for you. The coffee is very good too, and you can sit outside at tree-shaded picnic tables to savor your treats. These guys are in cahoots with Troubadour Bread & Bistro in town.

Mother's Beach

Russian River, Forestville

The quintessential summer river float featuring tall redwoods and deep swimming holes

ANCESTRAL HOMELANDS
Pomo, Miwok, Graton Rancheria, and Wappo

TYPE OF SWIM
River

ACTIVITIES
Swim, paddle, tube

Kid friendly, Dog friendly

BEST TIME TO VISIT
April to July. Later in the summer, check for algae alerts.

OPEN HOURS
7am to 30 minutes before sunset

CLOSEST CAMPSITE
Bend River Resort, Forestville

CLOSEST TOWN OF INTEREST
Guerneville (5.7 miles)

HOW TO GET THERE
Mother's Beach is about 15 miles northwest of Santa Rosa. Head north on Highway 101 for 6.5 miles and take the River Road exit toward Guerneville. After 9.8 miles, turn onto River Drive. The parking lot is immediately on the right.

ACCESS
Easy. It's 150 yards from the parking area to the beach.

LOCAL KNOWLEDGE
A convenient bus service, the Regional Parks River Shuttle, does a loop from Tom Schopflin Fields in Santa Rosa to Steelhead and Sunset Beaches in Forestville. In summer, it operates on weekends and holidays from 10am to 5pm. Day tickets are $5 per person.

Traveling with kids is equal parts challenging and rewarding. Whenever our guilt over dragging our two-year-old son around on our "work" trip began to negate our enthusiasm, we'd plan to arrive at a place like Mother's Beach on the Russian River—a magnet for swimmers, tubers, paddlers, and families.

Mother's (or Mom's) Beach, as the name suggests, is a wonderful place for families, but it's much more. This is a place for those who like to drift in the gentle current of a shallow, winding channel, discovering private beaches along a scenic, tree-lined river. It is a place where you can birdwatch from kayaks or drift on a tube with your friends, shooting the breeze for hours. In fact, floating down the Russian River has become one of Sonoma County's most popular summer pursuits.

The two-mile stretch from Steelhead Beach to Sunset Beach in Forestville is the best place to tube, and a convenient summer bus service (Regional Parks River Shuttle) delivers floaters and their vessels up and down the river to various drop-off points daily. While the drive is only a few minutes, it can take four hours or more to float the same distance. The water often moves at a crawl (half a mile per hour), which means you can travel faster walking than floating. Plan to arrive early—before 10am—and bring enough provisions for a full day on the water. Summer temperatures can soar above 90°F, even in the shadow of the looming redwoods and Doug firs.

For swimming, we like to wade around Forestville River Access, where a wide sandy beach allows easy entry. Water levels fluctuate dramatically from year to year due to long-term drought, but this spot tends to be reliably wet. We park in one of the designated beach lots in the neighborhood backstreets and walk the short distance to the water. Public life jackets are available at most of the entry points for kids, who play in the shallows with wagonloads of beach toys or chase tadpoles with fishing nets. Giant sturgeons glide past, friendly ducks appear at your side looking for food, and vultures sail overhead.

This section of the Russian River is just over an hour north of San Francisco, yet somehow feels infinitely far away. With its location just outside the coastal fog belt, the climate here is warm and dry. Although the area was once given over to vacation houses, now more than 80 percent of residents live here full-time, following a migration north from the city during Covid. The woodland setting is a soothing balm for locals and visitors alike. You can set up for the day on the pebbled beach and let the scene unfold before you, or wander upstream to a quieter outpost and sit under an umbrella reading a book with your feet in the water.

NEARBY

STUMPTOWN BREWERY
15045 River Rd, Guerneville

A dark-paneled, log cabin–style brewpub, Stumptown is a laid-back place to stop for a bite after a long day on the water. Sit out on the roomy deck overlooking the river for burgers, sandwiches, and craft beer on tap. Try the Rat Bastard IPA, the Donkey Punch Pils, or the Bush Wacker Wheat.

IRON HORSE WINERY
9786 Ross Station Rd, Sebastopol

A charming family-owned winery in a rustic redwood barn. Come for an outdoor tasting and enjoy panoramic views across Sonoma wine country to Mount St. Helena. On Sundays, sparkling wine and oysters are served up. Visits are by appointment only.

CAFE AQUATICA
10439 Highway 1, Jenner

Thirty minutes west of Mother's Beach is the coastal town of Jenner, with its waterfront Cafe Aquatica. Indoor seating is limited, but there's a picturesque deck overlooking the Russian River mouth out back where you can enjoy homemade focaccia and scones and a good cup of coffee.

Angel Island State Park

San Francisco Bay

A bicycle adventure to the beaches and ruins of this historic island

◎ **ANCESTRAL HOMELANDS**
Huimen

⊖ **TYPE OF SWIM**
Bay beach

✪ **ACTIVITIES**
Hike, cycle, swim

⊘ Kid friendly

⊗ No dogs

◖ **BEST TIME TO VISIT**
May to November

◔ **OPEN HOURS**
Day use is 8am to sunset. Campers have 24-hour use of the island and its facilities.

Ⓢ **COST OF ENTRY**
Park entry fee is included in the price of ferry tickets.

⬨ **CLOSEST CAMPSITE**
There are 16 state park campsites on Angel Island that are often reserved up to six months in advance.

⊕ **CLOSEST TOWN OF INTEREST**
Tiburon (15 mins by ferry)

⊘ **HOW TO GET THERE**
Access to Angel Island is by private boat or public ferry. Golden Gate Ferry operates a service from the San Francisco Ferry Terminal (30 mins), while Angel Island Ferry departs from Tiburon (15 mins).

⊖ **ACCESS**
Easy to moderate. Trails and roads are in excellent condition, but there are plenty of steep sections.

✳ **LOCAL KNOWLEDGE**
In the 1950s, the US Army bulldozed the top of Angel Island's Mt. Livermore to create a level launch site for Nike missiles. The missiles were removed in 1962, and in 2002 the top of the mountain was restored, raising the elevation by 16 feet. Crews pushed the original soil back into place and then resculpted the summit to an approximation of its original contours. The concrete launch pads are now used as picnic sites.

Angel Island is the largest natural island in San Francisco Bay, yet it is often overlooked by both locals and visitors. It wasn't on our radar either until we bumped into some friends at the Ferry Plaza Farmers Market and they let us in on the secret. They had loaded a backpack with pastries, cheeses, and fresh produce as they prepared to roll their bikes onto the ferry. A few weeks later we followed suit.

Angel Island strikes a perfect balance of nature and history. Its preservation was not due to incredible urban planning or altruistic foresight, but an accident of varied uses. History here spans at least 3,000 years of Hookooeko Coast Miwok life, followed by Spanish colonization, US military occupation, immigration processing and quarantine, and POW internment. In 1955, California State Parks acquired 38 acres around Ayala Cove, and subsequent expansions brought the entire island under the purview of State Parks by 1962. By then, the island had largely been reclaimed by nature.

There are no cars here. Instead, people explore beaches, Mt. Livermore, and historic ruins on bicycles (8 miles of bike trails) and on foot (13 miles of hiking trails). The passenger ferry deposits you in Ayala Cove, a sheltered sandy bay facing Tiburon. This is where all of the major amenities are located, and it's a good place to grab a map and plan your trip. If you want to see as much as possible, a bicycle is the best option (BYO or rent at Ayala Cove). We stop and start, jumping off to swim, hike, and peer into dilapidated buildings as we circumnavigate the island.

It's a steep climb out of Ayala. Huge, red-barked madrones shade the path until it levels out among drier oaks and shrubs. We like to ride south, directly to Perles Beach. A rough path drops to a narrow patch of sand as the Bay Bridge, SF skyline, Alcatraz, and the Golden Gate materialize out of the swirling fog. It is the best view of the city, yet you will hardly ever share it with another person.

From here we continue counterclockwise. The road climbs past more lookouts and picnic areas before reaching a high saddle. We leave our bikes for a quick side trip up Sunset Trail to the summit of Mt. Livermore (788 feet), before resuming our pedal down to the east side of the island at Fort McDowell. This mostly abandoned garrison features the huge "600-man barracks," officers' quarters that look like Spanish mansions, and the sheltered Quarry Beach. After peering through dusty windows, we head north to China Cove and back around to Ayala.

The whole circuit is about five miles, but you can easily spend an entire day exploring—even longer if you are lucky enough to reserve a campsite. There are so many intriguing nooks on this island that it always leaves you wanting more.

NEARBY

WOODLANDS MARKET
1550 Tiburon Blvd, Tiburon

The gourmet Woodlands Market carries premium organic produce, deli goods, and a hot bar with ready-made food—soups, salad, and rotisserie meats: the perfect place to stock up for a trip to the island. Also in this complex is Rustic Bakery & Cafe, for coffee and pastries pre-ferry.

SAM'S ANCHOR CAFE
27 Main St, Tiburon

After a day out, find a table out on the deck at Sam's Anchor Cafe and get another perspective on the island. Famous for its seafood menu— think fried calamari, steamed mussels, smoked lobsters rolls, and clam linguine—Sam's has been holding down this spot on Tiburon's Main Street since 1920.

SQUALO VINO
34 Main St, Tiburon

Squalo Vino (meaning "wine shark") is across from Sam's on Main Street. This intimate Italian wine bar offers over 90 wines by the bottle (both new- and old-world styles), alongside small bites like charcuterie and cheese, rustic bread and caviar.

Sunny Cove
Santa Cruz

A sheltered neighborhood beach in Santa Cruz's legendary Eastside surf scene

⊙ **ANCESTRAL HOMELANDS**
Popeloutchom (Amah Mutsun) and Awaswas

⊖ **TYPE OF SWIM**
Beach

✳ **ACTIVITIES**
Swim, surf, stroll

⊘ Kid friendly and dog friendly on leash

◐ **BEST TIME TO VISIT**
August to November

◔ **OPEN HOURS**
Sunrise to sunset

⊘ **CLOSEST CAMPSITE**
New Brighton State Beach (4.1 miles)

⊕ **CLOSEST NEIGHBORHOOD OF INTEREST**
Pleasure Point (2 miles)

↗ **HOW TO GET THERE**
The entrance to Sunny Cove is opposite 134 Sunny Cove Dr, Santa Cruz. You can also access the beach from the other side, opposite 295 Geoffroy Dr.

⊖ **ACCESS**
Easy. Park in the nearby streets and walk the short distance down to the beach.

✳ **LOCAL KNOWLEDGE**
Santa Cruz is the birthplace of surfing in mainland America. In 1885, three young Hawaiian princes introduced the sport to California right here at the San Lorenzo River mouth. In 1938, Duke Kahanamoku, the legendary Hawaiian waterman, held a surfing exhibition at Cowell Beach that led to a rapid popularization. In 1953, Santa Cruz local Jack O'Neill pioneered the neoprene wetsuit for surfing.

Santa Cruz has an outsized reputation. Even the name has become a brand. When we were kids, it was the epicenter of Nor-Cal cool and antiheroes. It was surfing and punk rock, skating and vampire bad boys. As we got older, we got to know another side: gentle, thoughtful people; hippies and college students; surf nerds. Some friends of mine shared a house in the neighborhood of Live Oak. They had an outdoor shower and grew vegetables. They surfed twin fins and played Bob Dylan vinyl on repeat. They knew all of the spots, and to this day, whenever we visit them, we always end up at Sunny Cove.

Just walking to the beach is a pleasure. This is a typical Santa Cruz neighborhood with its mix of exuberantly painted bungalows and wood-shingle craftsman cottages. Dense garden beds line the street, lavender and pineapple sage perfuming the air. Everyone around here seems to have a green thumb. We take note of the culinary herbs for later use as we continue toward the hulking Monterey pines that mark the beach entrance.

In a town known for surf, Sunny Cove is one of its rare, protected beaches. Low sandstone bluffs flank the cove, acting to buffer incoming swell. It's not guaranteed to be flat here, but the surf is always smaller than at nearby beaches. Marble green water shimmers in the afternoon sun. On a clear day the cove reminds us of those narrow calas in Majorca. Flat reef extends around the base of the bluff, and people leap into the water below, timing their jump to hit the top of incoming waves. Kids squeal with delight as the water chases them up the beach.

In the fall, the cove lives up to its name, but during summer we've spent many days here waiting for the fog to burn off. It pulses and flows with an eerie sentience, creeping inland overnight to swallow whole neighborhoods, then slowly retreating over the ocean in the afternoon, until, finally, the sun breaks through. Once it clears, you can see all of the way across the bay to the Monterey Peninsula and the mountains further south, looking like a chain of islands on the horizon.

On clear, warm evenings, people gather on the rocky headlands to watch the sunset or stroll along East Cliff Drive to Pleasure Point. Along the path, people ride on rusty beach cruisers, swerving distractedly as they watch knee-high waves roll across the reef. Knots of people chat and laugh as they climb the stairs from the beach. We love this side of Santa Cruz. It's one of those places where it feels like everyone is on vacation.

NEARBY

SANTA CRUZ FLEA MARKET
2260 Soquel Dr, Santa Cruz

Since 1971 the Santa Cruz Flea Market has been a weekend (Sat–Sun) ritual for many. Dealers, collectors, and bargain hunters flock here before 7am to peruse racks filled with preloved clothes, arrays of secondhand furniture, and tables of homemade food goods. It's a lot of fun if you're ready to rummage.

WALK PLEASURE POINT

A walk along Pleasure Point, one of California's most vibrant surf spots, always provides interesting sights. The paved path winds along the clifftop for miles. We suggest starting at Capitola Beach and heading along Opal Cliff Drive, finishing at Point Market on East Cliff Drive where you can grab a burrito.

PRETTY GOOD ADVICE
3070 Porter St, Soquel

From chef Matt McNamara of San Francisco's Michelin-star restaurant Sons & Daughters comes this casual take-out and outdoor dining spot in Soquel, a ten-minute drive from Sunny Cove. The menu—vegetarian, with GF, dairy-free, and vegan possibilities—includes hearty sandwiches, plant-based burgers, warming chili verde soup, and vegan soft-serve.

WINE COUNTRY

SAN FRANCISCO
TO NAPA VALLEY

This relaxed, food-oriented journey takes you from the Bay Area
north along the coast—think redwoods and beaches—then inland
to river swims, local breweries, and outdoor markets. There are
bakeries and eateries, there are wine country towns with more acres
of vineyards than residents, and most importantly, there are hot
springs to soak in.

Day 1

San Francisco to Stinson Beach

26 MILES / 1 HR + STOPS

Take Highway 101 north over the Golden Gate Bridge (it never gets old), then veer down into Sausalito, past the colorful houseboats—more than 400 across five residential marinas. Continue to **Muir Woods National Monument**, a primeval forest of old-growth redwood trees. Spend some time here, hiking the trails to Cathedral and Bohemian Groves along Redwood Creek. Stop for lunch at the Pelican Inn, an English-style pub in Muir Beach serving fish & chips, savory pies, and pints of beer. Continue to **Stinson Beach** for a swim, finishing at Parkside, a cool beachy venue with a coffee bar, bakery, boutique, and casual outdoor bar and restaurant.

Day 2

Stinson Beach to Sebastopol

78 MILES / 1 HR 45 MINS + STOPS

Follow Highway 1 north through Point Reyes, then cross to Highway 116 to reach the Russian River. Today you will undertake one of Sonoma County's favorite summertime pursuits: tubing down the river. Jump in at Steelhead and drift (or kayak) a few miles to **Sunset Beach**, surrounded by redwoods and Doug firs. This could take a few hours, so make sure you have the time. Catch the Regional Parks River Shuttle (summer weekends and holidays only) back to your starting point and drive to Sebastopol for dinner and drinks in the **Barlow District**—an outdoor market featuring locally sourced food, wine, beer, and spirits, and crafts.

Day 3

Sebastopol to Healdsburg

22 MILES / 25 MINS

From Sebastopol it's less than a half hour to Healdsburg—the focus of today's itinerary. It's going to be an eating, drinking, walking, and swimming day, our favorite combination. To kick things off, visit **Quail & Condor Bakery** for flaky pastries and excellent coffee. Continue on foot for a swim at Healdsburg Veterans Memorial Beach, where swimmers and families picnic and splash under the bridge at a busy, patrolled section of the snaking Russian River. When you've had your fill, wander back toward downtown along the old Great Northern train line to Fogbelt, a brewery set up in old cabooses. End your day at the Idlewild tasting rooms, just off Healdsburg Plaza. Or for something more casual, check out the cantina at the back of Mexican supermarket **Casa de Mole**.

Day 4

Healdsburg to Calistoga

24 MILES / 37 MINS

On your way out of town, stop into **Little Saint** for breakfast. This uplifting gathering place is dedicated to good food, wine, and art, and is worth visiting for dinner and live music in the evenings as well. Take Highway 108 through northern Napa wine country to Calistoga. It's a beautiful part of the world, filled with bucolic vistas of vineyards. For the

full (very indulgent!) hot spring experience, stay at Indian Springs (p.101), or try the funky Dr. Wilkinson's Backyard Resort and Mineral Springs. Sample local wine at any number of wine bars in town. For dinner, try Gott's Roadside in St. Helena—American classics with a modern twist—or if you're in the mood for authentic Louisiana barbecue, go to Buster's at the top end of Calistoga, where you'll get live jazz into the bargain.

Day 5

Calistoga to Morton's Warm Springs

38 MILES / 1 HR 5 MINS

Wake up in Napa wine country and you could be forgiven for thinking you are in the south of France. Wining and dining is a way of life here, with farm-to-table restaurants with their own organic kitchen gardens, and indie winemakers popping up among the established old Cabernet kings. From Calistoga, we drive south to the historic town of St. Helena. Start at **Model Bakery** for galettes and coffee. Ten miles further on is Yountville, home to the legendary French Laundry restaurant (bookings essential)—but for something more low-key, seek out the **Tacos Garcia food truck**. Visit local wineries and end the day soaking in Morton's Warm Springs, surrounded by a grassy forest setting.

Gold
COUNTRY

Gold Country

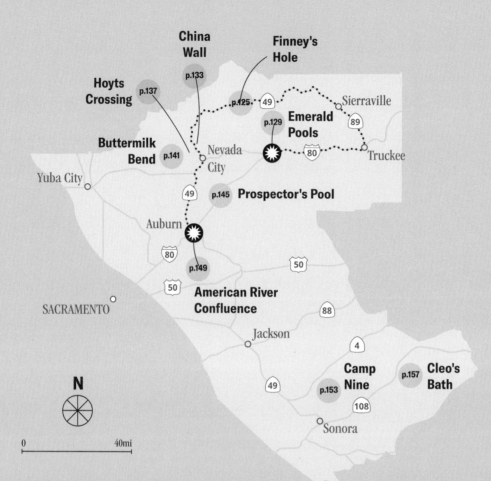

China Wall
p.133

Finney's Hole
p.125

Hoyts Crossing
p.137

Emerald Pools
p.129

Buttermilk Bend
p.141

Nevada City

Sierraville

89

49

80

Truckee

Yuba City

49

p.145 Prospector's Pool

Auburn

80

p.149

50

American River Confluence

SACRAMENTO

Jackson

50

88

4

Camp Nine
p.153

Cleo's Bath
p.157

49

108

Sonora

N

0   40mi

When to visit

June to October,
depending on the snowpack

Favorite Swim

Purdon's Crossing
(p.133)

Best Hike

South Yuba River Trail
(p.133)

Favorite Meal

**Three Forks Bakery and Brewery,
Nevada City (p.137)**

Over two-thirds of California's freshwater comes from the Sierra Nevada, most of it pouring down the range's gentle western slope to the Central Valley in rivers and streams. This water is arguably the state's greatest form of wealth, and it is therefore perhaps fitting that the discovery of gold on the South Fork of the American River in 1848 radically transformed its fate. The big story of the gold rush is the devastating and innumerable atrocities against the Indigenous Peoples of California. That cannot be overstated. Gold triggered the second-largest mass migration in US history as over 300,000 people poured in from around the world. Statehood came. Fortunes came (for some). Cities were built virtually overnight. For a brief moment, this narrow corridor in the Sierra foothills was the wealthiest place in the world.

When the boom ended, most of the people moved on, leaving behind many dozens of mining outposts with sprawling main streets, inviting clapboard saloons, and ornate Victorian homes. Those towns and the nearby wilderness are what make this area so extraordinary to visit. Downieville (p.125) has been revitalized as a mountain biking and swimming mecca. Near Nevada City, the shimmering South Fork of the Yuba River contains some of California's most stunning swimming holes, from Emerald Pools (p.129) near the Sierra crest all the way down to Buttermilk Bend (p.141) on the edge of the Sacramento Valley.

Oak-lined Highway 49 is the connective tissue of this region, rolling through golden grasslands to link sleepy former boomtowns along a trail of endless historic markers. At Auburn, it crosses the American River Confluence (p.149). Further south, the road is flanked by old apple orchards and vineyards. Scenic byways split off to wind up and over the Sierra, passing some of our favorite off-the-beaten-path swimming holes, such as Cleo's Bath (p.157) and Camp Nine (p.153). Everywhere you look, communities are slowly being rediscovered and reimagined, now celebrating the nature that they once exploited. This small, dense region continues to surprise us with its natural beauty and complicated legacy.

Best Saloon

**Golden Gate Saloon in
Holbrooke Hotel
(p.123, p.133)**

Cutest Town

**Downieville
(p.125)**

Road Trip

**Boomtown Legacy
(p.158)**

Finney's Hole

Downieville

◎ **ANCESTRAL HOMELANDS**
Nisenan and Wá-šiw (Washoe)

⌣ **TYPE OF SWIM**
River

✳ **ACTIVITIES**
Swim, hike, mountain bike, paddle, fish

⊘ Kid friendly, Dog friendly

◐ **BEST TIME TO VISIT**
June to October

⃤ **CLOSEST CAMPSITE**
Union Flat (5.8 miles)

⊕ **CLOSEST TOWN OF INTEREST**
Downieville

⬀ **HOW TO GET THERE**
About one hour north of Nevada City on Highway 49

⊖ **ACCESS**
Easy. Finney's Hole is at the exact center of town, under the green bridge.

✳ **LOCAL KNOWLEDGE**
According to (unsubstantiated) lore, the largest nugget of gold ever found in the United States was discovered by G. G. Finney in 1853 near Downieville. It weighed 5,009 ounces—313 pounds—and was valued at $84,302, or the equivalent of $3,278,731 in today's dollars. Today, the same amount of gold would be worth $9,730,450.

Downieville is a remote former boomtown located at the confluence of the Downie River and the North Fork of the Yuba River. Gold was discovered here in the summer of 1849, and by the mid-1850s it was California's fifth-largest town, with 15 hotels and gambling houses, four bakeries, four butcher shops, and who knows how many brothels. Although the population peaked some 170 years ago, Downieville has made the transition from nostalgic mining outpost to vibrant outdoor adventure destination. The source of this new fortune, not surprisingly, is the surrounding rivers and mountains.

Every July, the population of some 325 permanent residents swells to thousands for the Downieville Classic, an annual mountain bike race and festival. Activity revolves around the town center and rivers' confluence, where the clear blue-green water mixes to form a deep pool known as Finney's Hole. People lie on the sandy beach, swim, and lazily float in garish inflatable tubes. The weekend's festivities culminate with the Big Air River Jump, with bike riders launching off a ramp into the river as onlookers pack the banks and bridge to cheer them on.

The rest of the summer, things are more peaceful, and we spend the days wandering the river. About a half mile down from Finney's, at the end of River Street, the North Yuba swirls into a calm pool known as Willoughby's. Rainbow and brown trout will often outnumber people here, as they all bask in the refreshingly cold, clear water. There are a couple of low rocks to jump from, but if you are chasing a bigger thrill, the best jump rock is a further half mile downstream.

Be mindful of private property as you navigate the riverside trail. After a series of small rapids, the water runs directly into a huge rock outcrop. The top of the rock is polished by generations of foot traffic. Underneath it, the river carves out a wide, deep pool. If there were teenagers in town, you would find them leaping from these rocks. As it is, the youngest and boldest locals are likely the motley crew of volunteer firefighters we meet here one warm summer morning. They look like surfers with wetsuit tans: brown faces, necks, and hands, milky skin everywhere else.

When we see them back in town, we hardly recognize one another. That's the funny thing about meeting people when you are nearly naked. Downtown is already busy with visitors, and we blend in with the groups of mountain bikers, kayakers, hikers, and fly fishermen who stroll the wooden boardwalks. The narrow, tree-lined streets are faithfully preserved, yet the colorful historic buildings still have grit. We can't get enough of it.

NEARBY

LA COCINA DEL ORO TAQUERIA
322 Main St, Downieville

This beloved eatery is known by locals as "Feather's Place," after the owner and long-time Downieville resident Feather Ortiz. The menu features wholesome Mexican dishes with a focus on locally sourced, organic produce. Sit on the patio out back overlooking the river with a giant margarita.

SABRINA'S AT THE FORKS
308 Main St, Downieville

A casual breakfast spot, deli, coffee shop, and, later in the day, bar, Sabrina's is connected to the Downieville Outfitters bike shop, so is the default local meeting point in town. Enjoy homemade scones, readymade burritos from a hot cabinet on the counter, or sandwiches from midday on. Beer is also available on tap.

BOOMTOWN LOUNGE
200 Main St # B, Downieville

An intimate Old West–style speakeasy run by four friends in the historic Downieville downtown. Decked out with vintage furniture, and a courtyard with firepit out back for live gigs, Boomtown serves wines from Nevada City Winery, beer from local breweries, and Sabe cocktails. Warm up here after a cold river plunge.

Emerald Pools

Yuba River South Fork

⊙ **ANCESTRAL HOMELANDS**
Nisenan and Wá-šiw (Washoe)

⊖ **TYPE OF SWIM**
River and gorge

✳ **ACTIVITIES**
Swim, cliff jump

⊘ Kid friendly, yes at upper pools, no in lower gorge.
Dog friendly

◖ **BEST TIME TO VISIT**
July to September

⊗ **CLOSEST CAMPSITE**
Lake Spaulding Campground (4 miles)

⊕ **CLOSEST TOWN OF INTEREST**
Truckee (30 miles)

⊘ **HOW TO GET THERE**
Turn off I-80 onto Highway 20 at Yuba Pass. Drive
southwest for 3.7 miles, then turn right onto Bowman
Lake Road and continue for 1.5 miles until you cross
the Yuba River. Parking and trailhead are immediately
after the bridge on the right-hand side.

⊖ **ACCESS**
Easy to upper pool—flat, shaded, half-mile walk in
from the parking area. Challenging to lower pool—
scramble down the rock slabs to the river and gorge
below.

✳ **LOCAL KNOWLEDGE**
Bowman Lake Road provides access to a little-visited
part of Tahoe National Forest. It's a great place to
escape the usual summer crowds. Beyond Emerald
Pools, there are abundant off-the-beaten-path lakes
and campgrounds.

Emerald Pools are a series of swimming holes that perfectly capture
two distinct moods of the South Yuba River. The upper pool is
a calm, supersized swimming hole with dazzlingly clear water. The
lower pool is a cliff-jumping hot spot at the base of a narrow gorge.
Both are perfect in their own way.

Most people gravitate toward the upper pool. From the bridge on
Bowman Lake Road, it's an easy short walk upstream along a well-
traveled path. The forested trail ends abruptly at a deep, bowl-like
pool of sparkling green water. Rock slabs form a natural dam at the
bottom, ensuring that the pool remains full even in late summer when
there is very little flow.

Unlike the white-gray granite that we associate with the Sierra
and lower sections of the Yuba River, this pool is surrounded by
colorful metamorphic rock, with bright vertical bands of red, orange,
yellow, white, and gray. Water feeds in through a tiny slot canyon,
and people slosh through the shallow turquoise water examining the
swirling variegated stone.

The upper pool can get busy, especially on weekends. You can walk
upriver to find smaller tubs and more privacy or go downriver to the
impressive lower pool and gorge.

To reach the lower pool, go back out to Bowman Lake Road and
look for a well-defined use-trail about 200 yards west of the bridge
on the left-hand side of the road. (It's marked by memorials to people
who have died cliff jumping—a sobering message to all would-be-
visitors. Be careful.) Follow the trail down until you are walking
on open slabs, then veer right to find the gentlest slope to the river
below. It shouldn't ever feel too exposed. Once at the river, continue
downstream to the top of the gorge. You can't miss the 25-foot
waterfall with its huge pool.

The gorge is a stunning natural amphitheater, and there is a
performative quality to the way young men throw themselves into the
water. It's both beautiful and terrifying—a case study for the impacts
of testosterone on risk assessment. Morbid fascination compels us
to watch, yet it is hard not to shake the uneasy feeling of complicity.
We don't endorse jumping from great heights. There are a lot of other
ways to enjoy this beautiful place.

Our preferred mode is to climb down to the bottom of the pool
and swim up the gorge. We lounge on the sunny rocks and look up
at the crisp blue sky. The mist from the waterfall somehow activates
the hot dry air, allowing the sweet, resinous smell of ponderosa pines
and juniper to cascade over us in waves. It's the smell of the Sierra
foothills. It's the smell of the Yuba River. It's the smell of summer.

NEARBY

ALIBI ALE HOUSE
10069 Bridge St, Truckee

At this local ale house beers are brewed with
Lake Tahoe water, and sometimes with wild
yeast from local beehives or fresh juniper. The
offering rotates regularly, alongside cider, nitro
coffee, and kombucha. Sit at the big communal
table inside, or in the large outdoor beer garden
with its live music.

LITTLE TRUCKEE ICE CREAMERY
15628 Donner Pass Rd, Truckee

There's always a line out the door at Little
Truckee Ice Creamery. People queue for
delicious, house-made flavors crafted from
natural ingredients, such as the three-berry
cobbler, the ginger cookie cheesecake, or the
signature Truckee Trails—sweet cream with
pine-nut brittle and brownie.

DONNER PASS TRAIN TUNNELS

As you drive up I-80, stop to wander through
the historic Donner Pass Train Tunnels. This
two-mile stretch was the first railroad line to
traverse the Sierra Nevada range. The tunnel,
which closed to trains in 1993, now serves as a
makeshift gallery for graffiti artists. At night,
bring a flashlight or headlamp for best viewing.

"The mist from the waterfall somehow activates the hot dry air, allowing the sweet, resinous smell of ponderosa pines and juniper to cascade over us in waves."

Flawless pools, a river beach,
and a crumbling dam that looks
like a Salvador Dalí painting

⊙ **ANCESTRAL HOMELANDS**
Nisenan

⌣ **TYPE OF SWIM**
River

⋈ **DRESS CODE**
Nudity is common at China Dam

✦ **ACTIVITIES**
Swim, hike, fish

✓ Kid friendly, Dog friendly

◖ **BEST TIME TO VISIT**
June to September

① **OPEN HOURS**
6am to 10pm

⊘ **CLOSEST CAMPSITE**
Inn Town Campground, Nevada City (8.5 miles)

⊕ **CLOSEST TOWN OF INTEREST**
Nevada City (6.9 miles)

⊘ **HOW TO GET THERE**
From Highway 49 in Nevada City, take East
Bloomfield–Graniteville Road north for half a mile.
At a fork, veer left onto Lake Vera Purdon Road. After
2.6 miles, follow Purdon Road, continuing for 3 more
miles as it becomes a gravel road and winds down the
canyon to the bridge and trailhead. (Google Maps will
be your friend here.)

⊖ **ACCESS**
Easy. From the bridge at Purdon Crossing, it's a short,
mostly level walk to the swimming holes along this
section of the river.

✳ **LOCAL KNOWLEDGE**
The stretch of the South Yuba River between Purdon
Crossing and Edwards Crossing is generally accepted
to be clothing-optional.

Purdon Crossing
to China Wall

Yuba River South Fork

We could write a whole book on the Yuba River and its various
forks. The South Fork has miles of smooth granite boulders and
emerald water. It's just a matter of how far you want to go to find
your perfect swimming hole. For us, Purdon Crossing strikes the right
balance: it's far from any main road, so the trailhead is reliably quiet,
but you don't have to walk far to have a pool all to yourself.

Only about 20 minutes north of Nevada City, the historic steel
bridge at Purdon Crossing feels like the middle of nowhere. Built in
1895, it was once a vital link along the main road from Nevada City
to Downieville and the Northern Mines. While the river was once an
obstacle, it's now the main attraction.

Park along Purdon Road on the south side of the river or turn
right just before the bridge to reach the South Yuba Trail parking
area, about 200 yards up the access road. The trail hugs the bank of
the South Yuba River as it winds upstream under a dense canopy of
oak trees. Lush ferns, pipevines, blackberries, and poison oak round
out the quintessential Gold Country forest floor. (Growing up in this
environment you learn to identify the last two at a young age.)

After about a quarter of a mile, a use-trail drops down to Mother's
Beach. It's a wide, slow-moving section of river with a gentle, sandy
entrance. Because it is so accessible, this is typically the busiest
swimming area along the trail. The deep, cool water is irresistible. Just
above the main pool, small cascades create a series of personal spa
baths. You could happily spend the entire day here.

But we like to go further upstream.

Staying on the main path, continue until you're about one mile
from the trailhead. Look for an old wooden fence marking the turnoff
down to China Dam and a use-trail leading to a series of large, deep
pools flanked by high rock outcrops. The polished granite shines like
ivory in the sunshine, and everywhere that water touches is smoothed
into rounded, organic forms. Rocks appear to melt and flow as if in a
Salvador Dalí painting. Even the dam wall, once a mining diversion
dam, is so softened by the passage of time that it looks more like the
work of elves than of humans.

The water is an alluring peacock green, and we immediately
strip off our clothes and leap from the rocks. There are plenty more
pools upstream, but our willpower only carries us so far on a hot day.
We laugh with giddy joy as a slight current carries us downstream.
Swimming holes like this are the epitome of summer. They fill us with
goofy energy and remind us of the importance of play. After a visit we
are both exhausted and completely refreshed. That's the power of the
South Fork of the Yuba River.

NEARBY

SOUTH YUBA RIVER TRAIL

This moderately challenging 20-mile hiking
trail runs from Poorman Crossing to Purdon
Crossing along a segment of the Yuba River's
South Fork. A popular trail for hiking,
backpacking, and camping, the trail is open
year round, but (as always) check the weather
before setting out. Dogs are allowed on leash.

GOLDEN GATE SALOON
212 W Main St, Grass Valley

Saloon bars go hand in hand with the Gold
Country, as you imagine thirsty prospectors
downing shots of whiskey back in the day.
Nowadays things are a little more polished. The
food menu is contemporary—California with a
dash of Mexico—sourcing produce from local
farms. There are also hotel rooms upstairs.

EMPIRE MINE HISTORIC PARK
10791 East Empire St, Grass Valley

The Empire Mine was one of the oldest,
deepest, and richest mines in the state. It
operated for over 100 years, uncovering 5.8
million ounces of gold before closing in 1956.
Some of the mine's buildings and abandoned
shafts remain. The 856 acres of backcountry
forest also includes 14 miles of trails for hiking,
horse riding, and biking.

Deep clear pools under a historic highway bridge, and a famous nude swimming spot upstream

Highway 49 Crossing to Hoyts Crossing

Yuba River South Fork

◎ **ANCESTRAL HOMELANDS**
Nisenan

◎ **TYPE OF SWIM**
River

◎ **DRESS CODE**
Nudity is common at Hoyts Crossing

◎ **ACTIVITIES**
Hike, swim

◎ Kid friendly, Dog friendly on leash

◎ **BEST TIME TO VISIT**
June to September

◎ **OPEN HOURS**
Sunrise to sunset. No parking from 10pm to 6am

◎ **CLOSEST CAMPSITE**
Inn Town Campground, Nevada City (8.9 miles)

◎ **CLOSEST TOWN OF INTEREST**
Nevada City (7 miles)

◎ **HOW TO GET THERE**
From Nevada City take Highway 49 north for seven miles to the South Yuba River Crossing. A parking lot is on the right-hand side of the road before the bridge.

◎ **ACCESS**
There are pools directly under the bridge, accessed from the parking lot side by stairs leading down to the river. Upstream, the Hoyts Crossing pool and Lemke's Lagoon require a 1.2-mile walk up a gently sloped, shaded trail on the north side of the river. Cross the pedestrian bridge to reach the trailhead.

◎ **LOCAL KNOWLEDGE**
This section of the Yuba River is more treacherous than other parts in the spring/runoff season. Avoid swimming during this time. You may see experienced kayakers tackling the rapids here.

The first time we visited Grass Valley was to see Devendra Banhart play at the Center for the Arts. We spent a couple of days in the area, swimming under the bridge on Highway 49 and strolling laps through Nevada City's streets. For those who remember the psychedelic-folk era of the early 2000s—including Joanna Newsom (a Nevada City local), Neutral Milk Hotel, and Animal Collective—that music always feels like the perfect soundtrack for this part of California. These twin gold rush towns of Grass Valley and Nevada City have long had an allure for musicians and artists, offering the perfect balance of nature and culture. The streets are lined with hotels, bars, theaters, and saloons oozing historic charm, dulcet tunes, and good times.

Since that first visit, we've often used these towns as a springboard to explore the nearby swimming holes. As with our music selection, there is a constant tension between discovering something new and returning to our favorites. The stop at Highway 49 is definitely part of the greatest hits collection. Just seven miles northwest of Nevada City, the old highway bridge forms a graceful concrete arch 120 feet above a large, inviting pool.

Framed by pale granite boulders, the water is a brilliant green, and despite its depth, you can see right to the bottom. Swimmers sit in the shallows or scramble up onto huge rocks. There's plenty of space here for all, and seen from the bridge above, the colorful towels, umbrellas, and inflatable rings create a sumptuous summer scene. If you never ventured further upstream, you'd be perfectly satisfied.

But if you're like us, possessing a healthy FOMO about what may be around the corner, then we recommend heading just over a mile upriver to Hoyts Crossing. The shaded trail begins on the north side of the bridge. Small paths regularly splinter off to provide access to swimming spots all along the river below. Take your pick. When you reach a sign stating "no glass, no alcohol, no camping" and a free life jacket stand, you know you're close. Hoyts is a big open pool with a pebble beach surrounded by giant rocks, butterflies, willow trees, and unclad sunbakers. It's Nevada City's unofficial nudist beach.

Spend a day dipping in and out of this swimming hole and enjoying its shaded banks. Just beyond Hoyts is Lemke's Lagoon, which looks like an Olympic pool was plonked into a huge granite bowl. Naturists do long laps of breaststroke, then slide onto submerged slabs to chat in the sun. It's at this point that the nagging feeling to go further finally subsides. Every trip here reinforces our opinion that the Yuba River has some of the best swimming holes in California.

NEARBY

THREE FORKS BAKERY & BREWERY CO.
211 Commercial St, Nevada City

This cool all-day cafe is the perfect post-swim spot. House-brewed beer is served from giant barrels that sit above the bar, including Mother's Beach Blonde Lager, Purdon Porter, and Emerald Pool IPA (all named after local swim spots). The menu changes weekly based on what is in season and available locally.

KITKITDIZZI
231 Broad St, Nevada City

Kitkitdizzi is the Miwok word for bear clover or mountain misery, a fragrant endemic of the western Sierra Nevada. It is also the name of an eclectic shop, a colorful and uplifting space selling ethically sourced artisan and designer clothing, jewelry, art, and decorative objects, including handmade ceramics.

SUSHI IN THE RAW
135 Argall Way, Nevada City

For 20 years Kaoru "Ryu" Suzuki and his wife, Susan, ran this traditional Japanese restaurant in downtown Nevada City. In 2022, the local organic market California Organics took over the business, relocating the restaurant but staying true to its original ethos—using only the freshest ingredients for their made-to-order sushi rolls.

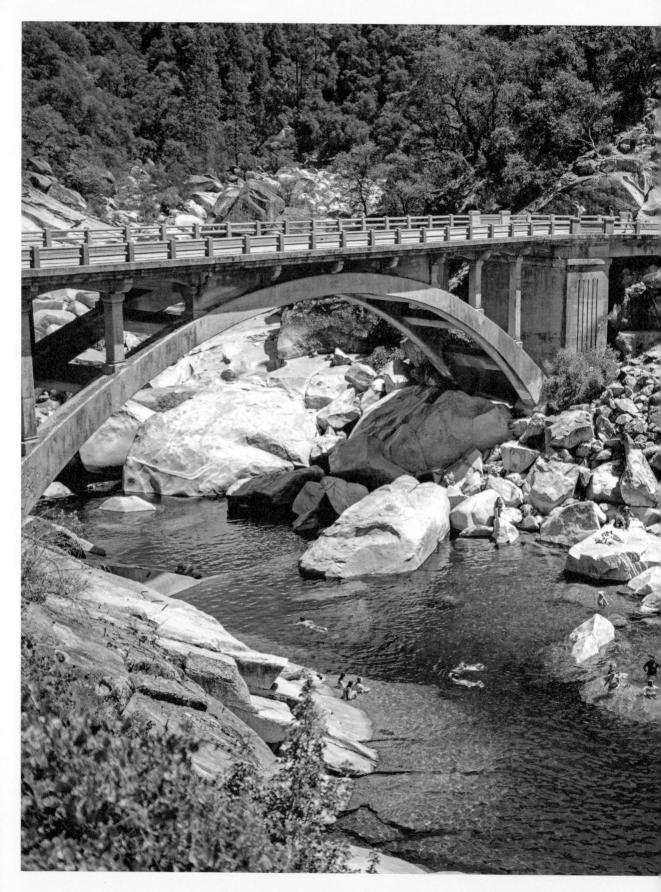

Buttermilk Bend

South Yuba River State Park

Sandy beaches and deep pools
on voluptuous riverbends

ANCESTRAL HOMELANDS
Nisenan

TYPE OF SWIM
River

ACTIVITIES
Hike, swim

Kid friendly, Dog friendly on leash

BEST TIME TO VISIT
June to September for swimming. March, April, May
for wildflowers. Always check water conditions.

OPEN HOURS
Sunrise to sunset

CLOSEST CAMPSITE
Windsong Ridge Village Campsite (2.6 miles)

CLOSEST TOWN OF INTEREST
Grass Valley (18 miles)

HOW TO GET THERE
From Nevada City, take Highway 49 west for 2.4
miles. Turn left onto Newtown Road and continue 3.9
miles until you reach a T-junction at Bitney Springs
Road. Turn right and drive 5.5 miles to Pleasant Valley
Road. Turn right and continue for 2.5 miles until you
reach Bridgeport. The parking lot and Buttermilk Bend
Trailhead are on the north side of the bridge.

ACCESS
Easy. It's a level 1.2-mile hike upstream along
the Buttermilk Bend Trail. You have to do some
scrambling down to the river, but it is pretty friendly.

LOCAL KNOWLEDGE
Wildflowers explode along the trail of Buttermilk
Bend in the spring, from March through mid-May. It's
an ever-changing feast of color, with golden poppies,
purple lupine and larkspur, white daisies, yellow
western buttercup, and pink shooting stars.

The mighty Yuba River winds through Gold Country leaving a trail of wet footprints. All along its course, it's a California classic and a swimmers' dream, which is why we feature it so many times in this book (see also Highway 49 Crossing to Hoyts Crossing [p.137] and Purdon Crossing [p.133]). Every location we encounter is an entirely different scene, but always linked by the river's ethereal emerald water. In the case of Buttermilk Bend, proximity to the Sacramento Valley and Yuba City also makes it one of the most easily accessible swims in the area.

Located in the rugged canyon of the South Fork, the swimming hole is named after the frothy cascades that resemble buttermilk. Giant polished boulders and green waterways flow through this region, creating deep pools for jumping, shallow pools for kids, rock slabs for sunbathing, and pebbly inland beaches that rival the best on the coast. What's not to love?

We start our day exploring the historic covered bridge in Bridgeport—the longest remaining single-span burr-arch truss bridge in the country. Setting aside the descriptive contortions that arrive at its uniqueness, it's a beautifully restored bridge and is well worth a walk-through. Plenty of people swim in the river underneath, but we like to go further upstream to get away from the crowds.

The 1.2-mile Buttermilk Bend Trail starts just up the road at the north parking lot and, hugging the high bluffs overlooking the water, follows the river's course into the foothills. In summer, the brilliant wildflowers of spring have long gone, but there's a new kaleidoscopic focus of dry shrubs, sunburnt grass, and orange leaves. Below, deep pools fringed with sandy coves tempt you down at every bend via steep, unmarked tracks.

In summer too, it's already hot by 8am, and the sky is cloudless. With little shade on the trail, we cover up in light clothes and wear shoes that can traverse both land and water. We're not the first to be enjoying the fine morning—people scramble with their dogs upstream, while others fish from rocks for rainbow trout and Chinook salmon. On prime curves along the riverbank, big groups set up colorful sunshades and lay out mouthwatering feasts of salads, barbecued meats, homemade tortillas, and cold drinks.

The gentle current and shallow entries at Buttermilk Bend make it a safe swimming destination for all abilities. Or you can just relax in small rapids, not moving but totally enjoying the refreshing water. It's a place to spend long summer days, hiking, swimming, and exploring the natural surroundings. It is, all things considered, pretty near perfect.

NEARBY

OUTDOOR YOGA—YUBA RETREAT
outdoor-yoga.org

Outdoor Yoga, a Bay Area community of yoga teachers, runs immersive retreats in various outdoor locations, from SF as far as the Yuba River and even Mexico. The Yuba Retreat is a soulful summer camp for women across three days, and includes plant-based meals and accommodation for two nights, as well as river swims and hikes.

MEZE
106 Mill St, Grass Valley

Alon Greenstein grew up in Israel, and when he moved to Grass Valley, he missed the simple, daily flavors of the Middle East— cumin, paprika, hummus, falafel, shawarma, and fresh pitas. So he and his wife, Tal, opened Meze, a casual restaurant serving fresh, flavorful Israeli dishes. They call it "high vibe food."

PANOY BISTRO
442 Colfax Ave, Grass Valley

This unexpected Laotian restaurant is the perfect place to refuel after a day on the Yuba. A mother-daughter team runs this authentic, low-key eatery on the outskirts of Grass Valley. Punchy plates of larb, big bowls of pho, and spicy khao poon noodles transport you to Southeast Asia, a Beerlao in hand.

Discover the Mother Lode of swimming
along this wild and scenic river

Prospector's Pool

Mineral Bar, Auburn State Recreation Area

◎ **ANCESTRAL HOMELANDS**
Nisenan

〜 **TYPE OF SWIM**
River

✺ **ACTIVITIES**
Swim, paddle, hike, fish, pan for gold

✓ Kid friendly, Dog friendly

◖ **BEST TIME TO VISIT**
June to September (depending on snowpack)

◷ **OPEN HOURS**
Day use area is open during daylight hours.

⑤ **COST OF ENTRY**
$10 day use parking fee, or free entry with a valid State
Parks Pass

⊘ **CLOSEST CAMPSITE**
Mineral Bar Campgrounds, located at trailhead

⊕ **CLOSEST TOWN OF INTEREST**
Colfax (3.9 miles)

↗ **HOW TO GET THERE**
From downtown Colfax, take S Auburn Street 0.3
miles to Highway 174. Turn left and cross the I-80
overpass, then turn right on Canyon Way and drive
south for 0.3 miles to reach Iowa Hill Road. Turn left
and follow Iowa Hill Road 3 miles, as it winds down to
the river and Mineral Bar Campgrounds.

⊖ **ACCESS**
Moderate. There are no trails north of Mineral Bar
Campgrounds, so you have to walk in the river
and along the banks to reach the pool, a mile-plus
upstream.

✳ **LOCAL KNOWLEDGE**
Unlike the South and Middle Forks of the American
River, which had tens of thousands of miners, only
about 2,000 prospectors inhabited the North Fork
during the gold rush. Eventually, the river's difficult
access and sparse gold return drove most on to more
profitable locations.

The bright, clear water of the North Fork of the American River
originates in the Sierra Nevada northwest of Lake Tahoe. From
there, the river carves through miles of rugged and remote wilderness,
scouring a deep canyon in its journey to the Sacramento Valley. Rock
walls rise more than 2,000 feet above the river for much of its length,
creating an impenetrable sanctuary that is one of the great refugia
for wildlife in the northern Sierra. Although the wild landscape has
resisted roads and development for centuries, there are a couple of
access points to the river along its length. For swimming and hiking,
Mineral Bar is our favorite.

The short, windy road down from Colfax descends over 1,200
feet to the river valley at Mineral Bar parking area. This is a popular
put-in/take-out spot for rafts during the spring and early summer,
marked by the old Colfax–Iowa Hill Bridge, a wire suspension
bridge built in 1923. By July, the water levels are typically too low for
whitewater rafting, and the calm water under the bridge becomes a
swimming hole known as the Bubble Bath, great for families with
young kids.

No matter how idyllic a roadside swimming hole may be, though,
we always feel compelled to hike upriver in search of privacy and
adventure. Indeed, this stretch of the North Fork of the American
is some of the friendliest river hiking around. We actually enjoy
trudging knee or waist deep in the water or directly on the banks,
crossing frequently to avoid obstacles. At almost every bend, the river
has scoured deep swimming holes, which we obligingly plunge into
before continuing upstream. It's easier than negotiating the dense
thickets of chaparral and scrub oaks that cover surrounding hillsides.

About 1.25 miles upriver, we reach our favorite swimming hole.
Here, wide slabs of greenstone on both sides channel the river into
a deep, still pool. We call it Prospector's Pool. Enormous trout lurk
in the shadows and flecks of sand (or is it gold?) glint in the sun. We
dive in and swim to the bottom. Alas, no gold, but the water is at least
20 feet deep, ideal for leaping from the surrounding rocks.

On the way back we like to chat with prospectors. They work with
an obsessive frenzy, but by the end of the day they are slowing down.
For some, sifting for gold, is a weekend hobby. For others, it's an act of
penance or solace. Some laugh and joke, while others tell us how they
are working through grief or regrets, processing thoughts one shovel
load at a time. It's hard work, and most of these prospectors won't sell
any of the gold they find. That's not the point. It's about getting lost
in a simple activity, alone with your thoughts in a beautiful place. We
won't be panning anytime soon, but we certainly recognize that same
desire within ourselves.

NEARBY
COLFAX

Colfax is a quaint one-strip town of historic
buildings with hand-painted signage and
convenient food options—a pizzeria, a taqueria,
and casual all-day cafes. Our preference,
though, is to head south on I-80 to Auburn,
where a gamut of delicious options await.
(See the Nearby section for American River
Confluence, p.149.)

THE BAKER AND THE CAKE MAKER
1102 Lincoln Way, Auburn

This artisanal bakery and cafe makes
handcrafted bread and pastries using organic
flours and top-quality seeds, grains, and nuts.
Think ciabatta and campagnes, baguettes
and levains. They also serve buttery pastries,
decadent iced cakes, and fresh fruit tarts.

HIGH-HAND NURSERY AND CAFE
3750 Taylor Rd, Loomis

This outdoor cafe doubles as a nursery selling
trees, shrubs, and garden requisites. As you sip
a drink, visit the historic fruit shed, the on-site
art gallery, and taste their house-made olive
oil. A recent addition is High-Hand Brewing
Company, with 12 beers on tap, plus signature
cocktails such as the PB&J Old Fashioned.

"No matter how idyllic a roadside
swimming hole may be, we always
feel compelled to hike upriver
in search of privacy and adventure."

American River Confluence
Auburn State Recreation Area

Big river energy where two beautiful rivers join to become one

ANCESTRAL HOMELANDS
Nisenan

TYPE OF SWIM
River

ACTIVITIES
Swim, hike, paddle, fish, mountain bike, pan for gold

Kid friendly, Dog friendly

BEST TIME TO VISIT
June to October, depending on water levels

OPEN HOURS
7am to sunset

COST OF ENTRY
$10 day use parking fee in the State Recreation Area

CLOSEST CAMPSITE
Ruck-A-Chucky Bar Campground (10 miles)

CLOSEST TOWN OF INTEREST
Auburn (3 miles)

HOW TO GET THERE
From Auburn, take High Street northeast, veering right as it becomes Highway 49. The road descends about 2.5 miles to the bottom of the gorge at the American River Confluence. There is paid parking on the north side of the river along Old Foresthill Road.

ACCESS
Easy. Cross the green bridge on Highway 49 to the south side of the river. You'll find a locked gate and trailhead immediately to the right. It's a short walk along the riverside trail to cross the arched "No Hands Bridge" and then scramble down the use-trails to the riverside beaches below.

LOCAL KNOWLEDGE
Water is released every morning at about 9am from the Oxbow Reservoir, reaching the confluence after a few hours. Be aware that water levels can change rapidly, and don't be alarmed if the river starts rising around lunchtime. We stick to areas that have access from both sides of the river, so we don't get stranded.

After their long journeys apart, the North and Middle Forks of the American River finally join just north of Auburn. There is something special about this meeting, a sort of alchemy that results from the mixing of these distinct bodies of water that is greater than the sum of its parts. Suddenly, at the confluence, these famously wild rafting rivers relax, and widen to become something new. The result is the best stretch of swimming in the Sacramento Valley.

While there are plenty of swimming holes in the area, we think the best are about half a mile downstream from the confluence, where the water is delightfully still and deep. To get here, look for the locked gate and trailhead just south of the Highway 49 bridge. After a short walk along the riverside trail, cross the arched "No Hands Bridge," then scramble down a use-trail to the riverside beaches below.

The river feels more like a lagoon in this stretch, its gentle current imperceptible. We easily swim upstream, then allow ourselves to slowly drift back to the entry point. Along the banks are plenty of shaded grottos and sandy beaches carved into the sturdy greenstone. Up above, numerous rock platforms provide altars for sun worship. People eagerly soak up the rays before leaping into the cool water below.

The shimmering blue-green water of the American River Confluence is the heart of Auburn State Recreation Area (SRA), a vast parkland that protects 40 miles of rivers and canyons along the North and Middle Forks. Many of the old supply roads, train lines, and trails used during the gold rush underpin the extensive recreational trail system.

The towering Forestville Bridge, meanwhile, is a legacy of a different period. Completed in 1973, it was meant to cross a huge reservoir behind one of the largest dams in the world. The proposed Auburn Dam, located two miles downstream from the bridge, was under construction for 15 years, starting in 1967, before construction was halted due to seismic and geologic concerns. The project was ultimately deemed unsafe and economically infeasible. Thankfully, the canyons were never flooded; instead, the land was placed under the protection of Auburn SRA.

Knowing that the American River Confluence could be underwater makes it feel all the more precious. On sweltering summer days (of which there are many in this part of California), there is no better place to escape the heat. This lucky stroke of conservation has become a sanctuary for water lovers. Get here early, bring a cooler, and stay all day.

NEARBY

THE POUR CHOICE
177 Sacramento St, Auburn

This craft coffee bar and taproom serves specialty coffee (cold brew, filter, espresso), along with light breakfast dishes like croissants and scones, avocado toast, and loaded banana bread (peanut butter and fresh banana between two slices of banana bread), salads and excellent sandwiches for lunch, and wine and beer in the evenings.

AUBURN BODEGA
937 Lincoln Way, Auburn

An unassuming neighborhood market and deli selling seasonal local produce, natural/organic groceries, bulk foods, coffee, bread, eggs—and more. They also make food to order, including sandwiches, bowls, soups, juices, and smoothies. The tuna melt and super veggie bro sandwiches are top hits.

AUBURN ALE HOUSE
289 Washington St, Auburn

Centrally located, this cozy craft brewpub feels like the heart of Old Town Auburn. Sample their small-batch beers, alongside a casual all-day bistro menu. Beer names such as Gold Country Pilsner and Fool's Gold Ale reflect the region's mining history. A second, smaller venue, the Auburn Annex, is just across the road at 103 Sacramento Street.

"At the confluence, these famously wild
raftering rivers relax, and widen to become
something new. The result is the best stretch
of swimming in the Sacramento Valley."

Monolithic rocks rise high above
this secluded river swim, deep in
a Gold Country gorge

Camp Nine

Stanislaus River, Calaveras County

◎ **ANCESTRAL HOMELANDS**
Central Sierra Miwok

〰 **TYPE OF SWIM**
River

✳ **ACTIVITIES**
Swim, hike

✓ Kid friendly, Dog friendly on leash

☽ **BEST TIME TO VISIT**
June to October

⏱ **OPEN HOURS**
7am to sunset

⑤ **COST OF ENTRY**
$10 day use parking fee in the State Recreation Area

⌂ **CLOSEST CAMPSITE**
Calaveras Big Trees Campground (26 miles)

⊕ **CLOSEST TOWN OF INTEREST**
Murphys (14 miles)

⇗ **HOW TO GET THERE**
The slightly longer way from Murphys (14 miles—
about 35 minutes) down Parrots Ferry Road to Camp
Nine Road was the better option for us in our 24-foot
RV. Nine of those miles are down a patchy, single-lane
paved road to the Collierville Powerhouse, where you
can park along the road.

⊖ **ACCESS**
Take the mint-colored footbridge over the river at
the Collierville Powerhouse and continue along the
trail about a quarter mile to deep pools and large
monolithic rocks.

✳ **LOCAL KNOWLEDGE**
The possibility of riches (gold!) attracted fortune
hunters and adventure seekers from around the
world to Murphys and Angels Camp. Gamblers,
opportunists, and renowned outlaws came in droves.
One colorful character associated with the mining
camps was Joaquin Murrieta, aka the Robin Hood of
the West, a legendary Mexican bandit whose exploits
are said to have inspired the story of Zorro.

Highway 4 in Calaveras County is one of the less visited areas in Gold Country. As anywhere on this side of the Sierra, a steady trickle of city transplants is slowly repopulating the old boomtowns such as Murphys, but it still feels relatively remote. We asked around about local swimming holes, and most people gave us polite but unhelpful responses. Eventually, however, a woman in an outdoor shop surreptitiously dropped a pin on our map. A co-conspirator. The satellite image showed a big pool at the end of Camp Nine Road.

The steep, narrow road is a patchwork of repairs making for a slow nine-mile drive, especially in a 24-foot RV. The landscape sizzles in the summer heat, and as you peer down into the gorge you can see the uppermost reaches of New Melones Lake. Thick, lifeless scar lines mark the receding water level of the reservoir. Thankfully, that's not our final destination.

The road dead-ends at the Collierville Powerhouse, a small hydro station that generates electricity for Calaveras County residents. Park there and cross the mint-green bridge, then continue along a dirt trail through golden grass and stately black oaks. After about a quarter of a mile you'll reach the North Fork of the Stanislaus River. Unlike the gorge immediately downstream, this landscape remains wild.

Follow interwoven access paths to the main swimming hole, where huge vertical slabs of rock, swirled with veins of red, orange, and white, rise out of the water like sculptures. A good rule of thumb for swimming holes is: the higher the rocks, the deeper the pool. The centerpiece of this pool is about 25 feet high.

We climb up the smooth surface, getting the best traction without shoes. At the top there is a flat perch large enough for a couple of people to sit or stand. We leap off, slapping the water with the soles of our feet. The drop is sheer and the water is deep. It's cool and fresh, and dark like a lake. Rays of sunlight pierce the surface to reveal the pebbled bottom far below—too deep to touch, but good to know it's there. For a moment we could have convinced ourselves this pool was bottomless.

The swimming hole overflows into a series of shallow rapids and sandy beaches. We lie in them, letting the fresh water wash over us as the sun slowly tracks across the sky. You can stay here all day and hardly see another person. If anyone asks, you didn't hear about it from us.

NEARBY

MURPHY'S POURHOUSE
35 Main St, Murphys

It's impossible to drive through Murphys and not spot the Pourhouse, a large, leafy beer garden with a series of picnic tables. There are 16 rotating beer taps, some pouring rare and unusual craft brews, and a small menu of gourmet sandwiches and hot dogs with toppings like bacon jam, candied jalapeños, and house-made BBQ sauce.

CALAVERAS BIG TREES STATE PARK
1170 Highway 4, Arnold

You never really get used to the sheer size of California's giant sequoias. In the 6,498-acre Calaveras Big Trees State Park, a few miles north of the town of Arnold, two groves contain hundreds of sequoias, 300 feet tall and thousands of years old. Come here to hike and camp under these peaceful giants.

LUBE ROOM SALOON
3431 Highway 4, Dorrington

Just north of Big Trees State Park in Dorrington is the Lube Room Saloon, a favorite place for travelers along Highway 4, serving up classic American food—burgers, sandwiches, soups, salads, pizzas. It's lively and fun here in the cluttered cabin furnished with taxidermied deer heads, old license plates, and a multitude of other Americana.

"Follow access paths to the main swimming
hole, where huge vertical slabs of rock,
swirled red, orange, and white, protrude
out of the water like sculptures."

Cleo's Bath

Stanislaus National Forest

A natural swimming pool on the granite plateau high above Pinecrest Lake

ANCESTRAL HOMELANDS
Tuolumne band of Me-Wuk Indians

TYPE OF SWIM
River

ACTIVITIES
Hike, swim, paddle, sail

Not kid friendly

Dog friendly

BEST TIME TO VISIT
May to September

OPEN HOURS
7am to sunset

COST OF ENTRY
$10 day use parking fee in the State Recreation Area

CLOSEST CAMPSITE
Pinecrest Campground (at trailhead)

CLOSEST TOWN OF INTEREST
Pinecrest (0 miles)

HOW TO GET THERE
Hike up 3.5 miles from Pinecrest Lake.

ACCESS
Moderate to challenging. The Pinecrest Lake Trail is mostly flat but becomes steep and challenging for the last quarter mile as you scramble up to Cleo's Bath.

LOCAL KNOWLEDGE
In winter, Pinecrest transforms into a village of snow-covered A-frames. You can snowshoe the trails, make snowmen, and ski at the local Dodge Ridge Mountain Resort, 1.5 miles down Dodge Ridge Road. Pinecrest is just as impressive to visit in winter as in summer. You just won't be able to swim.

In 2017, Dillon's dad and his wife moved to a small town just outside of Sonora. Through them we came to discover the many rivers, lakes, and trails of the nearby Stanislaus National Forest, and we often join them on their summer dog walks around Pinecrest Lake. From there it is only a 3.5-mile hike up to Cleo's Baths, one of our favorite foothills swims, where a series of natural infinity pools are fed by the South Fork of the Stanislaus River.

To get there, we take the Pinecrest Lake Trail counterclockwise along the shoreline, walking among large boulders, sugar pines, and holiday cabins. You can hardly tell by looking at it, but Pinecrest Lake is actually a reservoir. It's one of several built here in the 1850s to store water for the mining town of Columbia, 30 miles downstream. The marshy meadow of Strawberry Flat first became Lake Edna, which was enlarged and renamed Pinecrest Lake in 1914, during the logging era, to provide drinking water and power to lower-elevation towns.

After about 1.5 miles you'll reach the top of the lake, where the trail splits off to the east. Continue up this small valley, following blue arrows painted on trees and rocks for another mile or so. You will eventually see a small meadow and a sign pointing up toward Cleo's Bath. Here, the trail becomes steeper as it navigates up the granite escarpment. It's easy to follow, but you need to occasionally use your hands to grab trees and rocks. Think StairMaster meets bouldering.

This might spook some hikers, but for perspective, one of us did it with a baby on his back, and our 60-year-old step-mom thought it was exciting. In climbing parlance, it's a class-two scramble (minimal exposure, stable terrain, low risk), and it's less than a quarter mile up. If you're scrambling, you're almost there.

The Stanislaus National Forest neighbors Yosemite but is far less visited. Indeed, as you reach Cleo's Bath, it feels like one of those great Sierra places. Water cascades down a vast granite plateau to form successive pools. Clear, cool water flows through cracks and spreads into nearby soil to nourish delicate moss and ferns. It's a mountain oasis.

Late in the season, when the water levels are lower, the large pool splits into several smaller ones, including an infinity tub with views out over Pinecrest—a natural rooftop spa. People laze on smooth hot slabs, dipping in and out of the water to cool off. This is what life has come to—2 million years of human evolution and we're basically reptiles. Or perhaps this is what we've always been. Maybe the weirdest development is sitting at a desk.

NEARBY

MOVIES UNDER THE STARS
Pinecrest Lake

Through summer (May to September), Pinecrest's lakeside amphitheater screens movies beginning at dusk (around 8pm), with popcorn, drinks, and candy sold as refreshments. Eight-dollar tickets go on sale one hour before the show. Bring a blanket or warm wrap: the evenings can get quite chilly.

ALICIA'S SUGAR SHACK
24191 Highway 108, Twain Harte

On the way up to Pinecrest we like to stop in Twain Harte at the Sugar Shack, a classic counter-service cabin on the side of the highway. Alicia makes pastries—think sweet apple turnovers and coffee cake—and serves hearty breakfasts, sandwiches, and smoothies.

CONCERTS IN THE PINES
Eproson Park, Twain Harte

From mid-June to early September every Saturday evening at 6, the town of Twain Harte sponsors a fun-filled night with food vendors, drinks, and music—everything from big bands to solo singers, jazz, blues, and rock and roll. Check twainhartecc.com for details.

Road Trip

BOOMTOWN LEGACY

AUBURN TO EMERALD POOLS

Steeped in the legacy of the 19th-century gold rush, this region is peppered with cute, historic towns and flawless river swims in close proximity. Stops along this six-day road trip are so close, you'll rarely spend more than an hour in the car each day, and there is always a good meal or bar within striking distance.

Day 1

Auburn to Grass Valley

24 MILES / 30 MINS + STOPS

This road trip starts in the gold rush town of Auburn, just 45 minutes from Sacramento. Grab coffee and breakfast at The Pour Choice in the Old Town before setting off to explore nearby trails and swim at the **American River Confluence** (p.133) in Auburn State Recreation Area. It's less than a 10-minute drive. Park along the river and follow the Black Hole of Calcutta Falls Trail south to the swim under "No Hands Bridge." In the afternoon, head north along Highway 49 into Grass Valley for dinner at **Meze** and wander the lively streets in the warm summer-night air.

Day 2

Grass Valley to Nevada City via Hwy 49

20 MILES / 45 MINS + STOPS

Have a slow morning and get breakfast in town before heading north up Highway 49 for one of this area's preeminent swims at **Highway 49** and **Hoyts Crossing** (p.137), on the South Fork of the Yuba. This is where our love affair with that river really blossomed. Deep green pools below the highway are the most accessible, but walk just over a mile upriver to Hoyts Crossing for more secluded swimming—and the local nudist spot. Spend the day frolicking in clear rock-bottom pools and lazing in the sun. Then make your way into Nevada City for pizza and beer at **Three Forks**.

Day 3

Purdon Crossing to Downieville

34 MILES / 55 MINS

Only about 20 minutes north of Nevada City, the historic steel bridge at **Purdon Crossing** (p.133) feels like the middle of nowhere. Mother's Beach is typically the busiest swimming area along the trail, a wide, slow-moving section of river with a gentle, sandy entrance. Less than a mile up is China Dam, a crumbling dam wall where a secluded pool sparkles green. Strip off your clothes and leap from the rocks. It's easy to spend hours between these two spots. Then continue on Purdon Road through North San Juan to Downieville, a mountain biking town set at the confluence of the Downie River and North Fork of the good old Yuba River. Get a cocktail at **Boomtown Lounge** and dinner at **La Cocina del Oro Taqueria**.

Day 4

Downieville to Sierraville

37 MILES / 1 HR

Wake up in Downieville and take a refreshing dunk in the river right under the bridge in town at **Finney's Hole** (p.125). There are several swims within walking distance from Downieville's town center, but this one is our favorite, and the most convenient. Stop at **Sabrina's** for a breakfast burrito, then hit the road—Highway 49, that is—heading east an hour to Sierraville. Spend the rest of the afternoon and evening soaking at **Sierra Hot Springs**, on the cusp of an enchanted forest and alpine valley. Camping and accommodations are available at the lodge here, and all stays include access to the springs.

Day 5

Sierraville to Truckee

28 MILES / 36 MINS

Have an early-morning soak at Sierra Hot Springs before heading to **Truckee** for breakfast in the sunny courtyard of the Coffeebar roastery. There's lots to see and do in Truckee. Stop into Word after Word bookstore and wander the streets before the sun gets high in the sky, then head to **Donner Lake**, a few miles away, for a swim. Find a free public pier on the north side of the lake (there are 37 to choose from), and once the heat really starts to kick in, wander up to Little Truckee Ice Creamery for a cone. Finish the day with dinner and drinks back in Truckee at Moody's Bistro or Alibi Ale Works.

Day 6

Truckee to Emerald Pools

21 MILES / 25 MINS

For the final installment of this swimming pilgrimage through the Gold Country, after breakfast drive up to Donner Pass for lofty views over the lake. Wander through the historic Donner Pass Train Tunnels, a two-mile stretch of disused tunnel that forms a makeshift art gallery for graffiti artists. Then head east on I-80 past Sugar Bowl ski resort to the iconic **Emerald Pools** (pp. 129), back on the South Fork of the Yuba River. To close the loop, head to Nevada City on Highway 20 for one last meal—or jump on I-80 south to return to the Bay Area.

Central
CALIFOR

Central California

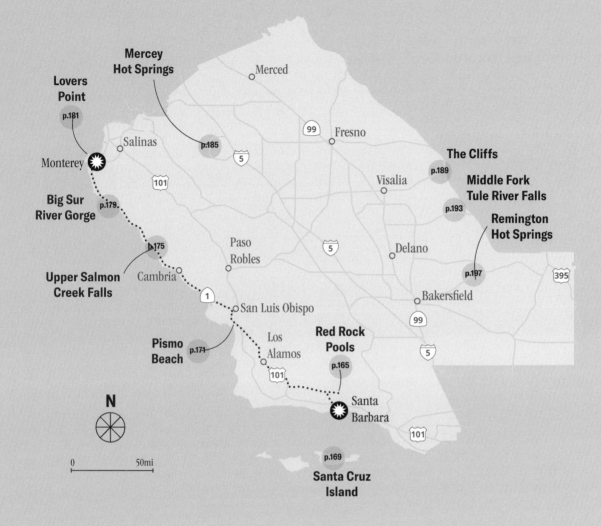

Mercey Hot Springs

Merced

Lovers Point
p.181

Monterey

Salinas

Big Sur River Gorge
p.179

p.185

[99] Fresno

[5]

[101]

The Cliffs
p.189

Middle Fork Tule River Falls
p.193

Visalia

Remington Hot Springs

p.197

p.175

Upper Salmon Creek Falls

Cambria

Paso Robles

[5]

Delano

Bakersfield

[395]

[99]

[1]

San Luis Obispo

[5]

Pismo Beach
p.174

[101]

Los Alamos

Red Rock Pools
p.165

[101]

Santa Barbara

N

p.169

0   50mi

Santa Cruz Island

When to visit

March to November

Favorite Swim

Big Sur River Gorge
(p.179)

Favorite Hot Springs

Remington Hot Springs
(p.197)

Cutest Town

Cambria
(p.175)

This chapter stretches from Santa Barbara to Monterey and across the San Joaquin Valley to the foothills of the Sierra Nevada. It's the perfect cross-section of the state, encompassing sunny beaches, cool redwood forests, giant sequoia groves, crystal-clear rivers, and quiet hot springs. Because much of the region is more than a day trip from San Francisco or Los Angeles, Central California is less traveled than other parts of the state. Life moves at a slower pace, and you'll find that there are noticeably fewer people everywhere you go.

The Central California coastline fosters one of the world's most diverse and productive marine environments, from the kelp forests of Santa Cruz Island (p.169) to the deep submarine canyon of Monterey Bay (Lovers Point, p.181). It's also home to California's most iconic road trip: 70 eye-popping miles of rugged coastline as the Pacific Coast Highway traces the edge of Big Sur's Santa Lucia range. People often don't stop long enough to have a good look around, but they're missing the many wonderful trails and swimming holes nestled among the dramatic ridges (Upper Salmon Creek Falls, p.175) and gorges (Big Sur Gorge, p.179) that define the landscape.

When fog blankets the coast in summer, the San Joaquin Valley and Sierra foothills are at their best. Back roads overflow with tomatoes, grapes, watermelons, apricots, and strawberries, to such an extent that our drives to Tule River (p.193) and Dinkey Creek (p.189) are often delayed by detours among the many farm stands. Gas station food trucks cater to the tastes of farmworkers and their families, serving up norteño-style burritos, Oaxacan tlayudas, and Salvadoran pupusas, to name a few. Which is to say, go to the gas stations, even if you drive an electric car.

In our opinion, Central California offers a perfect snapshot of the entire state. It's California at its most relaxed and authentic. Travel is friendly and accessible, with landscapes to suit every taste and season.

Best Brunch

Alta Bakery & Cafe, Monterey
(p.181)

Weekend Escape

Los Alamos
(p.165)

Road Trip

Central Coast
(p.198)

Red Rock Pools

Santa Ynez River, Los Padres National Forest

⊙ **ANCESTRAL HOMELANDS**
Barbareño Chumash and Santa Ynez Band of
Chumash Indians

∽ **TYPE OF SWIM**
River pools

✲ **ACTIVITIES**
Swim, hike, mountain bike, paddle, fish

⊘ Kid friendly, Dog friendly

◖ **BEST TIME TO VISIT**
May to August

⊘ **OPEN HOURS**
24 hours. Seasonal road closure may occur in winter
and spring due to high water levels on river crossings.

⑤ **COST OF ENTRY**
$10 day use and parking fee paid at First Crossing
Kiosk.

⊘ **CLOSEST CAMPSITE**
Fremont Campground (8.5 miles)

⊕ **CLOSEST TOWN OF INTEREST**
Santa Barbara (27 miles) and Los Olivos (29 miles)

⊘ **HOW TO GET THERE**
From Santa Barbara, take Highway 101 northwest for
10 miles. Exit at Highway 154 and drive about 10.5
miles, over San Marcos Pass, to Paradise Road. Turning
right, follow Paradise Road until it dead-ends at a
locked gate, another 10.5 miles. This final parking area
is at the Gibraltar Trailhead.

⊖ **ACCESS**
Easy. From the parking lot, it is about a half mile of
level, rocky trail to reach Red Rock Pools. The trail is
less defined thereafter, but you can follow the bank of
the river to more pools.

✳ **LOCAL KNOWLEDGE**
During high river flows, such as early spring or after
heavy rain, Paradise Road is closed to cars at First
Crossing. If safe, it may be possible to ford the multiple
crossings with bicycles and ride the five miles to the
trailhead.

Summer on the California coast is notoriously cool and gray. Frosty oceanic currents sweep down from the North Pacific, bringing cold moist air. When that air hits the coastal mountains and warm inland temperatures, it condenses to form the famous "marine layer." From late Gray-pril to Fog-ust, this charismatic swirling fog often blankets the coast. For people living around Santa Barbara, this means that the best summer beach days are not on the shore, but just over the Santa Ynez range, at Red Rock Pools.

From Santa Barbara, Highway 154 climbs over San Marcos Pass before descending into the beautiful Santa Ynez Valley. The gently rolling hills are known for their Syrah grapes and a thriving food culture (see the Road Trip, p.198). Take a sharp right onto Paradise Road and continue along the Santa Ynez River to the first vehicle ford at First Crossing. The canyon walls rise steeply over the next five miles, and the road hugs the river, crossing numerous times, until it dead-ends at a locked gate and Gibraltar Trailhead.

The Santa Ynez River is fed by a combination of surface water and springs. Sometimes it flows in a raging torrent, and other times it disappears underground only to resurface in big depressions like Red Rock Pools. Even if it looks dry at the trailhead, there is always a place to swim here.

It's an easy half mile along the Gibraltar Trail to the first and largest swimming hole. No matter what kind of cloud cover is visiting the coast, this spot is almost always hot and sunny. Be sure to carry lots of water. The parched, rocky mountains suck the moisture from you before you even have a chance to sweat. By the time the namesake red rock comes into view, we are desperate to strip down and throw ourselves into the cool, green water.

Shade from the towering rock tracks across the pool like a sundial. Lesser boulders rest in the water—sculpted recliners and diving boards. Kids scramble up the slippery rocks while adults shriek with glee, spinning tall tales of places they have jumped from, or of the turtle they once chased through an underwater tunnel. One grandfather has been coming here for 40 years. Another family hasn't missed a summer since 1994.

As more people arrive, we take the opportunity to move further downstream. There are another three river miles before the Gibraltar Reservoir, offering less boisterous spots to relax and swim. We find cozy sand-bottomed tubs shaded by willows, and roll out our towels on the soft bank. We've brought watermelon, dark chocolate peanut butter cups, tomatoes, bread and cheese—the essentials. We thumb through our books with sticky fingers. It's the perfect beach day.

NEARBY
SANTA BARBARA

There is a lot to do in Santa Barbara and its surroundings—from hiking in the Santa Ynez Mountains to strolling the downtown district. Check out the Funk Zone arts district, visit the farmers market (Tuesday and Saturday), ride bikes along the shore, or visit the old Spanish mission, built in 1786.

LOS BAÑOS DEL MAR
401 Shoreline Dr, Santa Barbara

This outdoor 50-meter pool right on the Santa Barbara shoreline was one of a handful of Olympic-sized swimming pools we found in California on our swim pilgrimage. And it's a real charmer. The historic chalk-colored building surrounded by tall palms is home to a spotless, sun-filled open-air facility.

LOS ALAMOS
Santa Ynez Valley

Los Alamos, a tiny four-block village in the Santa Ynez Valley, is a food destination, with wine tasting rooms, beer gardens, and critically acclaimed restaurants. Favorites include Bell's French-style farm-to-table bistro, Bob's Well Bread Bakery, Full of Life Flatbread, and Municipal Winemakers. Stay at the retro roadside motel Skyview, on the hill overlooking town.

"The parched, rocky mountains suck the moisture from you before you even have a chance to sweat. By the time the namesake red rock comes into view, we are desperate to strip down and throw ourselves into the cool, green water."

Santa Cruz Island

Channel Islands National Park

California's Galápagos Islands, just 20 miles off the coast

◎ **ANCESTRAL HOMELANDS**
Cruzeño Chumash

⊖ **TYPE OF SWIM**
Beach

✸ **ACTIVITIES**
Swim, snorkel, hike, kayak, camp

⊘ Kid friendly

⊗ No dogs

◖ **BEST TIME TO VISIT**
August to November

🕐 **OPEN HOURS**
24 hours

$ **COST OF ENTRY**
Free with Island Packers ferry ticket. For day trippers: $63 round trip for adults, $45 for kids 3–12 years old. For campers: $84 round trip for adults, $61 for kids. Children under 3 are free.

⃠ **CLOSEST CAMPSITE**
Scorpion Canyon Campground

⊕ **CLOSEST TOWN OF INTEREST**
Ventura

⊘ **HOW TO GET THERE**
Ferries to Santa Cruz Island from Ventura Harbor (or Oxnard) operate daily with Island Packers. The trip takes about an hour, with island dropoff points at Scorpion Anchorage and Prisoners Harbor.

⊖ **ACCESS**
Easy: straight off the boat, onto the pebbly beaches. For guided kayak and hiking tours on the island, contact Santa Barbara Adventure Company.

✳ **LOCAL KNOWLEDGE**
Biodiversity and conservation are a crucial part of life on the Channel Islands. Many plants and animals are endemic, including island species of prickly pear cactus, spotted skunk, big-eared bat, scrub jay, and fox (once at risk of extinction), as well as the now-extinct pygmy mammoth.

We've hardly left Scorpion Anchorage in our kayaks before someone asks our guide about the likelihood of seeing wildlife. Without turning around, he yells back: "100 percent." And immediately, a dark gray head pops up from the water right next to us. We all cling to the slimy tendrils of sea kelp to help stabilize our crafts and get a better look. The seal looks at us curiously, as if we are the spectacle, before disappearing into the underwater forest below.

Santa Cruz Island is part of the Channel Islands archipelago, a chain of eight mountainous islands that hug the California coast. Just 20 miles west of Santa Barbara, five of the eight—San Miguel, Santa Rosa, Anacapa, Santa Barbara, and Santa Cruz—make up Channel Islands National Park. The islands are defined by steep cliffs, giant sea caves, hiking trails over green bluffs to secluded beaches, and endemic flora and fauna with almost mythical histories. Santa Cruz is the largest island of the cluster and has some of the biggest sea caves in the world, carved by centuries of wave-powered erosion. Today, these littoral caverns are protected places where seals and seabirds live and breed. We paddle into the darkness with headlamps, sloshing around like pinballs, trying not to hit the cave walls.

Back out in the open water, our guide describes the Channel Islands's status as a marine sanctuary. This region has become one of the top dive destinations in the world, its rich kelp forests supporting an astonishing array of marine life—fish, seals, octopuses, sharks, and myriad invertebrates. The kelp forest comprises three layers: the canopy, the understory, and the forest floor, a mosaic of sandy flats and rocky reefs—"the sequoias of the sea," a beautiful hidden world. From our kayaks, we can only see the swirling fronds of the canopy, the tips of plants that grow over 100 feet tall. The rest of the morning sees us paddling along the northeast side of the island, in and out of caverns named Elephant Belly, Birth Canal, and Painted Cave.

For day trippers, kayaking is the best way to experience Santa Cruz Island and its dramatic landscape. Those arriving at Scorpion Anchorage will also find supreme swimming at the pebble beach right near the jetty. But to see more of the island, camping overnight will allow you time to access some of the 15 trails that range from short and easy (1–2 miles) to long and strenuous (8–10 miles). Trails to Smugglers Cove and Chinese Harbor will take you to the most secluded beaches.

Heading back to the mainland, our boat accompanied by a playful pod of dolphins, we look back at the islands from the water. The archipelago now appears as a distant mountain range. Clouds swirl around them as they slowly disappear behind us.

NEARBY

PATAGONIA FLAGSHIP STORE
235 W Santa Clara St, Ventura

Patagonia is such a global brand now, it's hard to believe there were ever humble beginnings. Environmentally conscious Yvon Chouinard launched it in the early 1970s. The first store, in the Great Pacific Ironworks in Ventura, still exists today, born out of a love of the outdoors and its proximity to good climbing and surf.

CARPINTERIA

Just 20 minutes north of Ventura is the small seaside suburb of Carpinteria. Ocean life reigns supreme here, with its surf beach and popular outdoor community pool (open year-round). A pedestrian-friendly strip offers restaurants and shops to explore. Try the Good Plough for hearty kale salads, bibimbap bowls, curries, and grass-fed beef burgers.

OJAI

Our favorite epicurean town, 25 minutes inland from Ventura. We love walking around Ojai in the summer—starting at the Duchess for coffee and pastries, food-shopping at Farmer and the Cook, dining at Rory's Place in the evening. The open-air Bart's Books is worth a visit. Ojai also has an impressive kids' playground.

Pismo Beach

Central Coast, San Luis Obispo County

A charming beach town from a bygone era

⊙ **ANCESTRAL HOMELANDS**
Chumash, 'Amuwu, Salinan, and Obispeño

⊖ **TYPE OF SWIM**
Beach

✱ **ACTIVITIES**
Swim, surf

✓ Kid friendly, Dog friendly on leash

◐ **BEST TIME TO VISIT**
March to November

⧖ **OPEN HOURS**
6am–10pm

◇ **CLOSEST CAMPSITE**
Oceano Campground, Pismo State Beach (3 miles)

⊕ **CLOSEST TOWN OF INTEREST**
Pismo

↗ **HOW TO GET THERE**
Three hours from LA, nearly four hours from San Francisco, along Highway 101. Once you arrive at Pismo, the best beach access is around 139 Main Street.

⊖ **ACCESS**
Easy. Park in town and walk a block or two to the beach.

✳ **LOCAL KNOWLEDGE**
In late October the vibrant orange-and-black monarch butterflies migrate to the Californian coast to rest in sheltered, warmer climes during the winter months. In Pismo, over 10,000 butterflies cluster annually in the limbs of a grove of eucalyptus trees at the south end of town, until about February. It's one of the largest colonies in the US. And…with a lifespan of only six months, the butterflies that leave will never return.

Some places you swim are personal. They are local knowledge or family secrets, directions scribbled on a napkin, a text message with a pin dropped on a map, sent from your best friend's brother. Others are more than obvious—fabulously touristy, popular for a reason, unforgettable and unmissable. Pismo Beach is the latter.

Pismo is no secret to any seasoned California beachgoer. Perhaps you've spent some time here, visited for a weekend, or even avoided the pulsing summer crowds entirely, preferring a smaller, more secluded swimming spot. But it is indisputable that Pismo Beach is special. It has all the beach vacation classics: clam chowder stands, palm readers, low-rise beachfront motels with dolphin motifs, and a pleasant Mediterranean climate. Souvenir stores clutter the first few blocks away from the beach, though the best stuff (good cafes, a yoga studio, a local vibe) is on Price Street, a little further into town. There is no denying the purpose-built tourist infrastructure that defines Pismo. But it's all at a scale that is somehow charming.

The beach itself is long, with some of the whitest sand we've seen in California. Just over 10 miles south of the friendly college town of San Luis Obispo, Pismo attracts tourists, students, and a low-key surf scene, which tends to collect around the spindly pillars of the 1,200-foot-long pier. Atop the pier, shiny Airstreams sell bait, candy, and snacks. Meanwhile, crowds of beachgoers populate the sand in fluorescent tents. When the wind picks up in the afternoon (as it always does), colorful kites fly high along the shore like a wayward flock of seabirds.

We like to explore the surrounding landscape on either side of the main beach. Walk up to the north end at low tide to find caves made of ancient white volcanic sediment. Here you'll see people lying in the shade under sea stacks or inspecting the swirling rock formations that look like petrified layer cakes. To the south is a grove of eucalyptus trees that periodically fills with monarch butterflies (see Local Knowledge), and beyond that, Oceano Dunes, 18 miles of picturesque white sand hills.

For better or worse, Pismo Beach is known as the "Hawaii of the Central Valley," so called for its proximity to Fresno and Bakersfield (2–2.5 hours). Not to throw shade, but we like it better than Malibu, which is the Hawaii of LA. Or maybe Hawaii is the Hawaii of LA? Either way, Pismo is great, and so is Hawaii. As with any good vacation spot, we're easily transported by its seaside buzz, the sand between our toes and the sweet smell of cinnamon in the air.

NEARBY
HONEYMOON CAFE
999 Price St, Pismo Beach

A 40-year-old cafe serving wholesome food—like veggie-filled omelets, rainbow salads, and tacos—with produce sourced from local farms. The Honeymoon Bagel is a favorite, and there's beer and wine. Next door is Harmony House Yoga studio and store—making for a very harmonious marriage.

ZORRO'S CAFE & CANTINA
927 Shell Beach Rd, Pismo Beach

Out of the Pismo Beach fray and up on the residential bluff of Shell Beach is Zorro's, a red-trimmed Mexican diner serving classic fare: big plates of eggy breakfasts, tacos, burritos, and enchiladas. Make it a meal by adding beans and rice, and drink $5 local beers. This place will leave you satisfied—and full.

SYCAMORE MINERAL SPRINGS
1215 Avila Beach Dr, San Luis Obispo

In neighboring Avila Beach, Sycamore is an alternative to the typical flashy spa resorts. This low-key wellness retreat is a peaceful escape, with hillside hot tubs, an oasis water lagoon, and mountain views. Their dog-friendly rooms are spacious and quiet, and all rooms include their own private outdoor mineral spring bath.

"Pismo Beach has all the beach vacation classics: clam chowder stands, palm readers, low-rise beachfront motels with dolphin motifs, and a pleasant Mediterranean climate."

Upper Salmon Creek Falls

Silver Peak Wilderness, Los Padres National Forest

◎ **ANCESTRAL HOMELANDS**
Xolon Salinan People

⊖ **TYPE OF SWIM**
Waterfall and creek

⊛ **ACTIVITIES**
Swim, hike

⊘ Dog friendly

⊗ No kids

◔ **BEST TIME TO VISIT**
May to October. In the summer this pool catches the
sun from about 12 to 3pm.

⊘ **CLOSEST CAMPSITE**
Spruce Camp is hike-in only (1.5 miles from the road,
half a mile before Upper Salmon Creek Falls). For a
waterfront campground, Kirk Creek is 17 miles north
along Highway 1.

⊕ **CLOSEST TOWN OF INTEREST**
Cambria (28 miles)

▥ **BEST MAP**
No map is required, but if you want to get a better
sense of what is around, then check out Nat Geo's Big
Sur/Ventana Wilderness/Los Padres National Forest
map.

↗ **HOW TO GET THERE**
The Salmon Creek Trailhead is located 3.7 miles north
of Ragged Point on a large horseshoe bend in the road.
Keep an eye out for dirt turnouts just beyond the traffic
guardrail. Walk back behind the guardrail to reach the
trailhead, which is well marked by a large brown sign.

⊖ **ACCESS**
Challenging. It's a decent hike to get up the Salmon
Creek Trail, and then a bit of a scramble down to the
creek. Allow yourself at least half a day to enjoy the
falls.

⊛ **LOCAL KNOWLEDGE**
It's important to make reservations well ahead
when traveling through Big Sur. There is limited
accommodation and virtually no phone reception, so
it's difficult to make last-minute arrangements.

The Santa Lucia Range rises spectacularly from the ocean to create one of the most iconic stretches of coastline in the world: Big Sur. From San Simeon to Carmel-by-the-Sea, a roughly 90-mile stretch of the Pacific Coast Highway (PCH) bravely hugs the steep slopes in an ill-fated battle against erosion. The secret to this coast, though, is to turn your back on the ocean. If you follow any of the countless ridges and creeks inland, there are trails, campgrounds, swimming holes, and even sunshine. Our favorite stop on the southern end of the highway is Upper Salmon Creek Falls. And, unlike the road, you will probably have it all to yourself.

Salmon Creek carves a narrow canyon in its brief, three-mile journey from the crest of the Santa Lucia range to the coast. Steep relief and hard bedrock create dramatic waterfalls and deep pools along the way. The 120-foot Lower Salmon Creek Falls is well known and only a short walk from the road. You could happily stop there, but if you're like us, you will be curious about what is hiding further upstream.

The hike to Upper Salmon Creek Falls follows the Salmon Creek Trail, taking you high above the PCH. After the first steep mile, the trail eases as you begin to follow the contours of the canyon walls. Oak forest closes in around you, and the distant rush of Salmon Creek far below is almost imperceptible.

Spruce Camp is the landmark to indicate that you are only about half a mile from the access trail, and soon you will get glimpses of the clear green water below. The first time we visited, we were just at the edge of turning around, feeling hot and hungry. We wondered if we had spent yet another half day chasing a fantasy. Then we spotted the well-used access trail splitting off to the left. Our woes were immediately forgotten. (This is not an official trail—which is to say, proceed at your own risk.)

The dirt path drops steeply about 100 feet, with small tree trunks and roots polished by generations of grasping hands. We mountain-goat side-step, with a couple of butt slides, to get down to the creek, finally scrambling over a large boulder to reach the edge of the pool. There, it's about waist deep, but the ground gently slopes to a 10-foot depression at the base of the waterfall. Take a few steps, then dive in.

The water, cool and clear, washes away the journey and suspends you in a calm timelessness. Fragrant bay trees arch over the pool, and shoots of green burst from every crevice. Small fish swirl around your feet, though none appear to be the namesake salmon. The only sign of humans is the well-worn path. This is our favorite kind of swim: the unexpected gem.

NEARBY

CAMBRIA

South of Salmon Creek Falls 27 miles is the wine country town of Cambria, a village strip dotted with colorful timber houses, B&Bs, fermentation stores, ice cream shops, cafes, pubs, and shops touting crystals and psychic readings. We like to settle in and sip Paso Robles wine at Robin's garden restaurant, a restored adobe home.

ESALEN INSTITUTE
55000 Highway 1, Big Sur

The holistic retreat and clifftop spa of Esalen is devoted to its education program, a creative laboratory hosting therapeutic, exploratory workshops focusing on human potential. If you aren't staying at the institute, a limited number of visitor passes allow you to enjoy a massage and a day on the property.

DEETJEN'S BIG SUR INN
48865 Highway 1, Big Sur

A historic restaurant and inn tucked into a bend in the road, Deetjen's looks like it was built by fairies over many generations. It's magical. Stop for breakfast (served every day) and sit out on the patio in the sun sipping coffee. Or settle into the cozy, rustic interior for a simple but hearty dinner (closed Wed–Thur).

Big Sur River Gorge

Pfeiffer Big Sur State Park

A glassy freshwater pool along the Big Sur River

◎ **ANCESTRAL HOMELANDS**
Esselen

⊖ **TYPE OF SWIM**
River

⊘ Kid friendly, Dog friendly on leash

◐ **BEST TIME TO VISIT**
May to October

⊙ **OPEN HOURS**
Day use is 8am to sunset

Ⓢ **COST OF ENTRY**
State Park entry is $10 per car

⬠ **CLOSEST CAMPSITE**
Pfeiffer Big Sur State Park campground. Booking ahead is essential (months, sometimes years in advance for summer visits).

⊕ **CLOSEST TOWN OF INTEREST**
Carmel-by-the-Sea (29 miles)

↗ **HOW TO GET THERE**
Drive into Pfeiffer Big Sur State Park and park at Day Use Lot #3. Walk up the fire road about half a mile, then follow a dirt track that peels off to your left, heading upstream. Rock hop over boulders and through small creeks and clear pools for a few hundred yards until you arrive at a large contained green pool. You'll know it when you see it.

⊖ **ACCESS**
Easy to moderate. Some riverbed rock scrambling for about a mile. Wear water shoes, sturdy sandals, or sneakers and be prepared to get them wet.

✳ **LOCAL KNOWLEDGE**
You may notice the name Pfeiffer a lot in this area. Michael and Barbara Pfeiffer, with their (eventually) eight children, were the first European family to settle in Big Sur, around 1870. They were loggers, farmers, and beekeepers, and in 1908 son John opened Pfeiffer Ranch Resort, now Big Sur Lodge. When he sold 680 acres to the State of California in the 1930s, that land became the centerpiece of the new state park, which was named after the pioneering family.

You could easily drive right past this spot in Big Sur, never knowing it existed. It's not secluded or private, or even a secret. In fact, it's very popular. IYKYK, and lots of people do know: they know to leave the coastal fog of summer behind and turn inland at Pfeiffer Big Sur State Park, a redwood forest along the Big Sur River, with an 11-acre campground providing 189 tent and RV sites as well as cabins.

This legendary stretch of road is located 350 miles north of LA and 150 miles south of San Francisco—meaning you've likely traveled a long way to get here. It's time to get out of the car and stretch your legs. Arriving at Pfeiffer Big Sur is like stepping into the an idealized summer camp. Families ride bikes along redwood-lined trails, long days are spent swimming in cool shallow streams, and every meal is eaten outside. Phone reception here is scarce (as in most of Big Sur), so you are left with the pleasant company of your travel companions and the surrounding wilderness to amuse you. And there is no shortage of the latter.

To get to the Big Sur River from Day Use Lot #3, walk up the fire road about half a mile to an unsigned dirt track that peels off to your left, heading upstream. From here, you'll be getting your feet wet. This classic river hike takes you over car-sized boulders and sometimes knee deep through the water, past people sitting along the riverbanks reading or swimming in their own serene pools. But to access what might be our favorite (there, we said it) swim in the state, a little more wading—a few hundred yards upstream—will bring you to the main event. You'll know it when you get there.

Here, the river flows through a narrow slot in the canyon to spill out and create a large, pebble-bottomed pool. The water is deep and shockingly clear. An easy beach-like entry at one side means it's friendly for kids, too. People jump off rocks, duck-dive for crawdads, and float on inflatable donuts (an essential item for any river or gorge). It was here at Big Sur River Gorge that we inherited a kiwi fruit floaty from some fellow travelers, which we kept for the rest of our trip. Most swimmers have packed a picnic (watch out for feisty yellowjacket wasps: they'll fight you for your lunch) and are prepared to spend several hours dipping in and out of the water or, with the help of a fixed rope, exploring higher pools further upstream. Though none is quite as glorious as this one.

This pool checks all our boxes: it's accessible, distinctive to the area, and you can easily spend a whole day here. It's a true summer spot, because unlike the beaches along the coast, this river gorge is always sunny, unaffected by Big Sur's foggy microclimate. If we had a rating scale, we'd be giving it an eleven out of ten.

NEARBY

NEPENTHE
48510 Highway 1, Big Sur

Nepenthe restaurant stands 808 feet high on a cliff overlooking the Pacific Ocean. Built in 1949 using native materials such as redwood and adobe, it has truly become one with the landscape. Even if you don't eat here, it's worth climbing to the terrace for its breathtaking views. The associated Phoenix Shop is also worth a look.

RIDGE, PANORAMA, AND BLUFFS TRAIL LOOP
Andrew Molera State Park

This 8-mile hike (4–6 hours) in Andrew Molera State Park starts from the Creamery Meadow Trailhead and climbs the steep Ridge Trail for sweeping views of the Big Sur hinterland. After a few miles, continue down to the shore and the level Bluffs Trail. You can access Molera Beach here or at the northern end.

POST RANCH INN
47900 Highway 1, Big Sur

A boutique hotel using bio-structural architecture to minimize impact on the environment, the 40-room Post Ranch Inn is a serene getaway perched atop the Big Sur cliffs. Here, guests can feel a part of nature while enjoying panoramic ocean and mountain views, nature walks, yoga classes, and a spa and pool.

Lovers Point

Pacific Grove

A pocket-sized cove beach with a concrete deck for sunbathing

⊙ **ANCESTRAL HOMELANDS**
Esselen

⊖ **TYPE OF SWIM**
Beach

⊛ **ACTIVITIES**
Swim, paddle, surf, scuba dive

⊘ Kid friendly, Dog friendly

◖ **BEST TIME TO VISIT**
Year round, but it can be foggy in summer

◔ **OPEN HOURS**
24 hours, but we recommend swimming during daylight.

⊕ **CLOSEST TOWN OF INTEREST**
Monterey (2.5 miles)

↗ **HOW TO GET THERE**
Ocean View Blvd, Pacific Grove

⊖ **ACCESS**
Easy. Stairs and ramps directly to the beach.

✳ **LOCAL KNOWLEDGE**
Originally known as Lovers of Jesus Point, Lovers Point and the quaint surrounding area of Pacific Grove were founded as a Methodist retreat back in 1875. A sanctimonious attitude persisted for a long time: Pacific Grove was California's last dry town, with the selling of alcohol illegal until 1969. Nowadays the streets are filled with small Victorian homes, and there's a compact downtown of shops and eateries along Lighthouse Avenue.

White sand and clear blue water trigger cascading explosions of pleasure deep within our reptilian brains. So, it's no wonder that we love the Monterey Peninsula. From Carmel River all the way around to Del Monte the beaches are defined by fine white sand that seems far better suited to Caribbean islands than the temperate post-industrial fishing towns and artist colonies of the area. The mossy climate clearly states, "This is a place for deep contemplation and study." While the landscape replies, "This is the promised land, indulge in its earthly pleasures." Maybe that's why we are drawn to Lovers Point: it's the place where these dueling identities coalesce.

Here, a narrow spit of quartz-rich Santa Lucia Granodiorite rocks (the source of the area's white sand) extends into Monterey Bay to form the distinctive sweeping arm of Lovers Point, protecting the beach against incoming ocean currents and waves. The site was christened "Lovers of Jesus Point" by the Methodist founders of Pacific Grove. They had successfully identified the promised land.

Today, swimmers leap from a tiered concrete break wall into the cold, clear water below. They lay out on the warm slab, soaking up the radiant heat. Summers tend to be cool and foggy, and locals wait patiently for these perfect September days when the sun re-emerges and the ocean is still warm. However, most people's favorite season is winter when clear, blue-sky days can stretch out for months. Cheerful regulars, dressed in neoprene caps and gloves, brave the icy water for their daily dopamine release. These cold-water devotees tout the anti-inflammatory, mmunity-boosting benefits of their ritual swims. Some stay in for almost an hour, emerging pink and pruny, immersed in bubbly conversation.

Walking trails extend out from the point and continue along the shore for miles in either direction, through grassy parks and past exuberant red-orange kniphofias. Looking across the bay it's common to see breaching whales and pods of dolphins. Seals and sea lions jostle for the flattest rock. This is one of the most productive and diverse marine environments in the world. Below the surface is a giant underwater canyon over 10,000 feet deep (twice the depth of the Grand Canyon), where nutrient-rich water rises from the depths, the source of Cannery Row's famed sardine and anchovy wealth. Though, these days, the marine life is protected and studied, more than harvested, thanks to the Monterey Bay National Marine Sanctuary and Monterey Bay Aquarium Research Institute.

It's more than just a beautiful place. Lovers Point invites you to swim and explore, or simply sit and observe. It's the very best of what the Monterey Peninsula has to offer.

NEARBY

PAVEL'S BAKERY
219 Forest Ave, Pacific Grove

We heard about Pavel's Bakery from some Bay Area acquaintances who come regularly to Monterey on the weekend. They mentioned Pavel's limited hours and told us to go early, between 7 and 8am, and order bear claw pastries and giant donuts. You'll only be disappointed if they are closed.

TIDAL COFFEE
400 Cannery Row, Monterey

If you find yourself wandering along tourist-filled Cannery Row, Tidal Coffee is where you want to stop for a cup. Craft coffee drinks and baked goods are served in a relaxed hotel cafe setting with bay views. And there are almost always lines out the door, which says something.

ALTA BAKERY AND CAFE
502 Munras Ave, Monterey

With a nod to California's Spanish and Mexican past, Monterey's downtown is filled with restored adobe buildings. None more impressive than the Cooper Molera Adobe. Within its walls is Alta Bakery and Cafe. Swoon over mouth-watering sweets, wood-fired pizzas, and colorful salads, and dine in the expansive garden out back. It's easily our top pick.

"Most people's favorite season is winter when clear, blue-sky days can stretch out for months."

Mercey Hot Springs

Diablo Range

○ **ANCESTRAL HOMELANDS**
Yokuts and Amah Matsun

∽ **TYPE OF SWIM**
Hot springs

⊠ **DRESS CODE**
Clothing optional in designated areas and private
rooms

✷ **ACTIVITIES**
Swim, paddle, surf, scuba dive

⊘ Kid friendly

⊗ No dogs

☾ **BEST TIME TO VISIT**
September to May

⏲ **OPEN HOURS**
Day use 12–5pm. For overnight guests, the pool
is open from 9am to 10pm, and tubs from 5am to
midnight.

Ⓢ **COST OF ENTRY**
$50 for a day pass (5 hours). Soaking is included in the
rate for overnight guests. Camping starts at $75 per
night, cabins at $215.

⃤ **CLOSEST CAMPSITE**
On-site

⬈ **HOW TO GET THERE**
13 miles west of I-5 on Little Panoche Road

⊖ **ACCESS**
Easy. All bathing areas are within a couple hundred
yards of the main entrance.

✳ **LOCAL KNOWLEDGE**
Word of the day: balneology—the healing ritual of
soaking in natural mineral water. Derived from the
Latin word balneum, "bath," balneology has been used
in health and wellness practices for hundreds of years
in Greece, Egypt, Germany, Russia, Arabia, China, and
Japan, as well as in many indigenous cultures around
the world. Here at Mercey Hot Springs you can study
the art of balneology all day long.

Hot-spring soaking is a pastime we are rather partial to. We have been known to drive days out of our way to find natural warm springs in the ground, or hike hours in the snow to arrive at a hot mountain pool, and we regularly create our own version at home. Few things compare to the simple, nourishing joy of submerging in hot water.

On our trip through California, we adhered to a regular balneology (see Local Knowledge) regime, and you will find the best locations we found scattered throughout this book. Although Central California (and specifically the Central Valley) is home to several large aquifers, the hot, mineralized bathing kind is uncommon. Mercey Springs in Little Panoche Valley is one, and it's a good one.

This isolated oasis sits low in a valley of the Diablo range, one of the last undeveloped regions in Central California. To get here you drive through pastureland—cracker dry in summer, sodden green in the winter rainy season—home to cows with more than a football field each to roam. Out the car window you might spot the odd house or tree, but you won't manage a single bar of phone reception.

Located 10 miles off the highway, the remote 277-acre property of Mercey Hot Springs, though modest, is immaculately maintained. Larry Ronneberg and Grazyna Aust have owned the resort, established in the 1890s, for nearly 30 years, slowly introducing modern, eco-friendly technology that powers basic cabins, two Airstreams, a tiny house, and a larger house for group accommodation. There are also powered sites for RVs, tent camping, and a raised platform for outdoor yoga. Running 100 percent off-grid, the resort has a diligent approach to its carbon footprint, drawing water from the ground and energy from the sun, as evidenced by the impressive solar array up on the ridge.

A communal swimming pool is the focal point of the property. What appears as a regular hotel pool sits at around 85°F and is kid friendly. Just beyond the main pool, individual open-air tubs can be filled using hot- and cold-water taps. These therapeutic springs require swimwear, though if you are naturally inclined, clothing-optional tubs can be found deeper into the property a few hundred yards away. There is also a bathhouse with several private rooms, and space for massage treatments.

Mercey is a popular weekend escape for Bay Area residents (just two hours away). Guests can explore the property further by wandering up trails to a disk golf course and a labyrinth. But if your body needs to unfurl after days of driving or a week at a desk, the best bet is to take a soak in the healing mineral waters.

"Few things compare to the simple,
nourishing joy of submerging in hot water."

Granite cliffs and deep pools at the gateway to Sequoia National Park

⊙ **ANCESTRAL HOMELANDS**
Nyyhmy (Western Mono/Monache)

⊖ **TYPE OF SWIM**
River

⊕ **ACTIVITIES**
Swim, rock jump, hike, climb, paddle, fish

⊘ Kid friendly, Yes-ish, but some sections less so

⊗ No dogs

◐ **BEST TIME TO VISIT**
June to September

⑤ **COST OF ENTRY**
$35 entry fee to Sequoia & Kings Canyon National Park, valid for 7 days. Free entry with an America the Beautiful or similar annual interagency pass.

⊘ **CLOSEST CAMPSITE**
Potwisha Campground, Sequoia National Park (3.0 miles)

⊕ **CLOSEST TOWN OF INTEREST**
Three Rivers (5.5 miles)

⤴ **HOW TO GET THERE**
Driving north from Three Rivers on Highway 198, the trailhead is located about 0.6 miles past the Sequoia National Park entry station. Look for a turnout on the right with room for 3–5 cars. The well-defined path traverses between the Southern Sierra Research Station and two concrete ponds. If you get to the Visitor's Center you have gone too far.

⊖ **ACCESS**
Easy. From the road, it's about a quarter mile down to the river. There is one steep section with good footing that will take you to the water's edge. From there, follow the trail a couple hundred feet upriver to reach the cliffs and rock jumps.

The Kaweah River begins its life high up in Sequoia National Park, and it tumbles nearly 10,000 feet over the next 20 miles to reach the foothills town of Three Rivers. It's one of the steepest watersheds in America, and at times it feels like it is barely contained by its own banks. For much of the year it roils with whitewater, surging across the granite bedrock and cartwheeling over waterfalls to scour the riverbed below. As the first flushes of snowmelt pass, rafters and kayakers come and go. Finally, just as the summer heat becomes unbearable, the water level drops to a safe level. The river slows down to reveal still, green pools and sandy beaches. Polished granite slabs sparkle in the sun. It's worth the wait.

The Cliffs is literally the gateway to Sequoia National Park, making it the perfect beginning and/or ending to adventures in this incredible wilderness area. For Three Rivers locals, this swimming hole is a de facto public space. It's easy to get to, only a five-minute walk from the road, and there is enough shoreline for people to spread out. A well-defined trail descends the steep hillside and then follows the river upstream a few hundred feet. The main pool is immediately recognizable for its high granite walls, which channel the river into a narrow chute. At the top end, a waterfall spills into the *cañoncito*, with excellent jumping rocks and ledges on both sides. It is reliably deep, but be sure to inspect the landing for yourself. You never know what trees or boulders may have washed into the swimming hole between visits.

We hold our breath as people scramble up the cliffs some 20, 40, and even 80 feet high. Eeek, we can't watch. But everyone resurfaces with whoops of laughter: kids and dads, college students, cautious travel writers. The shared experience allows conversation to flow easily. It's a stark contrast to a day at the beach, where people territorially mark their spot and maintain their borders. These river swims feel more communal. We encourage and congratulate one another, and extend a hand to pull others out of the water. Add a little bit of danger to any situation and suddenly we see the best of people. It's strange but true.

That said, it's not all about jumping. Immediately downstream the river widens and slows. The rock walls descend to shallow beaches shaded by sprawling buckeye trees. It's the perfect place to marinate with a good book. We sit waist deep in the water, making tiny adjustments to find the perfect equilibrium between cool river and hot summer air. If you get it right, you can stay in all day.

NEARBY

THREE RIVERS BREWING CO
41763 Sierra Dr, Three Rivers

This community brewery is open Thursday to Sunday, and they make everything from the usual IPAs and sours to rootbeer and micheladas. Enjoy a drink in the spacious courtyard backing onto the Kaweah River. Pupusas la Sabrosa parks here during the summer season to serve their mouth-watering pupusas, tacos, and burritos.

SEQUOIA COFFEE COMPANY
41669 Sierra Dr, Three Rivers

As you drive through Three Rivers on your way to a mountain adventure in the national park, stop for coffee and sandwiches at Sequoia Coffee Co. The sign out front will lure you with its promise of espresso, iced coffee, warm griddled donuts, smoothies, and sandwiches. We're fans of the tuna on rye with cucumber, sprouts, red onion, and cream cheese, but the JD Club is a good time too.

BUCKEYE TREE LODGE
46000 Sierra Dr, Three Rivers

This friendly, peaceful twelve-room and ten-cabin eco-lodge makes an excellent base to explore Sequoia National Park. The property is nestled among granite boulders and lush gardens on the banks of the Kaweah River and offers daily yoga classes and massage, a saltwater swimming pool, and a seasonal stargazing program. Owners Shannon and Christian are enthusiastic about nearby hikes and swims.

Middle Fork Tule River Falls

Sequoia National Forest

Cascades, waterfalls, and deep pools in the southern Sierra Nevada foothills

⊙ **ANCESTRAL HOMELANDS**
Yokuts

⊖ **TYPE OF SWIM**
River and waterfall

⊛ **ACTIVITIES**
Swim, hike, fish

⊘ Dog friendly

⊗ No kids

◖ **BEST TIME TO VISIT**
July to October, once water has dropped to a safe level

⊙ **OPEN HOURS**
Roads typically open between May and September, depending on the snowpack.

⊘ **CLOSEST CAMPSITE**
Wishon Campground (3.7 miles)

⊕ **CLOSEST TOWN OF INTEREST**
Springville (9.7 miles)

⇗ **HOW TO GET THERE**
From Springville, drive northeast on Highway 190 for 9.7 miles. The trailhead pullout is about 2 miles past the powerhouse bridge on a big bend in the road. The trail (Stephenson's Trail) descends from behind the Forest Service sign.

⊖ **ACCESS**
Moderate. From the parking area, follow the steep trail to the river and continue downstream along the north rim of the gorge. After about 800 feet you'll see the lip of the waterfall. It's a further 20 yards downstream for easy access to the swimming hole below. Altogether, the walk is about a quarter of a mile.

✳ **LOCAL KNOWLEDGE**
Check out the Wishon Fork of the Tule River for more swimming holes and a natural waterslide.

The Tule River originates in the southwestern slopes of the Sierra Nevada in the Golden Trout Wilderness. Clear, cold snowmelt from the Kern Plateau flows west across the rugged foothills, creating abundant waterfalls, cascades, and swimming holes along the way. Steep canyons make much of the river inaccessible, but there are a few classic spots where locals go to escape the oppressive summer heat. One of our favorites is Middle Fork Falls. It's only a short walk from the road but features a waterfall, deep swimming hole, and plenty of rock ledges to lie in the sun.

This is a pilgrimage that we save for late summer, when waves of heat wash over the Central Valley, when all the snow has melted and water levels have dropped to safe levels. The time of year when everywhere else feels parched and crispy is when the Tule River comes into its own—a cold, nourishing, green thread of life.

The steep, sandy trail descends from a Highway 190 turnout. After a single switchback, the trail cuts across the slope of the hillside to continue downstream to join a path along the north rim of the gorge. Turn right and continue for about 800 feet. The easiest river access is just down from the waterfall, where you will find well-defined use-trails. If at any point it feels dangerous or climbing is required, it's not the right way. Backtrack until you find an easy trail.

Once you reach the river, the air temperature immediately drops. Cool air washes over the surface of water and fills this tiny valley with a feeling of respite from the outside world. It is a sanctuary. Small trout dart around in the clear water. Delicate green ferns and grasses flourish, in stark contrast to the scratchy manzanita that populates the canyon walls. Stepping into the water takes you away from the outside world and allows you to fully inhabit this small oasis.

The river braids down the 30-foot waterfall into the deep plunge pool below. Plumes of mist pulse across the granite walls and scatter tiny rainbows through the air. We dive into the pool and let the force of the waterfall push us backwards. Even late in the summer the water is cold—almost enough to give you an ice cream headache. We climb up onto the smooth granite slabs, then sprawl across them to drink in every square inch of warmth. We cycle back and forth all day. Heating and cooling. Swimming and sprawling.

Eventually the sun passes behind the mountains. We hike out feeling renewed. There is a freshness to mountain swimming that you can't get on the coast. Whatever anxieties we've been carrying have long since been forgotten. In their place is simple hunger. Which leads to the final sacrament of this swimming pilgrimage—a good meal and a cold beer.

NEARBY

COWPUNCHERS CAFE
35585 Highway 190, Springville

This all-day eatery offers a wide variety of the usual roadside fare—omelets and pancakes, salads and sandwiches, burgers and "cowpies" (pizzas). Try the Buckaroo Breakfast, the Pull Up Your Boot Straps club sandwich, or the Rancher's Cut 14-ounce ribeye steak. It's down-home local food in a rustic log cabin venue.

WILD OAK COFFEE HOUSE
35692 Bridge Dr, Springville

For a coffee and pastry in the sunny courtyard, or salad and a sandwich, this is a good option. But the real draw is the homemade, hand-cranked ice cream. Served in a cup, it comes in flavors like honey vanilla, fried peach, roasted banana, lemon cheesecake, and mint. It's bloody beautiful on a hot summer day.

CALIFORNIA HOT SPRINGS
42177 Hot Springs Dr, California Hot Springs

Founded in 1882, this historic lodge is located inside Giant Sequoia National Monument. Amenities include two outdoor hot pools, a deli, and RV parking. At 3,100 feet, the property is above the fog but below the snow line, which means winters are mild and summers are warm and sunny. The ideal combination.

MIDDLE FORK TULE RIVER FALLS

Remington Hot Springs

Kern River/Bodfish

Artfully constructed riverside hot springs with old-school California hippy vibes

⊙ **ANCESTRAL HOMELANDS**
Tübatulabal and Yokuts

∿ **TYPE OF SWIM**
River hot springs

⊠ **DRESS CODE**
Nudity is common

‖ **ETIQUETTE**
Wild hot springs are fragile and sacred places. Please be respectful of the environment and other users by practicing Leave No Trace (p.x) ethics. In fact, leave it better than you found it by picking up any waste that you see. Likewise, allow the springs to be a quiet place, not a party place. Keep your voice low and avoid playing any music. Strictly no glass or soap in the springs.

⊘ Kid friendly, Dog friendly

◑ **BEST TIME TO VISIT**
September to April. Bathe between 9am and 5pm for the most privacy.

⊙ **OPEN HOURS**
24 hours. Tubs are emptied and cleaned on Tuesday.

⑤ **COST OF ENTRY**
Free

⟁ **CLOSEST CAMPSITE**
Hobo Campground (1.7 miles)

⊕ **CLOSEST TOWN OF INTEREST**
Kernville (18 miles)

⬀ **HOW TO GET THERE**
From Lake Isabella, head south along Highway 178 toward Bakersfield. After about 3.5 miles, turn left onto Borel Road and then right onto Kern Canyon Road. Continue south another 3.4 miles to the Remington Hot Springs parking area. You will pass Hobo Campground and Miracle Hot Springs on the way.

⊖ **ACCESS**
Easy. It's a short but relatively steep walk down to the hot springs.

✳ **LOCAL KNOWLEDGE**
Every Tuesday, volunteers empty all of the water and scrub each tub to remove any built-up dirt and algae. The result is astonishingly clear springs that not even the crustiest van-lifer can sully. Make their work easier by carrying out any trash that you find.

The warm, sweet smell of radiator coolant greeted us as we were driving up the highway toward Lake Isabella. By the time we realized what it was, a jet of steam shot from under the hood, and we knew we were cooked. It would take days to repair the radiator, if we were lucky. Looking around the scorched chaparral hills, we didn't feel lucky. Yet if we hadn't been forced to stop, we never would have found Remington Hot Springs.

Our tow truck driver delivered us to a mechanic who said he'd have us back on the road in a couple of days. Before long, we were sipping coffee and sharing a slice of pie at the diner next door. Our luck was improving. We pored over the map, revisiting our research on the Kern River with a new sense of optimism.

From where we sat, just below the enormous earthen dam that creates Lake Isabella, the options nearby were limited. But we found old notes about a couple of hot springs just south of town. Although it wasn't exactly hot-spring weather—outdoor temps were hovering around 100°F—we were on our third coffee refill, and pretty much anything sounded like a good idea.

The next morning, the only taxi in town dropped us in a parking lot with a plan to return a few hours later. Dazed heads peered out from dust-covered vans and RVs. Burning Man had ended a couple of weeks earlier and we'd been bumping into a bleary-eyed diaspora of "Afterburners" at swimming holes across the state ever since. We exchanged smiles and found the trail down the hill. A short walk brought us to some of the most beautifully constructed hot springs we've ever seen.

Remington Hot Springs sits like a series of blue jewels on the banks of the Kern River. The tubs are artfully constructed in organic shapes using large river stones for the walls, while smaller pebbles and marbles decorate their mosaic bottoms. There are four pools by the river, with a small tub 50 feet up the hill, known as "The Miners Tub."

The pools are arranged so that hot water flows from one to the next, each tub incrementally cooler than the last. It takes about half an hour for water to cycle through the system and overflow into the river. We stripped down and tested each pool, sometimes jumping into the river to reset. After months of driving and hiking, it was a relief to have this forced layover. Our achy bodies craved the hot mineral water, and we passed the time reading our books or chatting with people who came and went. After a while, the mechanic called. He was struggling to remove the old thermostat and would need another day. Yesterday that would have been a disappointment, but today it felt like a gift.

NEARBY

MIRACLE HOT SPRINGS
Kern River, Sequoia National Forest

Previously known as Hobo Hot Springs, Miracle is a similarly secluded set of man-made hot springs along the Kern River, not far from Hobo Campground. There's a nice day use area with river swimming access, so it can get quite busy on weekends. Expect nudity, free spirits, and drum circles.

NELDA'S DINER
5128 Lake Isabella Blvd, Lake Isabella

Lake Isabella isn't the most exciting place to be broken down for three days, but finding Nelda's Diner along the main drag was a welcoming respite. Settle into dove gray leather booths with pink trim and order shakes, floats, burgers, and a wide selection of house-made pies. It's the kind of place both locals and visitors love.

KERNVILLE

Just up the canyon from Lake Isabella is the river town of Kernville. Breweries, scenic drives, hikes, mountain biking trails, and rafting are a few of the draws of this charming village. Drink beer at Kern River Brewing or cocktails at Ewings overlooking the river; eat slices at Pizza Barn or bowls of pasta at That's Italian.

CENTRAL COAST

SANTA BARBARA
TO MONTEREY

This unpopulated strip of coast is a roadtripper's dream. Drive winding country roads through the epicurean wine towns of the Santa Ynez Valley, before you meet the dramatic coastal bluffs of Big Sur. Swim in freshwater rivers, stay in cabins in redwood forests, and finish up at the white-sand beaches of Carmel-by-the-Sea and Monterey.

Day 1

Santa Barbara to Los Olivos

57 MILES / 1 HR 30 MINS + STOPS

Santa Barbara is an excellent place to start any road trip. But first, be sure to visit the historic hilltop Mission, wander around downtown, and swim at **Los Baños del Mar pool**. Then get on the road and head 50 minutes inland to Los Padres National Forest and **Red Rock Pools** (p. 165), where, about half a mile from the trailhead, you will find several swimming holes along the **Santa Ynez River**. Plan to spend an afternoon there. Then continue west 30 miles to the tiny town of **Los Olivos** for a one-stop wine country experience, exploring tasting rooms, eateries, art galleries, and shops.

Day 2

Los Olivos to Cambria

94 MILES / 1 HR 30 MINS

From Los Olivos you could easily explore the other nearby towns in the Santa Ynez Valley, cute and kitschy in varying degrees. But **Los Alamos** is our first choice. Wine tasting rooms, beer gardens, and celebrated restaurants have made this once sleepy town into a food destination with a cult-like following. Stop in for breakfast at **Bob's Well Bread Bakery** before continuing an hour north to San Luis Obispo. It's a charming college town with great farm-to-table food and a thriving epicurean landscape. Have a coffee at Scout and visit the San Luis Obispo Museum of Art (SLOMA). Then continue the drive, heading 40 minutes along the coast to Cambria, where you can enjoy the evening with a bottle of Paso Robles wine. Robin's garden restaurant in a restored adobe home is a favorite.

Day 3

Cambria to Big Sur

68 MILES / 1 HR 40 MINS

Make sure to explore Cambria and its village strip dotted with colorful timber houses, fermentation stores, cafes, and crystal shops touting psychic readings. Then drive 15 minutes to the ornate Hearst Castle estate in San Simeon. A tour is the only way to see the property, and booking ahead is recommended. As you continue north, pull up at Elephant Seal Vista Point on San Simeon Beach to see hundreds of these behemoths hauled out on the sand. Breathe in the briny sea air, then carry on toward the craggy coast of Big Sur. Stop and hike to **Upper Salmon Creek Falls** (p. 181), a steep 4.2-mile round trip up the canyon to a waterfall and pool. Stop for the night in one of **Deetjen's Big Sur Inn's** cozy forest cabins under the redwoods along Highway 1.

Day 4

Big Sur to Carmel-by-the-Sea

31 MILES / 50 MINS

Wake up in the sleepy forest at Deetjen's and wander over to the restaurant for breakfast. Eggs benedict or fluffy buttermilk pancakes are likely candidates to start your day. In April/May, Big Sur is vibrant with wildflowers and flowing waterfalls. For sunny, cloudless days, visit September to November. But during summer, when the water and weather are warmest, **Big Sur River Gorge** (p. 179) is the place to be. Inland from the coast, the Big Sur River isn't affected by the summer fog. Here you will swim in the most impressive freshwater pools on this trip. Then follow the wild, unspoiled coastline north to Carmel-by-the-Sea, Bohemian artist enclave turned ritzy seaside village, and settle in for the night.

Day 5

Carmel-by-the-Sea to Monterey

12 MILES / 37 MINS + STOPS

It's only 12 miles to Monterey, but our route is going to take you most of the day. First, follow 17 Mile Drive through Pebble Beach, past several of its famous golf courses. This private community costs $10.50 to enter and hangs right over the Pacific Ocean. At the end of the drive you'll arrive in Pacific Grove; continue along the shore to **Lovers Point Beach** (p. 175), where we like to swim and warm up in the sun on the concrete wharf. Then head into downtown Monterey. It's a 2.5-mile walk along the coastal rec trail, if you have the time and energy, or a 10-minute drive. Visit the historic Cooper Molera Adobe and its **Alta Bakery and Café** for a late lunch out in the gardens—the perfect end to this delicious five-day itinerary.

Southern

CALIFORI

Southern California

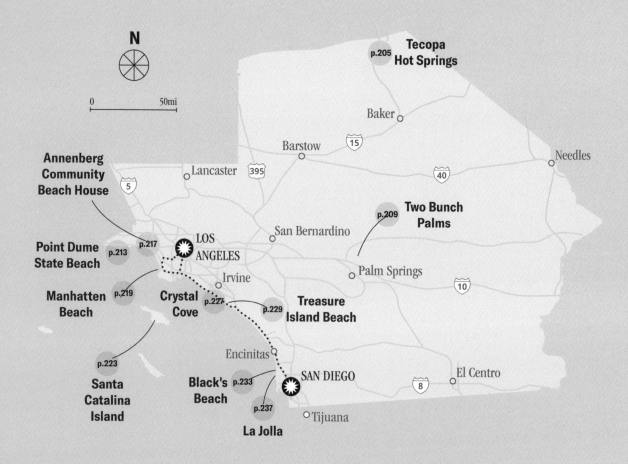

N

0   50mi

p.205 **Tecopa Hot Springs**

Baker

Barstow

15

Needles

Annenberg Community Beach House

Lancaster

395

5

40

San Bernardino

p.209 **Two Bunch Palms**

Point Dume State Beach   p.213   p.217

LOS ANGELES

Irvine

Palm Springs

10

Manhatten Beach   p.219

Crystal Cove   p.227

p.229   **Treasure Island Beach**

p.223

Encinitas

SAN DIEGO

El Centro

Santa Catalina Island

Black's Beach   p.233

8

p.237

Tijuana

La Jolla

Best Beach

Treasure Island Beach, Laguna Beach (p.229)

Favorite Meal

The Rooster and the Pig, Palm Springs (p.209)

When to visit

Year round

Southern California is surely one of the most photographed, filmed, and crooned about places in the world, so deeply woven into the 20th-century zeitgeist that it almost feels like public property. The brilliant sunlight, dusty chaparral, ubiquitous palm trees, and enigmatic Joshua trees, not to mention the boundless possibility of the Pacific Ocean, are all well known, even if you've never set foot in the state. Our goal here, thus, has been to explore both the familiar and the unfamiliar, searching from the coast to the desert for sanctuaries in this densely populated part of the state and breaking down what is real and what is make-believe.

Our favorite places are ones where you can find peace and privacy even when you least expect it. Nowhere better exemplifies this than San Diego, a laid-back city that has been spoiled by its exquisite coastline and climate. While people rightfully flock to La Jolla's (p.237) jewel-like coves, nearby Black's Beach (p.233) is a peaceful alternative, relaxed and secluded. There is so much to explore around San Diego, from Imperial Beach on the Tijuana border all the way up to North County's craggy coves and surf breaks, each coastal community with its own distinct culture and identity.

Orange County is world famous for its pristine beaches, and it doesn't disappoint. You can find astonishingly clear water at Crystal Cove (p.227), as well as the area's largest remaining open space and natural seashore. Its federally listed historic district includes a motley collection of 46 rustic 1930s-era seaside cottages, available for rent. We found ourselves drawn to this area again and again, especially neighboring Laguna Beach, which strikes a fine balance between glitz and charm. Laguna's hidden Treasure Island Beach (p.229) is our nominee for best beach in the state.

Beyond the coast, you can discover another aspect of Southern California's culture by making a trip into the high desert during winter or spring. Upscale Palm Springs is appropriately celebrated, but we found our favorite wellness oasis in neighboring Desert Hot Springs. Two Bunch Palms (p.209) is an indulgent mineral springs resort with lush native gardens and panoramic views over the Coachella Valley and San Jacinto Mountains. At the opposite end of the spectrum, we were completely won over by the remote Mojave Desert town of Tecopa (p.205). This hard-worn outpost has abundant hot springs, incredible stargazing, and a burgeoning food culture.

For a place that is seemingly so familiar, Southern California always surprises us. There is a depth and diversity of experiences to suit all tastes, and enough incredible landscapes to exceed any expectations.

Favorite
Desert Outpost

Tecopa Hot Springs
(p.205)

Cutest
Town

Encinitas
(p.233)

Road
Trip

Sunshine Coast
(p.240)

Tecopa Hot Springs

Nopah Range/Mojave Desert

ANCESTRAL HOMELANDS
Nuwui (Southern Paiute) and Newe Sogbia
(Western Shoshone)

TYPE OF SWIM
Hot springs

ACTIVITIES
Soak, hike

DRESS CODE
Nudity is common at many of the springs in this area
unless otherwise specified.

ETIQUETTE
Wild hot springs are fragile and sacred places. Please
be respectful of the environment and other users by
practicing Leave No Trace (p.x) ethics. In fact, leave
it better than you found it by picking up any trash
that you see. Likewise, allow the springs to be a quiet
place, not a party place. Keep your voice low and avoid
playing any music. Strictly no glass or soap in the
springs.

No kids, No dogs

BEST TIME TO VISIT
November to March

COST OF ENTRY
Free to $30/day

CLOSEST CAMPSITE
Tecopa Campground

CLOSEST TOWN OF INTEREST
Tecopa

HOW TO GET THERE
Tecopa is located just off Highway 127 (Death Valley
Road) about 51 miles north of Baker and 9.5 miles
south of Shoshone.

ACCESS
Easy. All springs are within a short walking distance
from roads and parking.

LOCAL KNOWLEDGE
A small man-made bath known as the "Tecopa Hot
Tub" is located along unpaved Furnace Creek Road.
Hidden by a collection of palms, the private tub fits
just two to three people, and has a constant flow of
warm water cycling through. You can drive right up to
it or walk via a path from the back of Delight's resort.
Make sure to return the pool cover after use.

Tecopa had long been on our list of destinations, but there was always some reason not to go—too far, wrong season, roads closed. It wasn't until a huge winter storm chased us from the coast that Tecopa became our unlikely refuge, the only place in the state, it seemed, that wasn't flooding. We waited out the tempest there, and when the sun finally reappeared, we soaked in the hot springs, sampled the local beers, ate slow-cooked meats, and guzzled date shakes. We were sold.

Tecopa is far from everywhere in California, sitting in the eastern part of the state just south of Death Valley National Park, where the sublime, otherworldly beauty of the Mojave Desert is like the tailings of the world's largest mine. Driving along Highway 127, you'll pass chloride green rocks, sulfur yellow hills, and black mountains scarred white by borax. The winter sun saturates the land, creating an intensely bleak allure. Against this dramatic backdrop, Tecopa sits atop a small rocky plateau, looking out over the surrounding saline desert wetlands.

In summer, temperatures regularly soar above 115°F and only a handful of brave locals stick around to look after the town. Instead, it is winter when Tecopa becomes a refuge for migratory birds and weary travelers, drawn to the remote tranquility of this desert outpost with so much sky and so little phone service.

Clusters of tall palms are scattered among low-slung utilitarian houses, trailers, and RVs. The town has an unapologetically hard-worn look, but it is more than meets the eye. If you stick around, you'll notice all the good food and drink: a couple of breweries, a barbeque joint, a five-table steakhouse, and a cafe. Artists, both fine and culinary, have found their way to this frontier community of eccentrics and nonconformists.

The large marshy pool on the north end of town is the biggest and most notable natural hot spring. Visitors coat themselves in silky clay, often gathering around sunrise and sunset to watch the light dance across the desert sky. Locals, meanwhile, are more likely to be found at Tecopa's utilitarian public bathhouse, where $10 will get you a day pass. The Japanese sentō-style setup consists of two single-gender baths with adjoining locker rooms. Nude bathing only.

For a mixed bathing experience, Delight's Hot Spring Resort is our go-to. Tiny cabins and vintage trailers surround a large outdoor geothermal pool with panoramic views of the Nopah range. There are also four private, enclosed tubs, each accommodating up to six people. Kitschy classical busts, friezes, and fountains adorn the common areas like a post-apocalyptic Caesars Palace. Like everything in this town, somehow it works.

NEARBY

TECOPA BREWING COMPANY
420 Tecopa Hot Springs Rd, Tecopa

One of two brewers in town (the other is
Death Valley Brewing), this modest dining
room and bar sits at the entrance into
Delight's. Though you can't miss the bold red
sign: BREWERY BBQ. In addition to house-
brewed ales and IPAs, they serve barbecue—
pulled pork, brisket, and ribs with sides of
cornbread, coleslaw, and homemade chili.

STEAK AND BEER
860 Tecopa Hot Springs Rd, Tecopa

Grass-fed beef and locally sourced organic
vegetables make up the small but robust dinner
menu at Steak and Beer. Sauteed cauliflower,
arugula salads, and a soup du jour are available,
but it's the giant steak—one-pound ribeye or
filet mignon—that people come for. This place
gets busy.

CHINA RANCH DATE FARM & BAKERY
China Ranch Rd, Tecopa

China Ranch is a hidden oasis down two miles
of narrow dirt road (think *Star Wars*' Tatooine).
Date shakes are the winning order here, but
you can also take home rare varieties of fresh
dates. Hike the short Mercer Trail to get a view
of the farm, or a three-mile loop trail along
Willow Creek to Amargosa Slot Canyon.

This luxuriant hot springs resort is a literal oasis near Palm Springs

Two Bunch Palms

Desert Hot Springs, Coachella Valley

◉ **ANCESTRAL HOMELANDS**
Ivilyuqaletem (Agua Caliente band of Cahuilla)

⊖ **TYPE OF SWIM**
Private hot springs resort

⊛ **ACTIVITIES**
Soak, spa, yoga, meditation

⋈ **DRESS CODE**
Swimwear required in all common-area pools and tubs.

⊗ No kids, No dogs

◖ **BEST TIME TO VISIT**
January to April

⌚ **OPEN HOURS**
24 hours for guests

⑤ **COST OF ENTRY**
Entry is for hotel guests only. Rooms start at $265 a night.

⊕ **CLOSEST TOWN OF INTEREST**
Desert Hot Springs

↗ **HOW TO GET THERE**
67425 Two Bunch Palms Trail, Desert Hot Springs

✳ **LOCAL KNOWLEDGE**
Two Bunch Palms opened to the public in 1940 as a "desert spa," but journal entries dating back to 1840 tell people to "look for the two palms to find rest and water." Among its rumored owners was Chicago mobster Al Capone. If he didn't actually own it, he may well have frequented it. He is said to have used the property as his west coast hideout and a place to stash his cash. His legacy is so enduring, the resort named a suite after him.

As long as there have been people living in California they have come to the palm-filled canyons of the Coachella Valley seeking water, food, and refuge. Tall mountains rise out of this desert plain, providing shelter from prevailing winds and making this area much more fertile than you might expect. The local Cahuilla people have called this land home for thousands of years, and today it is a haven for health, wellness, and revitalization. Visitors come year round from LA, Brooklyn, and beyond.

Coachella is known for its annual psychedelic music and arts festival and for glamorous, midcentury-modern Palm Springs, with its glitzy downtown. But don't overlook its lesser-known, more modest neighbor of Desert Hot Springs. This is where you can find relatively secluded places to soak, though they are mostly on private properties—resorts and B&B-type accommodations. Both towns are located on the San Andreas fault, where a water basin with wells approximately 1,200 feet deep resides underground—a literal oasis in the desert. As the highly mineralized water moves to the surface, it cools to about 100°F, making it ideal for swimming. It is this water that resorts such as Two Bunch Palms tap into for their luxuriant pools and hot tubs.

Set on 77 lush acres with sweeping mountain views, this adults-only resort is a place you come to treat yourself. (It's not a drop-in kind of place, and you can only access the pools as a paying guest.) Most stay for a minimum of two nights, so there is time to soak in the cool saltwater pool, the large grotto, and the 15 common-area open-air tubs. A wellness spa, yoga classes, tennis courts, a tea and wine bar, and a restaurant serving cleansing SoCal cuisine round out the offerings. Gravel paths flanked by bougainvillea, aloe vera, and Washingtonia (California's native fan palm) weave between rooms and pools, as guests wander the property in bathrobes. Their day of pampering is likely punctuated by a tranquil morning soak, lunch by the pool, and an evening floating and stargazing. It's nourishing and rejuvenating, and completely indulgent.

If you've visited Palm Springs before, you may be familiar with the chic desert town's dedication to architectural swimming pools, be it at a scenic hotel or a private midcentury home. Winter is the time to come, with warm, sunny days that beckon you to swim—even in a hot spring in the desert.

NEARBY

WINDMILL MARKET
17080 N Indian Canyon Dr, North Palm Springs

With 95 percent of dates grown in the US coming from this region, it only makes sense that they're making shakes out of them—some 200–300 a day at this unassuming roadside grocer. The recipe is simple: blend vanilla ice cream with Medjool date puree and milk. Don't overthink it. It's delicious.

PALM SPRINGS

Highlights of this swank desert town include the Palm Springs Art Museum, poolside drinks at the Ace Swim Club or (for something fancy) the Parker, coffee at Ernest Coffee, or street-style Vietnamese at The Rooster and the Pig. Take an architectural tour to see midcentury-modern homes in all their sun-drenched glory.

INDIAN CANYONS
38520 S Palm Canyon Dr, Palm Springs

The Indian Canyons, at the base of the San Jacinto Mountains, are the ancestral lands of the Agua Caliente Band of Cahuilla Indians. The area offers 60 miles of hiking trails, ranging from short and easy to long and strenuous, through native fan palm oases and along meandering mountain streams. Entry fee is $12 for adults.

Point Dume State Beach

Malibu

The most laid-back beach in the most over-the-top location

The most laid-back beach in
the most over-the-top location

ANCESTRAL HOMELANDS
Ventureño (Chumash)

TYPE OF SWIM
Ocean

ACTIVITIES
Swim, surf, climb, hike

Kid friendly

No dogs

BEST TIME TO VISIT
May to November

OPEN HOURS
Sunrise to sunset

COST OF ENTRY
A parking fee may apply, depending on where you arrive.

CLOSEST CAMPSITE
Leo Carrillo State Park Campground (8.8 miles)

CLOSEST TOWN OF INTEREST
Malibu

HOW TO GET THERE
From Malibu, turn off Pacific Coast Highway onto Westward Beach Road. Continue for about 1.3 miles as it reaches the beach and then bends south along the coast. The road dead-ends at a large parking lot.

ACCESS
Easy. Beach access is from the parking lot at the end of Westward Beach Road. You can also reach the headland from above via Cliffside Drive, though parking is limited.

LOCAL KNOWLEDGE
Our top three favorite movie scenes filmed at Point Dume:
1. Jackie Treehorn's beach party in *The Big Lebowski* (1998)
2. Austin Powers and Felicity Shagwell arriving at Dr. Evil's private volcano island wearing matching white bikinis in *Austin Powers: The Spy Who Shagged Me* (1999)
3. The classic final scene from *Planet of the Apes* (1968—the Charlton Heston version), featuring the Statue of Liberty: "Oh my god. I'm back. I'm home…"

Malibu epitomizes the best and worst of Southern California: the delightful sunshine, mountains, beaches, and surf, on the one hand; the excess, exclusivity, and extreme inequality, on the other. To be honest, we don't get it. Or at least we didn't, until we visited Point Dume. Forget the houses, the celebrities, the mythology. The best thing about Malibu is its nature.

The towering rock monolith at the southern end of Westward Beach is the remnant core of an ancient volcano. It's a singular feature on the coast, and a sacred place for the Chumash people who lived here in a precolonial village called Sumo. The rocky headland offers excellent views to both east and west, which made it particularly useful for communication between coastal people. No doubt it was premium real estate even then.

Below the headland is a semi-secret beach known as Pirates Cove. Hidden from view, it can only be accessed by traversing the rocky shoreline from Westward Beach—ideally, at low tide. Unlike the long, broad beaches nearby, Pirates is cozy and quiet. High orange cliffs encircle this small patch of sand, and the Pacific Ocean shines in radiant blues and greens. If there were neatly arranged umbrellas and chairs, you could easily mistake it for Portugal's Algarve coast.

Even on the busiest summer weekends, Pirates Cove is reliably peaceful. However, on days with strong surf, we seek out more protection by hiking over the headland to Big Dume Beach. A small network of trails traverse the point, making concentric circles to the summit. From here you can catch glimpses into the exclusive properties of Cliffside Drive—the blushing terracotta of Tuscan-style estates and polished metal of modernist homes. From mid-February to May you might even spot migrating gray whales as they travel up the coast from winter birthing grounds in Baja California to summer feeding grounds in Alaska.

Follow the trails to the east side of the point, where you'll find a long stairway leading down to the almost-guaranteed seclusion of Big Dume Beach. This narrow strip of sand runs for miles underneath high cliffs. Outer reefs make it a reliable surf spot in winter and protect the beach from strong currents in summer. There are a handful of parking spaces above, but you should generally plan on walking half a mile or so to get here. It's just far enough that most people don't bother. Which is fine with us.

Sitting on the beach, looking across Santa Monica Bay at the haze of LA, we finally understand the appeal. Malibu is extraordinarily close to the city, but feels completely disconnected. Despite immense pressure from development and population growth, it has managed to retain the character of a small coastal town.

NEARBY

TRANCAS COUNTRY MARKET
30745 E Pacific Coast Hwy, Malibu

This retail complex is made up of chic barn-like structures housing surf stores, coffee shops, and hip boutiques. Vintage Grocers is the focal point, a community-minded market selling high-end organic produce and other comestibles. Ideal for grabbing some fancy beach snacks and trying to spot an A-lister or two.

MALIBU SEAFOOD
25653 Highway 1, Malibu

There's no shortage of good seafood along the Malibu coast. But for price and quality, it's hard to beat Malibu Seafood. The cafe menu offers shrimp, lobster, and good old fish and chips, which you can eat at picnic tables with ocean views. Fresh fish is also available at the fish market.

OLD PLACE
29983 Mulholland Hwy, Agoura Hills

Up in the Santa Monica Mountains, this 19th-century general store turned saloon and steakhouse is a favorite among Malibu locals and in-the-know Angelenos escaping the city. The menu features American comfort food—steamed clams, oak-grilled steaks, beef stew, chicken pot pie, and cobbler. With a limited number of dine-in tables, reservations are a must.

Annenberg Community Beach House

Santee Monica

Estate, turned luxury hotel, turned glittering public pool overlooking Santa Monica Beach

◎ **ANCESTRAL HOMELANDS**
Chumash and Tongva (Gabrieleno)

◯ **TYPE OF SWIM**
Public pool

✱ **ACTIVITIES**
Swim, sunbathe

✓ Kid friendly

✕ No dogs

◖ **BEST TIME TO VISIT**
June to September

◔ **OPEN HOURS**
12–6pm Mon to Thurs, 10am–6pm Fri to Sun during summer (subject to change, so double-check). The pool is open Memorial Day weekend (late June) through Labor Day (early September). Between October and May, the pool may be open occasionally on warm-weather weekends or holidays. Check the website for details.

$ **COST OF ENTRY**
$4 ages 1–17, $10 ages 18–59, $5 ages 60+

⊕ **CLOSEST TOWN OF INTEREST**
Santa Monica

↗ **HOW TO GET THERE**
415 Pacific Coast Highway, Santa Monica. Parking on-site costs $3 per hour or $12 for the day.

✳ **LOCAL KNOWLEDGE**
Guests can visit the grounds and go on free guided 20-minute tours of the Marion Davies Guest House on weekends (Friday–Monday) between noon and 2pm. No reservations required.

Only a few man-made pools made it into this book. Not because we don't like them—we love them—but because in California we think the natural spots are superior. Still, there are always exceptions to the rule. Annenberg Community Beach House, located on five acres of Santa Monica beachfront, is one, and in our opinion an easy inclusion here. Annenberg is a pool devoted to the idea of leisure—not swimming for exercise, but for the weightless, sun-kissed joy of it. It's a value we, too, celebrate.

The property was originally developed in the 1920s as an opulent estate by newspaper magnate William Randolph Hearst (of Hearst Castle—this guy had some cash) for actress Marion Davies, his mistress. The mansion had more than a hundred rooms, and the estate included an ornate marble swimming pool overlooking the ocean, around which Hearst and Davies entertained such Hollywood luminaries as Charlie Chaplin, Greta Garbo, and Clark Gable.

In 1947 the property was purchased from Davies and converted into a hotel, Oceanhouse, and a members-only beach club, the Sand & Sea. The hotel soon failed, but the beach club remained in operation until 1994, when the Northridge Earthquake caused serious structural damage. The philanthropic Annenberg Foundation now stepped in, donating $27.5 million to rehabilitate the site. The historic Marion Davies Guest House and marble pool were restored, and new recreation and indoor/outdoor events spaces were built, including an art gallery with year-round cultural programming. It reopened in 2009 as the Annenberg Community Beach House.

Today, this immaculate facility is home to a heated 110-foot saltwater pool, with restored decorative mosaic tiling and stone paving. Orange beach umbrellas and lounge chairs are arranged along one side for guests to laze in the dappled shade, while stoic lifeguards keep watch from a raised seat over kids splashing in the water. The Pool House, fronted by a series of 30-foot modernist concrete pillars, contains changing rooms and, on the second floor, a glass-enclosed events space and open-air terrace. From here you can look out to the expansive beach (think Baywatch), where cyclists and rollerbladers spin past on the 22-mile Marvin Braude Bike Trail.

The property also includes the North House, set within gardens and terraces shaded by palms and melaleuca trees, with sculptures and a waterfall that masks the sound of the highway. On the beach out front there are amenities such as a children's play area, a cafe (see Nearby), and beach volleyball courts. There's so much to do and see at Annenberg. But it's the balmy water of the sunlit pool that we find most enticing.

NEARBY

BACK ON THE BEACH CAFE
445 Pacific Coast Hwy, Santa Monica

Right out front of Annenberg is Back on the Beach, open daily for breakfast (until 2pm) and lunch, and dinner some nights. Dishes include breakfast pasta (eggs and bacon sausage), shakshuka, and a granola sundae. Sit with your toes in the sand under umbrellas and look out toward Santa Catalina Island (p.223).

REEL INN MALIBU
18661 E Pacific Coast Hwy, Malibu

Seven minutes up the PCH toward Topanga Canyon is a funky roadside fish shack serving fresh seafood—halibut, mahi mahi, seabass, grilled, sauteed, or blackened. Add sides, and find a booth. The interior is a busy mix of neon signs, road bikes hanging from the ceiling, and fish tanks with wacky underwater scenes. It's an experience.

THE SURFRIDER HOTEL
23033 E Pacific Coast Hwy, Malibu

This surf-inspired, 1950s-style boutique hotel with 20 rooms located on Malibu's famous Surfrider Beach is light and airy, complete with outdoor terraces and hammocks. The Roof Deck Bar and Restaurant (open only to guests), with its panoramic views, serves organic farm-to-table food and craft cocktails. Amenities include complimentary breakfast and surfboard and wetsuit hire.

Manhattan Beach

South Bay

⊙ **ANCESTRAL HOMELANDS**
Tongva (Gabrieleno)

⊖ **TYPE OF SWIM**
Beach

✻ **ACTIVITIES**
Swim, surf, run, bike

⊘ Kid friendly

⊗ No dogs

◖ **BEST TIME TO VISIT**
The warmest months are July to October, but the water and weather are pleasant year-round.

⊙ **OPEN HOURS**
24 hours, but we recommend swimming only during daylight hours.

⊕ **CLOSEST TOWN OF INTEREST**
Manhattan Beach

⊘ **HOW TO GET THERE**
On Highway 1 southwest of downtown LA and just north of Hermosa Beach and Redondo Beach.

⊖ **ACCESS**
Easy, via stairs to the beach

✳ **LOCAL KNOWLEDGE**
In 1912 Charles and Willa Bruce bought the property known today as Bruce's Beach, located at 26th Street and Highland Avenue, to create a resort for Black beachgoers during a time of racial segregation. Black entrepreneurs were so successful that in 1924 the city caved to aggrieved white residents and seized the land under eminent domain. Nearly a century later, in 2022, the land was returned to the Bruces' descendants. Signage at Bruce's Beach tells this history in more detail.

As we cruise up and down the coast, we always return to Manhattan Beach. There's a coastal community feel here, a boardwalk that extends for miles, and the sort of early-morning beach culture that we like. Beach volleyball is big, surfing too, and depending on the season, you'll see lots of swimmers. Summer is when the crowds flock, but the mild year-round climate accommodates water lovers at all times of year. We like winter when days tend to be sunny and fog free. Ocean swimming here is for those who understand rip currents.

Located along the western edge of the Los Angeles basin, LA's beaches are an important part of the commercial, financial, and cultural sprawl that is Southern California, and a key aspect of its identity. Manhattan Beach (together with its southern neighbors Hermosa and Redondo) has the pace and the feel of a vacation community. As you exit the busy highways, and sloping streets funnel you toward the water and the centerpiece 926-foot-long pier, a laid-back feeling takes over.

The 22-mile Marvin Braude Bike Trail winds along the oceanfront between Pacific Palisades and the South Bay. Here, this flat, scenic cycling superhighway follows the footprint of a historic trolley line that once connected Manhattan, Hermosa, and Redondo Beaches. Alongside the bike path are beach volleyball courts, where bronzed, gym-hardened bodies dig, spike, and smash the ball with energetic grace. Up above, an elevated pedestrian path, the Strand, allows walkers to stroll past palatial modern mansions.

Where Venice and Santa Monica Beaches draw the tourist crowds, the bohemian spirits, and the celebrity culture, Manhattan feels like a local community of beachgoers, families, and outdoor enthusiasts. On the beach itself, baby blue lifeguard towers stand every few hundred feet, stoic and protective, while tall palms sway in the breeze and planes sail overhead, en route to LAX. The residential back streets are a haven for the wealthy, their deluxe homes with verdant courtyards facing onto pedestrian-only walkways. It's a fun place to wander on foot before indulging in the lively downtown area around Ocean Drive and Manhattan Avenue, where boutiques, cafes, pizzerias, bars, ice cream parlors, and upscale eateries are all part of a thriving dining scene. For us, a sunny day near the ocean here feels a little bit like home.

NEARBY

MANHATTAN PIZZERIA
133 Manhattan Beach Blvd, Manhattan Beach

We almost never pass up this hole-in-the-wall pizzeria for a slice (or two) on the way to the beach. New York–style pies, subs, and calzones come out piping hot and oozing with cheese, delivered to picnic tables on the sidewalk out front. Douse in chili oil and soak up the beachside scene. Open late.

SUGARFISH
304 12th St, Manhattan Beach

There's lots of good sushi in LA, but this celebrated, much-hyped sushi chain has special clout. Chef Kazunori Nozawa is committed to using ultra-fresh seafood across his menu of traditional rolls, sashimi, and nigiri, served with sake. No reservations.

KANSHA CREAMERY
18515 S Western Ave, Gardena

Kansha makes natural, artisanal ice cream, churned fresh five days a week by brother and sister duo James Tatsuya and Elaine Yukari. Their ever-changing list of flavors is uniquely delicious—for example, lemon olive oil sherbet, sesame banana, kumquat marmalade, and balsamic caramel. They also do a wicked matcha parfait sundae. It's well worth the 10-minute detour to Gardena.

Santa Catalina Island

Long Beach

ANCESTRAL HOMELANDS
Pimu Tongva (Gabrieleno)

TYPE OF SWIM
Ocean

ACTIVITIES
Swim, snorkel, dive, paddle, sail, hike, mountain bike

Kid friendly

No dogs

BEST TIME TO VISIT
August to November

COST OF ENTRY
Just the cost of your ferry ticket

CLOSEST CAMPSITE
Hermit Gulch Campground (1.3 miles from downtown Avalon)

CLOSEST TOWN OF INTEREST
Avalon

HOW TO GET THERE
The Catalina Express ferry operates daily round-trip service to Avalon from their Long Beach, Dana Point, and San Pedro terminals. San Pedro is the only port that offers service to Two Harbors. Adult fares start at $84 round trip.

ACCESS
Easy. Swim spots around Avalon are all easily walkable. Access to more remote parts of the island requires a shuttle or private taxi service, which can be costly.

LOCAL KNOWLEDGE
Stay awhile. Most visitors come and go in a single day. By staying longer you will get to experience all of the quiet moments that happen between ferries. In any case, you need a few days to explore all the island's riches beyond Avalon.

The ferry from Long Beach to Catalina Island takes about an hour: 15 minutes to leave behind one of the busiest ports in America, 15 minutes of open water, and 30 tantalizing minutes as the mountainous island materializes on the horizon. High ridges lead to steep canyons that terminate in sandy coves. Densely packed pastel houses fill Avalon's bowl-like valley. Sailboats sway gently in the harbor.

As we step off the ferry we instinctively reach for our passports. Avalon has the aged, compact feel of a European village. Or maybe a pre–Cold War Cuban resort. Either way, some recalibration is required. A two-stroke engine roar mixes with the electric whoosh of golf carts swarming the streets—proof that even in a 2.9-square-mile town, Americans will always find a way to drive.

The island was purchased in 1919 by the Wrigley family (chewing gum tycoons), who built it into a holiday destination. The simple clapboard homes, narrow streets, and art deco monuments have hardly changed in the century since. As ever, visitors are drawn to the pristine marine environment, mountainous wilderness, and psychological distance from the rest of the world.

The water around Catalina Island is extraordinary. Directly in front of the famed casino is one of the most popular dive and snorkeling sites in California - Casino Point. Visibility commonly ranges from 30 to 80 feet. The dive park incorporates a few sunken ships and nearshore debris. Magnificent kelp forests swarm with bat rays, octopus, kelp bass, and bright orange Garibaldi. Check out the nearby Descanso Beach Club to rent masks and snorkels for the day.

While Avalon is a dense nugget of tourism, the rest of the island is almost entirely wilderness, affording a snapshot view into Southern California's undeveloped past. Catalina Island Conservancy protects and manages 88 percent of the island. Wild bison, introduced in 1924 for a film production, roam the interior. Catalina Island foxes are back from the brink of extinction, as are the resident bald eagles. To get out of town, you need to book transportation through the Conservancy or a private taxi. Or you could simply walk out of Avalon via the Trans-Catalina Trail, which traverses 38.5 miles to finish at Two Harbors.

We love to camp at Little Harbor, a small palm oasis on the west coast with black sand beaches. This was a traditional village site for the Pimu Tongva, who used the sheltered harbor to launch their plank canoes, called *te'aat*. The cove's southwesterly orientation, protective rock reef, and protruding headland keep its waters relatively calm—perfect for snorkeling. It's a place to swim, read, and enjoy the company of family and friends. Nothing more is needed.

NEARBY

ORIGINAL ANTONIO'S PIZZA
114 Sumner Ave, Avalon

This vibey pizzeria serves cheesy deep-dish pies in a casual setting. Movie posters from bygone eras cover the walls, cold beers fill the fridge, and there's a jukebox in the corner. The venue is not to be confused with the larger Antonio's Pizzeria & Cabaret on the waterfront. This one is the original.

NDMK FISH HOUSE
109 Clarissa Ave, Avalon

Sourcing ingredients—especially fish—locally is a big part of the appeal of this casual seafood cafe (think endemic). Classics like fish and chips and fish tacos are featured, alongside made-to-order sushi rolls, poke bowls, and ceviche. They serve Over Town Brewing Co. beer on tap, as well as sake and Sabe cocktails.

ZANE GREY PUEBLO HOTEL
199 Chimes Tower Rd, Avalon

Built by novelist Zane Grey as a vacation home in 1926, this hillside property sits high above Avalon Bay. The estate has since been transformed into a luxury experience, with a mix of contemporary and old-world furnishings, an outdoor swimming pool, and a panoramic terrace with views of the harbor.

"While Avalon is a dense nugget of tourism, the rest of the island is almost entirely wilderness."

Crystal Cove

Laguna Beach, Orange County

A much-loved coastal reserve with rustic holiday shacks

◎ **ANCESTRAL HOMELANDS**
Tongva (Gabrielino) and Acjachemen (Juaneño)

⊖ **TYPE OF SWIM**
Beach

⊛ **ACTIVITIES**
Swim, surf, dive, fish, view tide pools, hike

⊘ Kid friendly, Dog friendly but dogs are only allowed on paved areas and must be on a leash.

◐ **BEST TIME TO VISIT**
April to November (but you can swim here year round)

◔ **OPEN HOURS**
6am to sunset

⑤ **COST OF ENTRY**
Free to enter, but parking is $5 an hour or $15 for the whole day.

⋀ **CLOSEST CAMPSITE**
Moro Campground (2.6 miles)

⊕ **CLOSEST TOWN OF INTEREST**
Laguna Beach (4.6 miles)

⬈ **HOW TO GET THERE**
Crystal Cove State Beach is located along Highway 73 between Corona del Mar and Laguna Beach. Park at Los Trancos parking lot.

⊖ **ACCESS**
Easy. A 0.3-mile path takes you straight from the parking lot on a pedestrian path through a tunnel under the highway to the beach. Shuttle buses operate regularly here too.

❋ **LOCAL KNOWLEDGE**
Surf, sun, and sand really sell Orange County, and the reality will not disappoint: the water is warmer, the swimsuits smaller, and the summers are less foggy than in Northern California.

Crystal Cove's history stretches way back. The Tongva and Acjachemen established villages in Moro Canyon and lived here for over 9,000 years before the arrival of Europeans in the late 1700s. It soon became a farming area, with the canyon's seasonal pastures used to graze cattle. In the 1920s, Japanese farmers moved onto the land and built homes, barns, a community center, and a school, taking advantage of the cove's favorable climate to grow beans, celery, tomatoes, and other vegetables. Around this time, too, people began traveling the brand-new Pacific Coast Highway to visit the beach for leisure. Crystal Cove started serving as both a tropical backdrop for films and an idyllic place to pitch tents or rent basic vacation beach cottages. Nowadays, tent camping is only permitted at Moro Campground, but 46 restored beach shacks remain dotted along the shoreline (available for rent via a lottery system)—a charming reminder of days gone by.

Access to the beach is via the Los Trancos parking lot. From there, you can walk a third of a mile to the beach, passing under the highway, or jump on a shuttle. Upon arrival you'll find the visitor center, a gift shop, and the Beachcomber restaurant with its Bootlegger bar (for a drink later). Set in a converted cottage, Beachcomber offers waterfront dining. It is very popular, and you may have to put your name on a list and have a swim while waiting for a table. Nearby, an aquamarine hut overlooking the water serves as a meeting point amid the array of mismatched, weather-beaten shacks in all their sun-kissed glory.

Crystal Cove is the region's largest section of open space. The broad sandy beach itself stretches for 3.2 miles below 80-foot bluffs and salt-sprayed sand dunes. Hikers can enjoy various trails that climb rugged chaparral-filled arroyos to the ridge. For us, surfing, swimming, sunbathing, and exploring aquarium-like tide pools fill the day's agenda. Meanwhile, offshore a fragile underwater world thrives, spanning 1,150 acres of designated marine conservation area. It is common to see dolphins frolicking in the surf and gray whales on their epic annual (December–April) migration between Alaskan waters and the lagoons of Baja California.

There's so much to Crystal Cove and surrounding Laguna Beach, it's hard to capture in a snapshot. Smack dab between LA and San Diego, the area celebrates its distance from the big cities, but also its accessibility to them. It's where wealthy Angelenos move to get more space and less traffic. It's where year-round visitors and weekenders channel an energetic, suntanned reality among beautiful beaches and beautiful people. It is beach life epitomized.

NEARBY

CRYSTAL COVE SHAKE SHACK
7703 East Coast Hwy, Newport Beach

Never has there been a more picturesque place to eat burgers. This 1940s-style open-air diner serves breakfast and casual fast food. We don't stray from the classics—cheeseburgers, fries, and vanilla shakes with whipped cream and a cherry on top. Order at the counter and take a buzzer: your deep-fried fantasy will be ready in minutes.

LAGUNA ART MUSEUM
307 Cliff Drive, Laguna Beach

Opened as a humble space to showcase local art over 100 years ago, Laguna Art Museum is now a focal point for culture in Southern California. A slick, modern gallery along Cliff Drive, LAM has a rotating schedule of exhibitions and events, including storytime Saturdays and wine tastings.

HOTEL LAGUNA
425 S Coast Highway, Laguna Beach

There are big plans to turn the landmark Hotel Laguna into deluxe beachfront accommodations once again. In the meantime, their restaurants—Larsen (fancy bistro) and Fin (sushi and sake)—and an excellent bar are open for business. Stop in for a cocktail and soak up the water views at sunset.

Treasure Island Beach

Laguna Beach

Stunning sandy coves beneath a clifftop garden paradise

○ **ANCESTRAL HOMELANDS**
Tongva (Gabrieleno) and Acjachemen (Juaneño)

⊖ **TYPE OF SWIM**
Beach

⊕ **ACTIVITIES**
Swim, snorkel, walk

⊘ Kid friendly, Dog friendly on leash only. From June 15 to September 10, dogs are allowed only before 9am and after 6pm. The rest of the year dogs are allowed during regular beach hours (6am–10pm).

◐ **BEST TIME TO VISIT**
March to November

⊙ **OPEN HOURS**
6am–10pm

◇ **CLOSEST CAMPSITE**
Moro Campground (5.9 miles)

⊕ **CLOSEST TOWN OF INTEREST**
Laguna Beach

⊘ **HOW TO GET THERE**
Treasure Island Beach is directly in front of the Montage Resort at 30801 South Coast Hwy, Laguna Beach.

⊖ **ACCESS**
Easy. You can access the beach through the Montage Resort (all-day paid parking available) or walk up from Aliso Beach, a lovely half-mile stroll.

✳ **LOCAL KNOWLEDGE**
Visit at mid to low tide to access all of the little coves and tide pools.

Okay, we will admit it: Orange County has the best beaches in California. The combination of the Mediterranean climate, exceptional water quality, rugged bluffs, and secluded coves is simply irresistible. The beaches are not only beautiful, but plentiful. We've scoured all 42 miles of this dramatic coastline and are continuously blown away. Even so, it's hard to beat the hidden gem that is Laguna Beach's very own Treasure Island.

We didn't know what to expect from Laguna, our frame of reference being early 2000s teen dramas and reality TV. However, we were pleasantly surprised to learn that it maintains a small-town feel and proudly embraces its artist/hippy/surfer legacy. These days there is no shortage of glitz, but the place still exudes plenty of charm. One of the best things about it is that conservation areas abound. The town backs onto 22,000 acres of protected hills and coastal canyons, while its idyllic shoreline is included in the Laguna Beach State Marine Reserve.

Treasure Island Beach is a poorly kept local secret. One thing that helps it stay under the radar is that it cannot be seen from the road. It is accessed by walking north along Aliso Beach or, our favorite, through the Montage Resort, which allows you to explore the headland known as Treasure Island Park. The curving path slowly reveals garden vignettes and viewing points with alcoves for sitting. Bright pink bougainvillea and purple pride of Madeira mingle with fleshy agave and prickly pear cactus under stately palm trees. Plein-air artists ply their craft and families picnic on grassy lawns. The magical garden spell is only briefly broken by the screams of our toddler in the outdoor shower.

Wooden stairs lead down to the beach, where the deep, clear water is breathlessly still. The southerly aspect and offshore rocks protect this little cove from most surf and currents, making it an excellent place to swim and snorkel. Visitors sit under umbrellas around the lifeguard tower, where the young rescuer does endless pull-ups. He unleashes a megawatt smile as he lowers his sunglasses to wink at a group of older swimmers who gather here daily (*ding*).

Long bands of rock jut into the ocean, distinguishing smaller coves beneath the high bluff. At low tide you can scramble along the shoreline or swim between beaches. Continue south through the natural rock archway to a huge reef platform full of tidepools. Colorful worlds teem with life just below the surface of the flawless turquoise water (look but don't touch). A few yards away a gentle ramp leads back up to the gardens, inviting another loop of the coast. It's not actually an island, but "treasure" suits it perfectly.

NEARBY

AhbA
31732 S Coast Hwy, Laguna Beach

This cozy neighborhood restaurant really hums on weekends when it opens for brunch (Saturday and Sunday. only), offering up burritos, shakshuka, Caesar salads, and mimosas in the courtyard out front. AhbA is open for dinner every night but Monday, serving seasonal California fare alongside craft beer, natural wine, and handmade cocktails.

Laguna Coffee Company
1050 S Coast Hwy, Ste B, Laguna Beach

Owned and run by mother-daughter duo Rene and Tomi Miller, this micro roaster and cafe serves specialty espresso drinks in a sun-filled shopfront. The food menu includes baked goods (croissants, banana flaxseed muffins, peanut butter cookies) and healthy hummus plates, salad bowls, and avocado toast.

1000 Step Beach
Laguna Beach

A steep set of incognito stairs—233 to be precise—lead you down from the Pacific Coast Highway to a glistening cove beach with pocky rock formations and, at the south end, caves (usually closed in summer for safety reasons). Rinse sand off in the beach shower at the base of the stairs before you climb back.

Black's Beach

Torrey Pines State Natural Reserve

San Diego's treasured wilderness
with secluded cliff-bottom beaches

⊙ **ANCESTRAL HOMELANDS**
Kumeyaay

⊖ **TYPE OF SWIM**
Beach

✢ **ACTIVITIES**
Swim, hike, surf (winter)

⊘ Kid friendly

⊗ No dogs

◖ **BEST TIME TO VISIT**
May to September. *Low tide only.*

⊘ **OPEN HOURS**
The entrance station is open from 8am to
approximately half an hour before sunset 365 days
a year.

Ⓢ **COST OF ENTRY**
$10 per car or free with valid State Parks Pass

⊕ **CLOSEST TOWN OF INTEREST**
Encinitas (8 miles)

↗ **HOW TO GET THERE**
12600 North Torrey Pines Road, La Jolla

⊖ **ACCESS**
Moderate. It's about a one-mile walk from the top of
Torrey Pines State Natural Reserve to Flat Rock Beach
below, around the corner from Black's Beach. You can
also approach from La Jolla Shores to the south or
Torrey Pines State Beach to the north. *Low tide only.*

✳ **LOCAL KNOWLEDGE**
Spring rains transform Torrey Pines into an exuberant
bouquet of wildflowers. Early May is the best time to
see the towering spires of Shaw's agave, the delicate
yellow of California sun cups, and blazing orange
swaths of California poppies—among many others.

We love San Diego—the people, the culture, the pace, the weather, and of course, the coastline. From the broad white strand of Imperial Beach to North County's craggy coves and surf breaks, the endless perfect beaches still feel like a secret from the outside world. It's all part of the area's humble, friendly identity. Despite being a major city, San Diego somehow feels like a collection of unhurried small towns and neighborhoods. You would think that with such abundance it would be difficult to find consensus, but most locals will readily admit to having a soft spot for Black's Beach, between La Jolla and Del Mar—especially if you're looking for a secluded swim.

Black's, named for the family that once had a farm on the bluff above, consists of about four miles of undeveloped coast beneath high sandstone cliffs. The beach is unusual by Southern California standards in that access is very limited and it's virtually invisible from the road. Therein lies both the challenge and the appeal. You can park on the mesa above and walk down via steep trails, or else take a long walk along the beach from either end. It's just the right level of effort to ensure that there are never too many people.

We always approach from the top, at Torrey Pines State Natural Reserve. The beloved park feels as barren as an Atacama Desert moonscape—and yet it supports over 400 varieties of native plants and wildflowers. Coastal sage scrub, maritime succulents, and chaparral line the high broken cliffs and deep arroyos, which provide one of the world's only sanctuaries for the enigmatic, wind-sculpted *Pinus torreyana*. Gravel trails wind among plant communities and past stunning coastal lookouts before funneling hikers down a metal staircase to Flat Rock Beach below.

Turn left and walk south around the headland to reach the long, open stretch of Black's Beach. Be sure to time your visit with low tide, when the sandy beach is widest. This guarantees more space to walk around obstacles and allows you to keep a distance from the tall cliffs, which periodically collapse. We try to stay at least 15 feet from the base.

Warm earth tones—reds, oranges, and yellows—saturate the pockmarked 300-foot cliff face, which extends above miles of empty beach. The north end of Black's is designated clothing-optional, which should not be read as exhibitionist. It's the kind of place where people find a private patch of sand in order to enjoy the feeling of the sun and water on their bodies. If you have never had a nudie swim in the ocean, this is the place. The calm turquoise water is as warm as it gets in California. As you stretch out in the summer sun, it's easy to forget you are in the middle of a sprawling city.

NEARBY
Lofty Coffee Company
90 N Coast Hwy 101, Ste 214, Encinitas

This specialty coffee shop serves brewed drinks (the beans are roasted just across the road), pastries, and simple cafe food. The breakfast croissant with sausage, egg, arugula, cheddar, and cactus jam is an excellent choice, whether to go or dining in.

Mexican food in Encinitas
Encinitas has a concentration of Mexican food of various styles. It's hard to just pick one, so here are a few: Taco Stand (Mexican street food in a refined sit-down venue), Juanita's (a no-frills post-surf taco shop), Raoul's Shack (hefty burritos via window service), and Haggo's Organic Taco (healthy burrito bowls).

The Crack Shack
407 Encinitas Blvd, Encinitas

A family-friendly chain serving all things chicken and egg. We like the Firebird sandwich—a lightly spiced fried thigh with crispy onions, pickles, and ranch sauce. And don't skimp on the fries; they're cooked in chicken fat. There's also a bar and a bocce court.

La Jolla

San Diego

A stunning series of cove beaches in San Diego's poshest seaside suburb

◎ **ANCESTRAL HOMELANDS**
Kumeyaay

⊖ **TYPE OF SWIM**
Beach

✱ **ACTIVITIES**
Swim, snorkel, scuba dive, paddle

⊘ Kid friendly, Dog friendly with restrictions. Dogs are allowed on beaches only before 9am and after 4pm (November–March) or in busier months (April–October) after 6pm. They must be leashed.

◖ **BEST TIME TO VISIT**
July to October

◐ **OPEN HOURS**
24 hours, but swimming is only recommended during daylight hours.

⊕ **CLOSEST TOWN OF INTEREST**
Village of La Jolla

⊘ **HOW TO GET THERE**
From downtown San Diego, take I-5 north about 13 miles (25 minutes) to the La Jolla exit. Park along Coast Boulevard or in the residential backstreets.

⊖ **ACCESS**
Easy. From Coast Boulevard stairs provide access to La Jolla Cove, Shell Beach, and La Jolla Children's Pool.

✳ **LOCAL KNOWLEDGE**
The native Kumeyaay called this spot *mat kulaaxuuy* ("land of holes"), most likely referring to the sea caves in the bluffs. The name La Jolla probably comes from the Spanish: *la joya*, or "the jewel."

It's impossible to write about swimming in Southern California and not mention La Jolla. To many, this is the literal jewel ("la joya") in the crown of San Diego's swims. This prosperous coastal enclave, once an artist colony, just 25 minutes north of downtown, sits atop a stunning set of small cove beaches, strung together like a necklace. Sherbet pink condos and muted pastel hotels cluster along the foreshore here, Spanish mission–style architecture mingling with ultra-modern. La Jolla attracts an older holiday crowd who enjoy cortados and shrimp cocktails in the sun. It's a vibe.

As you walk toward the shore, a salty, fishy musk thickens the air like fog. On closer inspection, the smell is a distinctive mix of pelican guano and sea lion piss. The barking pinnipeds engage in endless jostling for flat rocks and sunshine, their skin glistening as they swing. Throngs of neoprene-clad swimmers push past the shorefront market—vendors of Oaxacan *animalitos*, jewelry, hats and novelty tees—as school buses unload on Coast Boulevard, the children ready to hit the tide pools. For better or worse, La Jolla is a popular destination. But it can handle it.

The thing is, La Jolla is popular for a reason. Its beaches are sublime. With white sand juxtaposed against impossibly clear water, it reminds us a little of Mallorca. At 9am the marine layer is still low, but snorkelers, stand-up paddleboarders, and kayakers have already left the shore to explore the rock caves and the seal colony. By 11am, it's a completely different place. The fog has burnt off, the air has warmed up, and you can see all the way across the bay to La Jolla Shores.

People congregate at La Jolla Cove, Shell Beach, and Children's Pool, but there are lots of little coves in between, and further along the palm-fringed boulevard. The small coves tend to get crowded quickly, with limited real estate for beach towels. But what people really come here for is the water, notoriously cool and refreshing. Even in summer, this upwelled section of the Pacific Ocean never gets much warmer than 60–63°F. It's perfect for a good strong swim, but it's also just right for the local sea life to thrive. In fact, it's not uncommon to come face to face with a curious seal bodysurfing in the shallows. At Shell Beach, tide pools are home to anemones, sea snails, and crabs. The spectacle of marine life on these busy beaches is truly impressive.

The best part about La Jolla is that everything is walkable. You could comfortably spend days wandering around the streets in a swimsuit and sarong, bouncing from beach to bar, boutique to restaurant, without even washing the sand out of your hair.

NEARBY

BRICK AND BELL
928 Silverado St, La Jolla

Brick and Bell is famous for its scones (try the sweet and tart cranberry one) and lox bagels, not to mention its delicious dirty chai—try it iced in summer. Oh, and did we mention cortados? Sit under the trees and soak up the balmy SoCal weather, any month of the year.

BOBBOI NATURAL GELATO
8008 Girard Ave #150, La Jolla

There's nothing like the pairing of gelato and the beach. This tiny parlor serves an array of frozen treats made with organic ingredients. Flavors rotate based on the season, but might include charcoal vanilla, banana and dulce de leche, dragon lemon and rose honey, or more classic options like pistachio and stracciatella.

LEILANI'S CAFE
5109 Cass St, San Diego

The menu at this funky Hawaiian eatery includes fruit smoothies, quesadillas, salads, and poke bowls. Or you might get adventurous and try My Kalani—a kalua pork and rice dish served with Portuguese sausage, fried eggs, and macaroni salad—or Leilani-style Spam Musubi (Hawaiian sushi). It will transport you straight to the sunny shores of O'ahu.

SUNSHINE COAST

LA TO SAN DIEGO

This Southern California road trip is quintessential, providing
surf, sun, and sandy dreamscapes all the way south from
LA to San Diego. The trip is short and sweet (120 miles) and
can be done in five days or less. No matter what time of year,
there will be swimming—we promise!

Day 1

LA/Manhattan Beach

For us, almost every trip to California begins and ends in LA. When we're heading out of town on a road trip, we like to strike the coast first. **Manhattan Beach** (p.219) eases us in. We get an ice cream at Kansha Creamery in Gardena on the way through, then hit Manhattan Beach Boulevard and The Strand walkway along the beach, jumping in for a swim. After a day enjoying metropolitan beach life, finish up with a slice from Manhattan Pizzeria or sushi at Sugarfish.

Day 2

Manhattan Beach to Laguna Beach

50 MILES / 1 HR 35 MINS

The drive from the outskirts of LA south to Laguna Beach isn't the prettiest. Do it early so you can make the most of your time in Orange County on its glorious beaches. Head into Laguna for a coffee at **Laguna Coffee Co.**, then backtrack to **Crystal Cove State Park** (p.227). Surf or swim, wander around the rustic rental shacks on the water, explore the tide pools, and grab lunch up at Shake Shack overlooking the beach. In the afternoon, drop into the eclectic Laguna Art Gallery, and end the day with a sunset cocktail at Hotel Laguna.

Day 3

Laguna Beach

4.6 MILES / 10 MINS

We like to spend a couple of days around Laguna Beach with its dreamy seascapes. Sheltered cove beaches are peppered along the coast here, and there are lots of discoveries just off the highway. 1000 Steps is a blink-and-you'll-miss-it staircase leading down to a surf beach below multimillion-dollar mansions, whereas **Treasure Island** (p.229) offers stunning sandy coves beneath pretty clifftop gardens. It's a kind of paradise. Get a meal at **AhbA** (on weekends they do brunch). It's such beautiful decadence to spend your days salty and sand-crusted.

Day 4

Laguna Beach to Encinitas

55 MILES / 1 HR

The drive from Laguna Beach to Encinitas is just an hour, but there is plenty to see as you pass by the surf beaches of Dana Point, San Clemente, and Carlsbad. **Moonlight Beach** in Encinitas is a magnet for wave seekers, swimmers, and sunbakers. We get coffee and breakfast sandwiches up the hill at Lofty Coffee. A handful of miles south is Black's Beach in **Torrey Pines State Natural Reserve** (p.233), another favorite. The two-mile craggy clifftop path winds down parched arroyos to the long empty strand. We finish up by heading back into Encinitas for fish tacos. There's plenty of great Mexican fare around here, but our pick is fancy street food from the **Taco Stand**.

Day 5

Encinitas to San Diego

26 MILES / 35 MINS

Taking advantage of SoCal's idyllic weather, roll down the windows and cruise into the beachy enclave of **La Jolla** (p.237) on your way south. We conclude this road trip in San Diego, but suggest you spend at least a few days here. It's an incredible place, rich with history, culture, art, music, and good food. Cute neighborhoods with craftsman-style houses and cool cafes surround **Balboa Park**. This 1,200-acre urban sanctuary features gardens, museums, Mission Revival–style pavilions, and the wonderful San Diego Zoo. It's all possible on foot, so take your time.

Index

1000 Step Beach, Laguna Beach 229, 232

Ace Swim Club, Palm Springs 209
Agoura Hills 213
AhbA, Laguna Beach 229, 241
Ahwahnee Hotel, Yosemite Valley 91
Alibi Ale Works, Truckee 129, 159
Alicia's Sugar Shack, Twain Harte 157
Aliso Beach 229
Alpine Drive Inn, Burney 31
Alta Bakery and Cafe, Monterey 181, 199
American River Confluence, Auburn State Recreation Area 149, 159
Anacapa Island 169
Andrew Molera State Park 179
Angel Island State Park, San Francisco Bay 111
Annenberg Community Beach House, Santa Monica 217
Ansel Adams Wilderness/Inyo National Forest 75
Arcata 39
Arnold 153
Auburn 145, 149, 159
Auburn Ale House, Auburn 149
Auburn Bodega, Auburn 149
Auburn State Recreation Area 145, 149, 159
Auburn to Emerald Pools road trip 158–59
Avalon 223
Axe & Rose Public House, McCloud 5
Ayala Cove 111

Back on the Beach Cafe, Santa Monica 217
Baker, The, and the Cake Maker, Auburn 145
Balboa Park, San Diego 241
Barlow District 119
Bart's Books, Ojai 169
Bay Area, The 94–119
Bear Creek Spire 81
Bell's, Los Alamos 165
Bidwell Park, Chico 27
Big Chico Creek, Bidwell Park, Chico 27
Big Dume Beach 213
Big Hole 27
Big Meadow Brewing Company, Bridgeport 67
Big Pine 85
Big River Estuary, Mendocino 39
Big Sur 175, 179, 199
Big Sur River Gorge, Pfeiffer Big Sur State Park 179, 199
Bishop 81, 85
Bishop Pass 85
Black Hole of Calcutta Falls Trail 159
Black Oak Coffee Roasters, Ukiah 9
Black's Beach, Torrey Pines State Natural Reserve 233, 241
Bluffs Trail, Andrew Molera State Park 179
Bobboi Natural Gelato, La Jolla 237
Bob's Well Bread Bakery, Los Alamos 165, 199
Bodfish 197
Bodie State Historic Park, Bridgeport 67, 91
Boomtown Lounge, Downieville 125, 159
Box Lake 81
Boy Scout Tree Trail 39
Boyden Cavern & Kings Canyon Lodge 87
Brick and Bell, La Jolla 237
Bridgeport 67, 71, 91, 141
Brokeoff Mountain Trail, Lassen Volcanic National Park 35

Bruce's Beach 219
Buckeye Hot Springs, Bridgeport 71
Budd Lake, Tuolumne Meadows, Yosemite National Park 59, 91
Bumpass Hell, Lassen Volcanic National Park 35
Burney 31
Buster's, Calistoga 119
Buttermilk Bend, South Yuba River State Park 141

Cafe Aquatica, Jenner 38, 109
Calaveras Big Tree State Park, Arnold 153
Calaveras County 153
California Hot Springs 193
Calistoga 101, 119
Calistoga Inn, Calistoga 101
Calistoga Roastery & Bakery, Calistoga 101
Cambria 175, 199
Camp Nine, Stanislaus River, Calaveras County 153
Capitola Beach 115
Carlon Falls, Tuolumne River South Fork, Stanislaus National Forest 55, 91
Carlsbad 239
Carmel-by-the-Sea 175, 179, 199
Carmel River 181
Carpinteria 169
Casa de Mole, Healdsburg 105, 119
Casino Point 223
Castle Lake, Shasta-Trinity National Forest 23
Castle Peak 23
Catalina Island 223
Catalina Island Conservancy 223
Cathedral Lakes 91
Cathedral Lakes Trailhead/John Muir Trail 59
Cathedral Peak 59
Cathedral Range 59
Cecile Lake 75
Central California 162–99
Channel Islands National Park 169
Chester 35
Chico 27
Chilnualna Falls Trail 63
China Cove 111
China Dam/Wall 133, 159
China Ranch Date Farm & Bakery, Tecopa 205
Chinese Harbor 169
Chocolate Lakes 85
Cleo's Bath, Stanislaus National Forest 157
Cliffs, The, Sierra National Forest—Shaver Lake 189
Coachella 209
Coachella Valley 209
Cocina Michoacana, Groveland 55
Cockscomb 59
Colfax 145
Collierville Powerhouse 153
Concerts in the Pines, Twain Harte 157
Cook's Beach 38
Cooper Molera Adobe, Monterey 181, 199
Copper Top BBQ, Big Pine 85
Cowpunchers Cafe, Springville 193
Crack Shack, The, Encinitas 233
Creamery Meadow Trailhead, Andrew Molera State Park 179
Crescent City 19
Crowley Lake 81

Crystal Cove, Laguna Beach, Orange County 227
Crystal Cove Shake Shack, Newport Beach 227, 241
Crystal Cove State Park 227, 241
Curry Village 91

D. L. Bliss State Park 45, 91
Dana Point 223, 241
Deadwood Supply, Mount Shasta 23
Death Valley National Park 205
Deetjen's Big Sur Inn, Big Sur 175, 199
Del Monte 181
Del Rio Woods, Russian River, Healdsburg 105
Delight's Hot Spring Resort, Tecopa 205
Desert Hot Springs 209
Desolation Wilderness/Eldorado National Forest 49
Devil's Elbow, Trinity River, Willow Creek 15
Devils Postpile 75
Diablo Range 185
Dinkey Creek General Store, Shaver Lake 189
Dodge Ridge Mountain Resort 157
Donner Lake 159
Donner Pass 159
Donner Pass Train Tunnels 129, 159
Dorrington 153
Downieville 125, 159
Dr. Wilkinson's Backyard Resort and Mineral Springs, Calistoga 101,
    119
Duchess, The, Ojai 169

East Lake, Hoover Wilderness/Inyo National Forest 71
East Side Bake Shop, Mammoth Lakes 77
Echo Peaks 59
Ediza Lake 75
Eel River Cafe, Garberville 13
Eldorado National Forest 49, 53
Emerald Bay Boat Camp 45
Emerald Bay State Park, Lake Tahoe 45, 91
Emerald Pools, Yuba River South Fork 129, 159
Empire Mine Historic Park, Grass Valley 133
Encinitas 233, 241
Ernest Coffee, Palm Springs 209
Esalen Institute, Big Sur 175
Ewings, Kernville 197

Fannette Island 45
Farmer and the Cook, Ojai 169
Ferndale 13, 39
Finney's Hole, Downieville 125, 159
Flat Rock Beach 233
Forestville 109
Forestville Bridge 149
Fort McDowell 111
French Laundry, Yountville 119
Freshies, South Lake Tahoe 91
Fresno 189
Full of Life Flatbread, Los Alamos 165

Garberville 13
Gardena 219, 241
Gateway Cafe, The, Meyers 49
Gem Lakes 81
Giant Sequoia National Monument 193

Gibraltar Reservoir 165
Gibraltar Trail 165
Gladys Lake 75
Gold Country 122–59
Golden Gate Saloon, Grass Valley 133
Gott's Roadside, St. Helena 119
Grana, Chico 27
Grand Canyon on the Tuolumne 59
Grant Grove Village 87
Grass Valley 133, 137, 141, 159
Grecian Pools, Wawona, Yosemite National Park 63
Green Lake/East Lake, Hoover Wilderness/Inyo National Forest 71
Grizzly Loop Trail 63
Groveland 55
Gualala 97
Gualala River Redwood Park, Gualala 97
Gualala Seafood Shack, Gualala 97
Guerneville 109

Haggo's Organic Taco, Encinitas 233
Harvest Market, Mendocino 39
Hatchett Creek Falls, Big Bend Road, off Highway 299 31
Healdsburg 105, 119
Hearst Castle, San Simeon 199, 217
Heart Lake 23, 81
Hermosa 219
High-Hand Nursery and Cafe, Loomis 145
Highway 49 Crossing to Hoyts Crossing, Yuba River South Fork 137,
    159
hikes around Silver Lake 53
Hilltop Hot Springs, Mammoth Lakes 77
Hiouchi 19
Hiouchi Cafe, Crescent City 19, 39
Honeymoon Cafe, Pismo Beach 171
Hoopa 15
Hoover Wilderness/Inyo National Forest 71
Hotel Charlotte, Groveland 55
Hotel Laguna, Laguna Beach 227, 241
Hoyts Crossing 137, 159
Humboldt Redwood State Park 13, 39

Iceberg Lake 75
Idlewild Wines, Healdsburg 105
Indian Canyons, Palm Springs 207
Indian Springs, Calistoga 101
Inyo National Forest 71, 75, 81
Iron Horse Winery, Sebastopol 109
Island Lake, Desolation Wilderness/Eldorado National Forest 49
Izakaya Gama, Point Arena 97

Jedediah Smith Redwoods State Park 19, 39
Jenner 38, 105, 109
John Muir Trail 59, 75, 85
John Muir Wilderness/Inyo National Forest 81
Jolly Kone, Bridgeport 67, 91
Juanita's, Encinitas 233
June Lake Loop 71, 91

Kansha Creamery, Gardena 219, 241
Keough's Hot Springs, Bishop 85
Kern River 197
Kern River Brewing, Kernville 197

Kernville 197
Kings Canyon National Park 87
Kirkwood 53
Kirkwood Inn, Kirkwood 53
Kit Carson 53
Kit Carson Lodge, Kit Carson 53
Kitkitdizzi, Nevada City 137
Kohm Yah-mah-nee (Lassen Peak) 35

La Cocina del Oro Taqueria, Downieville 125, 159
La Jolla 237, 241
La Jolla Children's Pool 237
La Jolla Cove 237
La Jolla Shores 231, 237
Laguna Art Museum, Laguna Beach 227, 241
Laguna Beach 227, 229, 241
Laguna Beach State Marine Reserve 229
Laguna Coffee Company, Laguna Beach 229, 241
Lake Isabella 197
Lake Tahoe 45, 91
Lassen Peak Trail, Lassen Volcanic National Park 35
Lassen Volcanic National Park 35
Lee Vining 59, 71, 91
Leggett 13, 39
Leilani's Cafe, San Diego 237
Little Harbor 223
Little Lakes Valley, John Muir Wilderness/Inyo National Forest 81
Little Panoche Valley 185
Little Saint, Healdsburg 119
Little Truckee Ice Creamery, Truckee 129, 159
Lofty Coffee Company, Encinitas 233, 241
Long Beach 223
Long Lake 81
Long Valley 77
Loomis 145
Los Alamos 165, 199
Los Angeles 219, 241
Los Angeles to San Diego road trip 240–41
Los Baños del Mar, Santa Barbara 165, 199
Los Olivos 165, 199
Los Padres National Forest 165, 175, 199
Lovers Leap, Twin Bridges 49
Lovers Point Beach, Pacific Grove 181, 199
Lower Salmon Creek Falls, Los Padres National Forest 175
Lube Room Saloon, Dorrington 153

McArthur-Burney Falls, McArthur-Burney Falls Memorial State Park 31
McCloud 5
McCloud River Falls Trail, Shasta-Trinity National Forest 5
Mack Lake 81
McKinley Grove 189
Malibu 213, 217
Malibu Seafood, Malibu 213
Mammoth Lakes 75, 77, 91
Mammoth Mountaineering Supply Gear Exchange, Bishop 81
Manhattan Beach 219, 241
Manhattan Pizzeria, Manhattan Beach 219, 241
Mariposa Grove, Wawona 63
Markleeville 91
Marsh Lake 81
Marvin Braude Bike Trail 217, 219

Matthes Crest 59
Meat Market & Tavern, McCloud 5
Mendocino 38–39
Mendocino to Smith River road trip 38–39
Mercey Hot Springs, Diablo Range 185
Mexican food in Encinitas 233
Meyers 49
Meze , Grass Valley 141, 159
Middle Fork Tule River Falls, Sequoia National Forest 193
Mike & Tony's, Mount Shasta 23
Minaret Lake, Ansel Adams Wilderness/Inyo National Forest 75
Minaret Lake Loop 75
Mineral Bar, Auburn State Recreation Area 145
Miracle Hot Springs, Kern River, Sequoia National Forest 197
Mist Falls Hike, Kings Canyon National Park 87
Mobil, The/Woah Nellie Deli, Lee Vining 59
Model Bakery, St. Helena 119
Mojave Desert 205
Molera Beach 179
Monitor Pass 91
Mono Cone, Lee Vining 71
Mono Lake 91
Montage Resort, Laguna Beach 229
Monterey 181, 199
Monterey Bay Aquarium Research Institute 181
Monterey Bay National Marine Sanctuary 181
Moody's Bistro, Truckee 159
Moonlight Beach 241
Morgan Pass 81
Morton's Warm Springs 119
Mosquito Flat 81, 91
Mother's Beach
    Russian River, Forestville 109
    Yuba River 133, 159
Mount Dade 81
Mount Livermore 111
Mount Morgan 81
Mount Price 49
Mount Shasta 23
Mount Shasta City 23
Mount Whitney 85
Mountain Rambler Brewery, Bishop 85
Movies Under the Stars, Pinecrest Lake 157
Muir Beach 119
Muir Rock, Kings Canyon National Park 87
Muir Woods National Monument 119
Municipal Winemakers, Los Alamos 165
Murphys 153
Murphy's Pourhouse, Murphys 153
Myrtle Beach 19

Napa Valley 101, 119
NDMK Fish House, Avalon 223
Nelda's Diner, Lake Isabella 197
Nepenthe, Big Sur 179
Nevada City 129, 133, 137, 159
Newport Beach 227
Nopah Range/Mojave Desert 203
North Palm Springs 207
North San Juan 159
Northern California 2–39

Ojai 169
Old Place, Agoura Hills 213
1000 Step Beach, Laguna Beach 229, 241
Orange County 227, 229, 241
Original Antonio's Pizza, Avalon 223
Osprey Cafe, Willow Creek 15
Outdoor Yoga–Yuba Retreat 141

Pacific Grove 181, 199
Pacific Palisades 219
Palm Springs 209
Palm Springs Art Museum, Palm Springs 209
Pamoo (Travertine Hot Springs), Bridgeport 67, 91
Panorama Trail, Andrew Molera State Park 179
Panoy Bistro, Grass Valley 141
Paradise Valley 87
Parker Palm Springs, Palm Springs 209
Parkside, Stinson Beach 119
Patagonia Flagship Store, Ventura 169
Pate Valley 59
Pavel's Bakery, Pacific Grove 181
Pebble Beach 199
Peg House, Leggett 13, 39
Pelican Inn, Muir Beach 119
Perlita's Mexican Restaurant, Crescent City 19
Pfeiffer Big Sur State Park 179
Pinecrest 157
Pinecrest Lake Trail 157
Pirates Cove 213
Pismo 171
Pismo Beach, Central Coast, San Luis Obispo County 171
Placerville 49
Pleasure Point 115
Point Arena 97
Point Dume State Beach, Malibu 211
Point Market 115
Point Reyes 119
Poorman Crossing 133
Post Ranch Inn, Big Sur 179
Potem Falls, Shasta-Trinity National Forest 31
Potholes, The, Silver Fork American River, Eldorado National Forest 53
Pour Choice, The, Auburn 149
Pretty Good Advice, Soquel 115
Prospector's Pool, Mineral Bar, Auburn State Recreation Area 145
Pub N Grub, Shaver Lake 189
Purdon Crossing to China Wall, Yuba River South Fork 133, 159
Pyramid Peak 81

Quail & Condor, Healdsburg 105, 119
Quarry Beach 111

Rainbow Pool, Groveland 55
Raoul's Shack, Encinitas 233
Reading Peak 35
Red Rock Pools, Santa Ynez River, Los Padres National Forest 165, 199
Redding 31
Redondo 217
Redwood National Park 19
Reel Inn Malibu, Malibu 217
Remington Hot Springs, Kern River/Bodfish 197
Richardson Grove State Park, Garberville 13
Ridge, Panorama, and Bluffs Trail Loop, Andrew Molera State Park 179

River Song Natural Foods, Willow Creek 15
Robin's Restaurant, Cambria 175, 199
Rock Creek Lakes Resort, Bishop 81
Rooster, The, and the Pig, Palm Springs 209
Rory's Place, Ojai 169
Rosalie Lake 75
Rubicon Trail, The, D. L. Bliss State Park 45, 91
Russian River 105, 109, 119

Sabrina's at the Forks, Downieville 125, 159
Sacramento 159
Sacramento Valley 141, 145, 149
St. Helena 119
Salmon Creek Trail 175
Salmon Hole 27
Sam's Anchor Cafe, Tiburon 111
San Clemente 241
San Diego 233, 237, 241
San Diego Zoo, San Diego 241
San Francisco 38, 111, 119
San Francisco Bay 111
San Francisco to Napa Valley road trip 118–19
San Luis Obispo 171, 199
San Luis Obispo County 171
San Luis Obispo Museum of Art (SLOMA), San Luis Obispo 199
San Marcos Pass 165
San Miguel Island 169
San Pedro 223
San Simeon 175, 199
San Simeon Beach 199
Santa Barbara 165, 169, 199
Santa Barbara Island 169
Santa Barbara to Monterey road trip 198–99
Santa Catalina Island, Long Beach 223
Santa Cruz 115
Santa Cruz Flea Market, Santa Cruz 115
Santa Cruz Island, Channel Islands National Park 169
Santa Monica 217
Santa Monica Bay 213
Santa Monica Mountains 213
Santa Rosa 109
Santa Rosa Island 169
Santa Ynez River 165, 199
Santa Ynez Valley 165
Schat's Bakery, Ukiah 9
Scorpion Anchorage 15
Scout, San Luis Obispo 199
Sea Ranch 38, 97
Sea Ranch Chapel, Sea Ranch 38
Sebastopol 109, 119
Sequoia National Forest 193, 197
Sequoia National Park 87
Shadow Lake, Lassen Volcanic National Park 35, 75
Shasta-Trinity National Forest 5, 23, 31
Shaver Lake 189
Shaver Lake Coffee and Deli, Shaver Lake 189
Shea Schat's Bakery, Mammoth Lakes 75, 91
Shell Beach, La Jolla 237
Shelter Distillery, Mammoth Lakes 77
Shingletown 35
Sierra Hot Springs, Sierraville 159
Sierra National Forest—Shaver Lake 189

Sierra Nevada 42–91
Sierra Nevada Brewery, Chico 27
Sierraville 159
Silver Fork American River, Eldorado National Forest 53
Silver Lake 53, 71
Silver Lake Cafe, June Lake 71
Silver Lake Lodge, June Lake 91
Silver Peak Wilderness, Los Padres National Forest 175
Six Rivers National Forest 19
Smith River Confluence, Six Rivers National Forest 19, 39
Smugglers Cove 168
Soquel 115
South Bay 217
South Fork Eel River, Humboldt Redwood State Park 13, 39
South Lake Tahoe 45, 53, 91
South Yuba River State Park 141
South Yuba River Trail 133
Southern California 202-241
Springville 193
Squalo Vino, Tiburon 111
Standish-Hickey State Recreation Area, Leggett 13
Stanislaus National Forest 55, 157
Stanislaus River 153
Steak and Beer, Tecopa 205
Steelhead Beach 109, 119
Stinson Beach 119
Stoble Coffee Roasters, Chico 27
Strawberry 49
Strawberry General Store, Twin Bridges 49
Stumptown Brewery, Guerneville 109
Sugarfish, Manhattan Beach 219, 241
Sunny Cove, Santa Cruz 115
Sunset Beach 109, 119
Sunset Trail 111
Surfrider Beach 217
Surfrider Hotel, The, Malibu 217
Sushi in the Raw, Nevada City 137
Swinging Bridge, Wawona 63
Sycamore Mineral Springs, San Luis Obispo 171
Sycamore Pool 27

Taco Stand, Encinitas 233, 241
Tacos Garcia food truck, Yountville 119
Tecopa 205
Tecopa Brewing Company, Tecopa 205
Tecopa Hot Springs, Nopah Range/Mojave Desert 205
Tenaya Lake 91
Terrace Lake 35
Thai Dish, Ukiah 9
That's Italian, Kernville 197
The Baker and the Cake Maker, Auburn 145
The Bay Area 94–119
The Cliffs, Sierra National Forest - Shaver Lake 189
The Crack Shack, Encinitas 233
The Duchess, Ojai 169
The Gateway Cafe, Meyers 49
The Mobil/Woah Nellie Deli, Lee Vining 59
The Potholes, Silver Fork American River, Eldorado National Forest 53
The Pour Choice, Auburn 149, 159
The Rooster and the Pig, Palm Springs 209
The Rubicon Trail, D. L. Bliss State Park 45
The Surfrider Hotel, Malibu 217

Three Forks Bakery & Brewery Co., Nevada City 137, 159
Tiburon 111
Tidal Coffee, Monterey 181
Toms Place 81
Toms Place Resort, Crowley Lake 81
Torrey Pines State Beach 233
Torrey Pines State Natural Reserve 233, 241
Trancas Country Market, Malibu 213
Trans-Catalina Trail 223
Travertine Hot Springs, Bridgeport 67, 91
Treasure Island Beach, Laguna Beach 229, 241
Trinity River, Willow Creek 15
Trinity River Farm, Willow Creek 15
Truckee 91, 129, 159
Truckee to Groveland road trip 90–91
Tule River 193
Tuolumne General Store, Tuolumne Meadows 59
Tuolumne Meadows, Yosemite National Park 59, 91
Tuolumne River South Fork, Stanislaus National Forest 55
Twain Harte 157
Twin Bridges 49
Twin Lakes 49
Two Bunch Palms, Desert Hot Springs, Coachella Valley 209
Two Harbors 223

Ukiah 9, 39
Upper Salmon Creek Falls, Silver Peak Wilderness, Los Padres National Forest 175, 199

Ventura 169
Vichy Springs, Ukiah 9, 39
Vikingsholm 45, 91

Walk Pleasure Point 115
Wawona, Yosemite National Park 63
Wawona Hotel, Yosemite Valley 63
Westward Beach 213
White Mountains Cafe, McCloud 5
Wild Oak Coffee House, Springville 193
Wild Willy's Hot Springs, Long Valley 77, 91
Willow Creek 15
Windmill Market, North Palm Springs 209
Women's Grove, South Fork Eel River, Humboldt Redwood State Park 13
Woodlands Market, Tiburon 111
Wrights Lake 49

Yahi Trail 27
Yak's Shack, Mount Shasta 23
Yama Ramen, Mammoth Lakes 75
Yosemite National Park 59, 63, 91
Yosemite Valley 63, 91
Yountville 119
Yuba City 141
Yuba River 141
Yuba River North Fork 125, 159
Yuba River South Fork 129, 133, 137, 159

Zane Grey Pueblo Hotel, Avalon 223
Zorro's Cafe & Cantina, Pismo Beach 171

Acknowledgments

This book is the result of many people and forces working together over millions of years.

Thank you to plate tectonics for creating California and to erosion for making it perfect. Thank you to the radical thinkers who fought for (and continue to fight for) the idea of public lands. May we never take that gift for granted.

Thank you to our son, Leo Sunny, for joining us on this great adventure and sitting in a car seat and backpack more than would ever be advised by a healthcare professional. Thank you for sharing your unwavering enthusiasm for life and reminding us to be in the moment. We're sorry we didn't do this at an age when you would remember it.

To the legends at Visit California: Xavi, Sarah, and Kirsten. This book would not have been possible without your support. Thank you for your enthusiasm and trust from the very beginning.

Thank you to our Hardie Grant Australia family—Megan, Melissa, Astrid, Roxy, and Emily—for your ongoing collaboration. You afford us the privilege to live out our dreams.

Thank you to the team at Evi O. Studio—Evi, Pamela, and Susan—for your unwavering attention to detail and willingness to push the design to create the best-looking book possible. This project is as much yours as it is ours.

To our editor Anne Canright, thank you for sharpening our edges, enduring our bad jokes, and reining in our hyperbole. We couldn't have picked a more qualified person for this job.

Thank you to Lyric Dodson, our proofreader, for being one of the few people that will ever read this book cover to cover.

Thank you to Professor JoEllen Anderson for your thoughtful feedback regarding Indigenous Peoples of California.

Thank you to Lorraine and Caroline, at Hardie Grant USA, and Natalie for your tireless efforts to make sure our book is seen by as many people as possible. All our work is for nothing without you.

Thank you to Ford Motor Company and the unionized American labor who built our 1994 Econoline engine. While just about everything else in the motorhome seemed to fail, the engine always purred like a tigress.

Thank you to Trader Joe's Smoked Trout Fillets, Crunchy Chili Oil, Dark Chocolate Peanut Butter Cups, and Everything but the Bagel seasoning: the four pillars of a complete diet.

This book would not have been possible without our friends and family who shared this journey with us. In order of appearance: Uncle Cal; Alicia; Rosie (and Willa); Lizard; Eric and Amanda; Margo, David, and Sunny; Val and Andrew; Dan and Anita; Lee-Man and Erich; Alfredo; Ryan; Mary, Everett, and Alton; Annie; Allen and Dave; Gavin and Willa; Liz, Logan, Reid, and Porter. Every tow truck driver and mechanic who came to our rescue.

Thank you to the countless visitor information center employees, parks staff, and anyone else who patiently endured our endless questions.

Last, but certainly not least: Thank you, dear reader, you wonderful human. By purchasing this book you have already demonstrated great judgment. We hope that you find joy in these pages and that this book is a springboard for your own adventures and memories.

About the Authors

Places We Swim California is the third book by couple Caroline Clements and Dillon Seitchik-Reardon. Their previous titles are *Places We Swim* (2018) and *Places We Swim Sydney* (2020). Caroline is from Melbourne, Australia, and is a writer and editor. She is currently studying psychology. Dillon grew up in New Mexico, USA, and bounced between California and Australia for many years before settling in Melbourne. He is a writer, photographer, and gardener. Together they have written for publications such as *The New York Times*, *The Guardian*, *The Infatuation*, and *Vogue*. They live on Gayamaygal Country in Sydney, Australia.

Photo credits

Copper Top BBQ image by Matthew Kerly-Otten (Sierra Nevada chapter intro p.43)

Idelwild Wines image by Leigh Ann Beverly (Bay Area chapter intro p.94)

Holbrooke Hotel image by Kat Alves (Gold Country chapter intro p.123)

Pig and the Rooster image by Bianca Simonian (Southern California chapter intro p. 202)

All other photos in this book are by Dillon Seitchik-Reardon.

Published in 2024 by Hardie Grant Explore, an imprint of Hardie Grant Publishing

Hardie Grant Explore (Melbourne)
Wurundjeri Country
Building 1, 658 Church Street
Richmond, Victoria 3121

Hardie Grant Explore (Sydney)
Gadigal Country
Level 7, 45 Jones Street
Ultimo, NSW 2007

www.hardiegrant.com/au/explore

Maps in this publication have been made with Natural Earth. Free vector and raster map data @naturalearthdata.com.

A catalogue record for this book is available from the National Library of Australia

Hardie Grant acknowledges the Traditional Owners of the Country on which we work, the Wurundjeri People of the Kulin Nation and the Gadigal People of the Eora Nation, and recognises their continuing connection to the land, waters and culture. We pay our respects to their Elders past and present.

For all relevant publications, Hardie Grant Explore commissions a First Nations consultant to review relevant content and provide feedback to ensure suitable language and information is included in the final book. Hardie Grant Explore also includes traditional place names and acknowledges Traditional Owners, where possible, in both the text and mapping for their publications.

Places We Swim California
ISBN 9781741178296

10 9 8 7 6 5 4 3 2 1

Publisher
Melissa Kayser

Project editor
Megan Cuthbert

Editor
Anne Canright

Proofreader
Lyric Dodson

First Nations consultant
JoEllen Anderson, PhD

Cartographer
Emily Maffei, Jason Sankovic

Design
Evi-O.Studio

Typesetting
Simone Wall

Index
Max McMaster

Production coordinator
Simone Wall

Colour reproduction by Simone Wall and Splitting Image Colour Studio

Printed and bound in China by LEO Paper Products LTD.

The paper this book is printed on is certified against the Forest Stewardship Council® Standards and other sources. FSC® promotes environmentally responsible, socially beneficial and economically viable management of the world's forests.